D1190479

WITHDRAWN

WOMEN IN BECKETT

WOMEN IN BECKETT

PERFORMANCE AND CRITICAL PERSPECTIVES

EDITED BY LINDA BEN-ZVI

UNIVERSITY OF ILLINOIS PRESS
Urbana and Chicago

For my children, Oriella and Arik

This book is printed on acid-free paper.

Angela B. Moorjani's essay, "The Magna Mater Myth in Beckett's Fiction: Subject and Subversion," was originally published in *Beckett Translating/Translating Beckett,* ed. Dina Sherzer et al. (University Park: Pennsylvania State University Press, 1987).

The actors have provided photographs from the following sources: of Madeleine Renaud, photo © Arch. Phot. Paris/S.P.A.D.E.M.; of Delphine Seyrig, photo © by Marc Enguer-and; of Shivaun O'Casey and Aideen O'Kelly, photos © 1987 by Tom Jenkins; of Hanna Marron, three photos by Mula and Haramaty, Tel-Aviv; of Irena Jun, the first photo from Zygmunt Rytka, Warsaw, and the second by Wojciech Plewinski, Krakow; of Brenda Bynum, by Charles Rafshoon, courtesy of Theater Emory, Atlanta, Ga.; of Billie Whitelaw in *Rockaby,* Louise Richardson, and in *Not I,* courtesy of Stan Douglas and the Vancouver Art Gallery, Vancouver, B.C., which also provided the jacket illustration.

Library of Congress Cataloging-in-Publication Data

Women in Beckett : performance and critical perspective / edited by Linda Ben-Zvi.
    p. cm.
    Bibliography: p.
    Includes index.
    ISBN 0-252-01658-0 (alk. paper)
    1. Beckett, Samuel, 1906–   —Characters—Women. 2. Women in literature.   I. Ben-Zvi, Linda.
PR6003.E282Z5727 1990
848'.91409—dc20   89–5126
                                                             CIP

Contents

INTRODUCTION ix

PART ONE: *Acting Beckett's Women*

ENGLAND

Billie Whitelaw, INTERVIEWED BY LINDA BEN-ZVI 3
Dame Peggy Ashcroft, INTERVIEWED BY KATHARINE WORTH 11

FRANCE

Madeleine Renaud, INTERVIEWED BY PIERRE CHABERT 15
Delphine Seyrig, INTERVIEWED BY PIERRE CHABERT 18

GERMANY

Eva Katharina Schultz 22
Nancy Illig 24
Gudren Genest 27

IRELAND

Shivaun O'Casey, INTERVIEWED BY ROSETTE LAMONT 29
Aideen O'Kelly, INTERVIEWED BY ROSETTE LAMONT 35

ISRAEL

Hanna Marron, INTERVIEWED BY LINDA BEN-ZVI 41

POLAND

Irena Jun, INTERVIEWED BY ANTONI LIBERA 47

UNITED STATES

Brenda Bynum, INTERVIEWED BY LOIS OVERBECK 51
Martha Fehsenfeld 55

PART TWO: *Re-acting to Beckett's Women*

FICTION

Patterns of Rejection: Sex and Love in Beckett's Universe
BY MARTIN ESSLIN 61

Beckett and the Heresy of Love
BY JAMES ACHESON 68

"Meet in Paradize": Beckett's Shavian Women
BY KRISTIN MORRISON 81

Clods, Whores, and Bitches: Misogyny in Beckett's Early Fiction
BY SUSAN BRIENZA 91

Stereoscopic or Stereotypic: Characterization in Beckett's Fiction
BY RUBIN RABINOVITZ 106

*Cartesian Man and the Woman Reader: A Feminist Approach
to Beckett's* Molloy
BY CAROL HELMSTETTER CANTRELL 117

The Magna Mater Myth in Beckett's Fiction: Subtext and Subversion
BY ANGELA B. MOORJANI 134

Homage to the Dark Lady: III Seen III Said
BY LAWRENCE GRAVER 142

FROM FICTION TO DRAMA

*Male or Female Voice: The Significance of the
Gender of the Speaker in Beckett's Late Fiction and Drama*
BY CHARLES R. LYONS 150

DRAMA: THE STAGE

The Femme Fatale on Beckett's Stage
BY RUBY COHN 162

The Transformational Grammar of Gender in Beckett's Dramas
BY SHARI BENSTOCK 172

Beckett and Sexuality (Terribly Short Version)
BY PETER GIDAL 187

"Her Lips Moving": The Castrated Voice of Not I
BY ANN WILSON 190

Portrait of a Woman: The Experience of Marginality in Not I
BY DINA SHERZER 201

Speaking Parisian: Beckett and French Feminism
BY ELIN DIAMOND 208

Female Subjectivity in Not I *and* Rockaby
BY LOIS OPPENHEIM 217

DRAMA: RADIO & TELEVISION

Beckett's Eh Joe: *Lending an Ear to the Anima*
BY ROSETTE LAMONT 228

Women in Beckett's Radio and Television Plays
BY KATHARINE WORTH 236

Not I: *Through a Tube Starkly*
BY LINDA BEN-ZVI 243

APPENDIX 249

CONTRIBUTORS 253

INDEX 257

Illustrations

Billie Whitelaw in *Rockaby* 8

Dame Peggy Ashcroft in *Happy Days* 13

Madeleine Renaud in *Happy Days* 16

Delphine Seyrig in *Footfalls* 19

Samuel Beckett directing
Eva Katharina Schultz in *Happy Days* 23

Eva Katharina Schultz in *Happy Days* 23

Nancy Illig in *Happy Days* 25

Gudren Genest as Nell in *Endgame* 27

Shivaun O'Casey on the set of *Happy Days* 34

Aideen O'Kelly as Winnie, with John Leighton
as Willie, in *Happy Days* 38

Hanna Marron in *Happy Days* 43

Irena Jun in *Footfalls* 49

Brenda Bynum in *Happy Days* 54

Martha Fehsenfeld in *Happy Days* 56

Irene Jun in *Footfalls* 169

Hanna Marron as Winnie, with Ori Levy
as Willie, in *Happy Days* 177

Billie Whitelaw in *Not I* 191

Peggy Sinclair 251

Introduction

This collection developed from a panel I chaired for the Samuel Beckett Society at a Modern Language Association meeting several years ago. The title, "Beckett's Portraits of Women: The Function of Gender in the Novels and Plays," focused on an area of Beckett's writing never before approached as a discrete topic. While studies examine individual Beckett fictions and plays in which women appear and while the ever-growing number of books on Beckett routinely devote sections to *Happy Days, Not I,* and *Footfalls,* as well as to the late fiction *Ill Seen Ill Said*—all of which have female protagonists—none of the criticism has, to my knowledge, concentrated specifically and systematically on questions of gender depiction in Beckett.

At first glance, gender might seem an irrelevant subject in Beckett's work. In *Malone Dies* Beckett's writer/protagonist makes the point when he sketches an outline of his work in progress: "Perhaps I shall put the man and the woman in the same story, there is so little difference between a man and a woman, between mine I mean." In a certain sense the same could be said of all Beckett's people. Men and women in the Beckettian world are both born "astride of a grave," as Pozzo and Vladimir recognize in *Waiting for Godot;* they live in a world where "everything oozes," as Estragon points out in the same play; and they are faced with the awareness that there is "nothing to be done" as almost all Beckett characters know.

The metaphysical human condition Beckett describes is not gender-specific. All characters exist in a grey umbra, where "perhaps" is the most surety they can muster; all struggle with the vagaries of memory, time, and the perception of self. Winnie's attempt to call up those "memorable lines" from a past, now only half-remembered, is repeated by numerous figures of both sexes. Time, "that double-headed monster of damnation and salvation" that Beckett described in his essay *Proust,* stalks indiscriminate of gender. And what the voice in *Fizzles* asks—"Did you ever say *I* to yourself in your life"—could be asked equally by men and women. Faced with life on "this bitch of an earth," Beckett's people all seek company, hew to habits, establish routines, and, when all else fails, talk to keep themselves going on.

Yet as much as they exist in a world of shared metaphysical uncertainty, they also exist in an everyday world—*this* world—shaped to a large degree by the societal constructs of gender that so often mark male and female behavior and shape personality. Characters may go *on,* but the word is not some vague directional pointer through a theoretical terrain. In Beckett it is an imperative, prodding the traveler along an all-too-familiar way, demarcated by alarm clocks, benches, bicycles, bedpans, tape recorders, and mirrors. In such a world, to live is to get up, brush one's teeth, and comb one's hair (or hairs); to survive is to "play" the roles assigned or—if in doubt or in rebellion—to improvise, but always to be aware of the script already written, in which gender too often shapes the part.

Beckett's writings reflect this gendered world, a fact critics tend to overlook in their rush to take the high ground. For example, "Astride of a grave" describes a metaphysical situation, but by choosing to omit the female from the description of birth, Beckett—or his character in *Godot*—makes a gendered comment. Time may affect both sexes, but the pressures on females to retain youth and beauty make their confrontations with the mirror more threatening and more devastating—and Beckett shows this. Even the phrase "this bitch of an earth," describing the scene of procreation and temporal decay, does not sidestep gender, since it indicates the coalescence of nature and the female, both denigrated by the phrase, spoken in a play in which no woman appears.

Such phrases and images are not random; Beckett is too precise a writer. They indicate his keen awareness of, and commitment to revealing, those elements that fix his people in place and tie them to stultifying gender roles. Therefore, he has adamantly opposed changing the sexes of his characters.[1] When asked if women could play the parts of men in *Waiting for Godot,* he said, "Women don't have prostates."[2] Beckett's refusal to cross cast should not be seen as exclusionary, implying that women do not experience the suffering of being the play depicts. Rather it indicates that *for the author* the *form* such suffering takes in the play is structured upon those behavioral roles socially sanctioned for males—bantering, bullying, declaiming—and that when Vladimir says, "All *man*kind is us," he is not using the term generically. In the same way, the later female-focused plays can be interpreted as depictions of female responses to the same suffering in the confines of stereotypic gender roles. Even in writings that are purposely ambiguous—in the short story "Enough," for example—Beckett still has a specific sex in mind. "They are both men," he has said.[3]

Just as shifts from one medium to another alter the intention of a Beckett work, since the form so intimately echoes the theme, so gender is scripted into the roles Beckett's characters play; and to deny the significance of gender questions would be to deny much that concerns Beckett as a writer.

With the exception of the abandoned *Human Wishes,* Beckett's plays date from 1947; with the also abandoned *Dream of Fair to Middling Women,* his fiction from 1932. Perhaps because the fiction has its genesis in an earlier period of Beckett's own personal and professional development, his early portraits of women in the fiction are far more stereotypic and scathing than any in the later drama, the author less distanced from the gender stereotype he is depicting.

Beckett's fiction is most clearly the domain of Males whose names, appropriately, often begin with the letter *M*—Murphy, Molloy, and Malone—or the inverted form, *W*—Watt. While the nameless spectres of the later fictions lose their letters with their corporeality, they still retain the gender markings of males. In the *nouvelles* the unnamed speakers are all men. The few memories that the speaker in *How It Is* recalls are of males—in childhood, maturity, and old age—presumably pictures of his own life that was. In *All Strange Away* and *Ping* the male, desiring the image of the female, remains, even when the world described is nearly subsumed in all-enshrouding white.

That is not to say that women are absent in the fiction. They are always present. In some works—like *Dream* and its published offshoot *More Pricks Than Kicks*—they even threaten to swamp the texts by their sheer numbers and grotesque forms. Most women in the fiction tend to fall into conventional, demarcated roles. They are usually lovers, mothers, and sometimes conflated images of both, devoutly to be avoided in the early works, futilely to be sought in the fictions after *How It Is.* Almost never depicted as independent figures, they are drawn in relation to the male protagonists of each work. It is *his* struggles with them, *his* fears of them, and *his* need for them which shape the actions and the portraits Beckett offers. Only in the last two fictions, *Ill Seen Ill Said* and *Worstward Ho,* do women become a focus of the piece, paralleling their importance in the plays. In the former work the unnamed woman is the central image the speaker describes; in the latter she is one of the trinity of fading spectres who still remain, residua of preceding Beckett fiction.

While the fiction is for the most part reserved for the male point of view—and some would even argue, as Charles Lyons does in this collection, that *Ill Seen Ill Said* preserves this gender dominance, with a male remembering the image of the Venus-like woman—the stage dramas, particularly the works after *Happy Days,* become the place where women emerge as full-drawn, independent figures in their own right. They are usually not aberrations of male desire and fear, not stereotypic images of myth and tradition, but real women living in the same world as Beckett's men, prey to the same metaphysical conditions but reacting in ways that are comments on their position as women in a given situation and a given society that has shaped them.

In fact, by count women dominate the Beckett stage. In the stage plays from *Happy Days* on, there are ten women, eight men, and in *What Where* five of indeterminate sex, designated "he" but bearing no other visual marks of gender. More significant than their numbers, however, is the power of their depiction. With the sensitive eye of a painter, Beckett creates portraits of women that go beyond simple gender identification. His women are among the most arresting and powerful that a dramatist—particularly a male dramatist—has ever sketched. Immediately the following stage images come to mind: Winnie sinking into her mound and her routines in *Happy Days;* the trio of women in *Come and Go* stepping in and out of the unlit darkness, marking with their movements the steps from youth to age; the solitary walker in *Footfalls* pacing herself to oblivion; the aged rocker in *Rockaby* saying less but demanding "more" of her fading life; and—the most searing gender image of all—Mouth in *Not I,* a gushing orifice spewing the words of her fragmented life, attempting to talk herself into being.

Beckett's portraits of women, however, offer more than the human form or a part thereof; they offer a visual concomitant to what it is to *be* female. Men may also be stuck: in routines that deaden their perceptions, in time that holds them fast, in the earth that will eventually cover them. They too need company, someone to hear them in the wilderness. But it is hard to imagine a male Winnie reacting as she does. Conditioned to "make the best of things," to "say one's prayers," recite one's "classics," take care of one's bodily functions, and repair one's physical appearance, Winnie goes through the rituals that society ascribes to, and allows, the female. Parasol, hat, and capacious bag are all the accoutrements she has inherited. Even her anger and her fear must be expressed indirectly in her fictionalized account of Millie, the surrogate figure who is allowed to scream as the proper Winnie is not.

Winnie could well be described as a caricature of the middle-aged woman from Borough Green, but Beckett prevents this interpretation by allowing her an awareness of her own predicament and her own limited means to ward off the despair she experiences. Her "on

Winnie" indicates her determination to do whatever she can, with whatever she has, to survive. Beckett's Winnie is thus not only a woman; she is the physical embodiment of the *condition* of being a woman in her society. Not a stereotype, she is the result of stereotypic views of women. Beckett suggests what culture offers as ballast for a woman like Winnie. Not much. And certainly not much more for her husband, Willie, also heir to gender-delineated roles. He can only muse over want ads that, as a male, he is expected to answer, and dress to play the part of the romantic gentleman come a-courting or, perhaps, a-killing. *Happy Days* illustrates the mythic, gendered tale of male mobility and female fixity, of the desire to leave and the desire to stay. The experiences of both are inscribed by their gender and circumscribed by a society as encasing as the earth in which she is buried and in which he burrows.

Beckett's sensitivity to the loss of freedom associated with typical gender roles is evident in *Happy Days*. But what is even more remarkable about Beckett is his ability to see this dilemma from the position of his female figure. It is she who is the protagonist, she who occupies stage front, her particular angle of vision the shaping vision of the play. Even in those plays in which gender is not a primary theme, it still becomes an important corollary to the main action. For instance, in the play *Catastrophe* Beckett goes to considerable lengths to illustrate how sexual harassment invariably accompanies political suppression and is another example of the catastrophe of a patriarchal, dictatorial regime.

In other plays Beckett continues to place women at the center of his work and to offer not only the female body but the female experience on the stage, an experience no longer shaped by relations to men. After Winnie and Woman 1 in *Play*, no other Beckett women are wives. When seeking an "other," most turn to their like, to their mothers. One has only to think of works such as *Footfalls* and *Rockaby* with their emphasis on mothers and daughters to realize how rare it is for a male playwright to touch on this relationship, depicted, when at all, by women writers. In Beckett's fiction, the father/son dyad appears repeatedly—a variation of the Joe Breen or Beam story in an early *nouvelle*; on the stage, after *Endgame,* the mother/daughter relationship takes precedence.

Other contemporary male playwrights have attempted to offer a female perspective. In Harold Pinter's 1978 play *Betrayal*, for instance, the two male characters, Robert and Jerry, wait for Emma, Robert's wife, to put the crying son to sleep. The talk turns to male babies and their difficulty leaving the womb. "But what about girl babies? They leave the womb too," Robert notes. "That's true. It's also true that nobody talks much about girl babies leaving the womb. Do they?" Jerry questions, causing Robert to retort, "I am prepared to do so."[4] Prepared he may be, but as the scene progresses it becomes clear that Robert—and presumably Pinter—has nothing to say, and the conversation soon returns to the world of men to which boy babies are heir, to their friendships, rivalries, and games. It is a world in which a woman like Emma is little more than a pawn fought over as the men fight over the outcome of a squash game. Several years later, when Pinter wrote the film script, he rewrote the scene, omitting even the attempt at explanation.

Another playwright, Sam Shepard, also comments on the need for male playwrights to depict the experience of being female. "I was determined to write some kind of confrontation between a man and a woman as opposed to just men," Shepard said in a recent interview. "I wanted to try to take this leap into a female character, which I had never really done. I felt obliged to, somehow. But it's hard for a man to say he can speak from the point of view of a woman. But you make the attempt."[5] Shepard's attempts can be seen in *Fool for Love* and *A Lie of the Mind.* However, both plays are still the plays of men, of sons and their fathers, existing in a paternalistic world in which women are beaten, victimized, and silenced. Eddie may listen to May's version of the story of their lives in *Fool for Love,* and he may seem to be denying his father; but in the end Eddie is still playing out the role of the controlling male, and May is still the reactive victim.

The depiction of women by playwrights of the preceding generation is often no better. One need only think of Arthur Miller's handling of Linda Loman in *Death of a Salesman.* She is wife, she is mother, but she is never a person in her own right. Unlike Winnie, she is never allowed to articulate her dreams, memories, or thoughts. She functions entirely as a cipher for the men in her life. Her signs are the laundry basket and the darned socks, just as the signs of the woman in the hotel room—another stereotyped figure at the other end of the gender spectrum—are her raucous laughter and her unclothed body. Both are images of women seen entirely from a male perspective. At the Loman family table only three places are set.

What makes Beckett different from these other male playwrights—and closer to Chekhov and Ibsen, if not in form, at least in scope—is his ability to depict the human condition, both male and female, without presenting women as disguised males, something Virginia Woolf early in the century chided even the best of male writers for doing.[6] Winnie, Mouth, and May are not males in disguise—in drag—or male desires of what women should be. They are real women while at the same time portraits of that societal construct labeled "Woman."[7]

In the introduction to a recent book entitled *The Female Body in Western Culture,* the editor, Susan Rubin Suleiman, writes, "Women, who for centuries had been the *objects* of male theorizing, male desires, male fears, and male representations, need to discover and reappropriate themselves as *subjects*" and to take back "what had always been theirs but had been usurped from them: control over their bodies and a voice with which to speak about it."[8]

In art this control and this voice need not be the province of female artists alone. Samuel Beckett, at least in many of his stage plays, presents both the body and the voice of woman. Beckett's human world is one that inscribes its figures in a frightening vise, but it is a world in which the word *human* subsumes both male and female bodies and voices and does not try to impose one upon the other.[9]

This collection concentrates on the women in Beckett's writing—describes them; studies their evolution and variations in the canon; discusses the forces that influenced their depiction; and illustrates, by use of a variety of critical tools, their significance in Beckett's writing and, more generally, their relation to the depiction of women in modern literature and in society.

Since description precedes analysis in the outline above, the book begins with a section of interviews with and statements by twelve international female actors and one director who have portrayed Beckett's women on the stage. They comment on what is required to take on the roles Beckett writes, how the experiences differ from those associated with playing other female parts, and their personal observations on the effect of the roles both on themselves and on their audiences. This section of the book offers a rare opportunity for English-speaking readers to learn how women from seven different countries have reacted to Beckett's portraits of women. Several discuss for the first time their reactions to the roles. Seven of the actors—Billie Whitelaw, Dame Peggy Ashcroft, Madeleine Renaud, Delphine Seyrig, Eva Katharina Schultz, Nancy Illig, and Gudren Genest—also describe what it is like to be directed by Beckett. One of the actors, Brenda Bynum, has directed Beckett plays herself, and one, Martha Fehsenfeld, has observed and written on Beckett directing others. Despite the differences in their backgrounds, many echo similar feelings: about the power of the roles, the emotional and physical commitments the works require, and the need to tap their own lives for inspiration, often drawing on their memories of their mothers in shaping their performances. The accompanying photographs of the women in their famous Beckett roles provide a comparison of the diversity of sets and costumes that have been used for specific plays, particularly *Happy Days*. The section also includes an interview with Shivaun O'Casey, daughter of Sean O'Casey, in which she discusses both her experiences directing *Happy Days* and the relation of Beckett's theater to that of her father.

The second part of the book moves to the difficult question of gender in the diverse Beckett canon. The essays are separated by genre and presented chronologically in general order of composition of the Beckett work under consideration, so that the reader can see the evolution of female depiction through Beckett's long career and also within a certain form as the genre itself changes. Less by design than happenstance, but one Beckett would probably enjoy, the contributors divide numerically: six men and twelve women, with nine critics—Acheson, Brienza, Rabinovitz, Cantrell, Moorjani, Graver, Benstock, Sherzer, and Oppenheim—specialists in narrative theory and fiction, and nine—Esslin, Morrison, Lyons, Cohn, Gidal, Wilson, Diamond, Lamont, and Worth—closely identified with issues of performance and drama.

No one theoretical approach is common to all the essays. Esslin and Acheson, for example, describe the traditional male artist/ persona's desire for and fear of woman and relate these concerns to the themes of love and artistic creation presented in the European literary tradition. Brienza and Cantrell offer feminist readings of the early fiction and argue the misogynist nature of the works, while Rabinovitz attempts to illustrate how Beckett offers multiple images—often grotesque—of both men and women. Morrison compares Beckett and Shaw in their evocation of the "life force"; Moorjani and Lamont discuss mythic elements of women; Cohn, the recurrent images of the femme fatale. Benstock connects a reading of *Happy Days* to central concerns of feminist literary scholarship; Oppenheim, a feminist reading of dramatic texts with the premises of "the philosophical critic working within the phenomenological tradition." Three of the essays in the drama section—by Wilson, Gidal, and Diamond—form a kind of mini-exchange around *Not I* and offer examples of the ways that feminist analyses can enlighten and often refocus contemporary discussions of drama, performance, and gender.

The richness of the approaches parallels the richness of the material studied and should offer new ways of thinking about Beckett. The goal of such a collection, I believe, is not to narrow the scope of the original works in light of a specific theme or of a particular approach, nor to ride hobby horses to override Beckett's texts for the sake of a given theory. Rather it is to suggest the pervasiveness and centrality of gender in Beckett and in all writing situated in the physical world and, by example, to indicate the exciting possibilities which open when questions of gender become central to a study of texts and performances. To ignore the roles of women, or of men, is to fall prey to an acceptance of the very stereotypes and limits the works reveal.

NOTES

1. In one instance early in the sixties, Beckett refused permission for two women, Estelle Parsons and Shelley Winters, to play Estragon and Vladimir, writing in response to their query, "definitely NO." However, the desire to cross cast has not abated, and neither has Beckett's objection to the gender shifts. In the summer of 1988, he tried to block a Dutch production that planned to use women. In the 1988 season the Denver Center Theater cast two women as Estragon and Vladimir. Beckett's disclaimer in the program reads, "Samuel Beckett wrote *Waiting for Godot* for five male characters and has never approved otherwise." In this production the women were dressed as men and the references to them retained the male pronoun. There was no attempt on the part of the director to make gender a question in the production by changing the sexes in the text. The effect of having women disguised as men was like that achieved early in the century when female actors played Hamlet in male dress, a far different effect than recent productions—the Mabou Mine's *Lear,* for example—in which characters actually changed gender.

2. Samuel Beckett, meeting with Linda Ben-Zvi, Paris, December 1987.

3. Beckett, meeting with Ben-Zvi. When I went on to ask him if the image of the two figures bent over, walking together, was the same as the image of the walking pair in "The Calmative" and the father/son dyad in *Worstward Ho,* he said, "Yes."

4. Harold Pinter, *Betrayal* (London: Metheun, 1979), 58. If there were any question about Pinter's lack of sensitivity to women, one need only see his adaptation of Margaret Atwood's *The Handmaid's Tale,* in which the woman's story disappears entirely and is replaced by a male fantasy of control and voyeurism.

5. Sam Shepard, quoted in Don Shewey, *Sam Shepard* (New York: Dell, 1985), 150.

6. See Virginia Woolf, "Men and Women," in *Women and Writing,* ed. Michele Barrett (New York: Harcourt Brace, 1979).

7. In *Alice Doesn't: Feminism, Semiotics, Cinema* (Bloomington: Indiana University Press, 1984), Teresa de Lauretis discusses the invention of a societally constructed concept of "Woman" and its relation to gender depiction of actual women. Also see Sue-Ellen Case, "Classic Drag: The Greek Creation of Female Parts," in *Theater Journal* (Oct. 1985): 317–27. In it she describes a possible theater "which might make the fiction of 'Woman' appear in . . . texts." It is possible, I am suggesting, to see many of Beckett's later stage plays as precisely such works: plays which present simultaneously the reality and the construct, allowing for the critique of both.

8. Susan Rubin Suleiman, "(Re) Writing the Body: The Politics and Poetics of Female Eroticism," in *The Female Body in Western Culture,* ed. Susan Rubin Suleiman (Cambridge, Mass.: Harvard University Press, 1986), 7.

9. This introduction was written before Samuel Beckett's death. Now that he is no longer able to oversee his productions or voice his wishes about shifts in gender, media, and texts, there will most likely be a whole spate of directors ready to "revise Beckett"—as in a recent New York production of *Catastrophe* that rewrote the ending to produce "a more optimistic conclusion." It failed miserably. The debate about authorial intentionality and directorial freedom in relation to cross casting and every other element of production is certain to become even more vocal. Yet, as the *Catastrophe* debacle proved, a new Beckett is not necessarily a better Beckett.

PART ONE

Acting Beckett's Women

Billie Whitelaw

INTERVIEWED BY LINDA BEN-ZVI

More than any other actress, Billie Whitelaw has become associated with the plays of Samuel Beckett. She has played nearly all the parts Beckett has written for women, and *Footfalls* was written for and dedicated to her. When I interviewed her in her home in early December 1987, she had just returned from Paris, where she had begun the task of preparing the role of Voice in the television play *Eh Joe*. She was also beginning work on the role of Ada in the radio play *Embers*. (Of Nell in *Endgame*, the only leading Beckett female part she has not done, she said, "The woman in the dustbin. I think I'll give that a miss.") In preparation for these latest productions, she is working directly with Beckett, as she has always done in the past. Even when he has not been the acknowledged director of the play, he has helped her on the particular nuances of the character and her speech cadences, tempos, and rhythms. Though she often professes to know nothing about the roles themselves—what these women "mean"—she offers important, sensitive insights into the parts and into the process required of an actor who wishes to play Beckett's women as the author intended them to be played.

Linda Ben-Zvi: Can you offer any general comments about your first reactions when you have read the women's parts Beckett has created?

Billie Whitelaw: Whenever I've read anything of Beckett's that I've been asked to do, the first thing that I've always wondered is how is it that everything he writes seems to be about my life. When I read *Happy Days,* I thought, what the hell was this man doing writing about me? He didn't even know me. Now having said that, Beckett's women are me, and therefore I don't know how I can discuss these women because they are all about me.

LB: In what sense?

BW: Well the most dramatic example of that is when I first read *Not I.* I was sitting on my orange Chesterfield up there. I read it through—not understanding one word of it, may I say, intellectually. And when I got to the end, I could not stop crying.... And yet if you were to say, why were you, I couldn't tell you other than I recognized—and I have said this before—the inner scream; I recognized a wound that's in there somewhere.

LB: David Warrilow has commented that to him Beckett's characters go beyond gender. Do you agree?

BW: Yes, that feeling that it aroused in me I'm sure is sexless and ageless. As I'm sure *Happy Days* could be about a man who was trying to hang up a shelf and getting the nails out of a tool box, and the hammer next, and then the drill, trying to get through his day; but I could be wrong; I most likely am. I just don't think of Beckett in terms of gender or age.

LB: Do you play the roles, then, as feelings that could emanate from men as women?

BW: Well, let us talk about *Not I,* which is to me the absolute essence of *it,* whatever *it* is. Most playwrights would write a three-act or a five-act play about this crazy lady, as it were, who is going out of her mind. But instead of writing about something, Beckett doesn't write *about* anything; he just writes *it.* With *Not I,* every night before I went on, while I was being taken up the scaffold, I used to go through a ritual and say, "All right now, Whitelaw, let the skin fall off; let the flesh fall off; let the bones fall off; all right, let it all go; keep out of the way; you physically keep out of the way." Therefore I lost all of the manifestations of my sex, and I was left with something—god knows what it was—that hand in the center of all of us. I don't know what that is, but that is what I had to get at and that is what I worked with. And I had to physically make the rest of me keep out of it, and then it would take off.

Although when we did *Happy Days,* which he directed, he made me quite a sexy little piece, he made me wear a sort of crazy Follies Bèrgère hat and strapless top with funny little feathers and things and very seductive.

LB: Did he say why he dressed you like that?

BW: No, it just amused him. Certainly a dusty, fading old lady in a twin set and a string of pearls I was not. Although I did wear this ludicrous makeup. My mouth was made up with a blob of red, and two little Dutch-doll globs of rouge on my cheeks. I wish to god I could have continued with Winnie. I was just about making that play my own, making Winnie my own, and then we came off.

LB: Did you feel that you weren't quite successful in the role?

BW: I could have been; it was all there. Of all the plays I've done, that needed working. I needed time to work my way into it because Beckett had so many notes that he gave me, and just technically it was like me talking and trying to boil a pan of milk at the same time—movement and speech, speech and movement, and putting things down, not only on a word, putting things down, say putting the toothbrush or the lipstick or the whatever down, on a syllable of a word, and he would describe it as—can't think of the word, a musical term—something for movement and voice like piano and voice, and the movement was very technically worked in and flowed absolutely like *perpetual mobile*. It flowed one to the other but each separate so the whole thing flowed but was also separate, and that took a lot of working out, and it meant while I was actually performing it a lot of the time I was directing myself, or I was jogging my memory and technically trying to do what Sam had asked me to do. Toward the end of the third or fourth week, I was becoming expert enough in the juggling that I was beginning to do it without thinking. I would love to think *Happy Days* would just pop into my memory box and it would take off. I still find that there are times when I hear myself talking like Winnie, or I make certain gestures that could be hers. You see, that's what I meant. There Sam is writing about me, and there I am actually doing Winnie for real: [singsong] "Dirty flannel for dirty face, into my bag, out of my bag!"

    LB: Do you find that the other women stay with you as Winnie has?

    BW: Because these characters are me, there is no alternative.

    LB: Can that be disturbing?

    BW: Yes. You bet. I have what is called "raging Beckettitus." I do actually have Beckettitus and, ironically, so does he, Beckett. Pierre Chabert and I were talking about this the other day in Paris, and he was saying, you have to distance yourself or you get the experience I had when doing *Not I*. Your head spins and the floor moves without you actually moving. Every damn play of Beckett's that I do involves some sort of physically or mentally excruciating experience. For instance, when I worked on Winnie, it took me three months to learn the part. I locked myself up in the top floor of my home. I knew the text before Sam and I started working together. You know how we work. We sit and look into each other's eyes and say the lines. It was very hard to learn; there were so many "Oh, well"s and "Ah, well"s. Sam would say, "Oh, you missed something there." He would keep reminding me, "No color." If I told him that I thought I sounded boring, he would say, "Let it be boring." You know it takes courage to go slow, to be boring. You have to have courage to work that way.

Yet it is so important to get the music right in Beckett, and I do think of the parts in terms of music. Beckett sometimes conducts me, something like a metronome. For example, I remember when we started working on *Happy Days,* I thought Winnie would say "Another happy day," sprightly. And Sam said—let me see if I can get it right—[*flat monotone*] "A-no-ther hap-py day." And in brackets I put in, "Oh, Christ, here we go. Another sodding twelve hours to get through. Right. Off we go. Christ, okay, sun is up, we've got till sundown to get through." And that is very different from the way I had originally heard it.

LB: And once you had that tone and tempo, was the process easier?

BW: Yes, yes. Look at the sun, look down at the sodding bag, and it gave the whole thing a kind of quality. The second half of *Happy Days* has a sort of desperation to it. The colors are from a different part of the pallette than those used in the first act. More grey and black. Because Sam and I have a kind of shorthand, he didn't have to tell me that. Yes, with these plays the music and tempos are essential. If you get them right, everything else falls into place.

LB: Are there similarities in the music of Beckett's plays?

BW: Yes. I recognize a lot of the rhythms, the more I do these plays, and similar images and similar words. One thing I remember in the Pennebaker film of me preparing for *Rockaby,* I turned to Alan [Schneider] and suddenly said, "I've said a lot of this before." There is a slight hint of *Not I,* for instance, in the second act of *Happy Days.* Of course the tempos are different. When I read *Footfalls* I thought, what the hell am I going to do with this? When I read *Rockaby* I thought, what the hell am I going to do with this? When I read *Not I,* I knew exactly what I had to get, how fast it had to go. When I read *Play* I knew exactly what I had to get, roughly what direction I was heading. While the tempos are different in each play, one must get the proper one.

Now, working as I am with *Embers,* I am thinking of the rolling in and out of the tide, of the waves coming to shore and receding. I've just started working on this one, and I'm not sure what I'll end up with, but this is my starting point. That is my idea—the breaking of waves. I tend to work in pictures. In *Embers* the woman may be a figment of the man's imagination, a weary voice that comes to him on the seashore. She does have a bit of humor, however. Hope I won't have my knuckles wrapped for giving her a little humor. She does make a joke, and she says, "Laugh, Henry, it's not every day I crack a joke."

LB: When you met with Beckett and began to read with him the lines from *Eh Joe,* did he offer any suggestions or comment on the character?

BW: He did mention the phrase "suppressed venom" in relation to the woman. She seems to be jealous of the other woman she describes, vindictive. He also said to remember that she is weary. And of course the phrase he always tells me, "No color." In the case of this woman, I must also try to remember that she is a voice in someone else's head, a disembodied voice.

The same is true for the woman in *Embers*. It is difficult to get the right tone that indicates that she is disembodied. I am working at placing my voice behind my nose, almost as if I have adenoids, but not quite. I must also stand very close to the microphone to get that sound, as if her voice is dripping into his head. Both women are not earthbound. And I must also go slowly, and I will emphasize particular syllables. I still have work to do on both plays.

If the music's right, the piece will work. Also the process cannot be done quickly. Noel Coward said acting consists of learning the lines, speaking clearly, and not bumping into the furniture. I do admire that kind of expertise in Coward, and I recognize that such acting is more than that. But with a Beckett work, the process is entirely different. It's only by reading it over and over and over, not understanding what the hell it's about, particularly emotionally, when nothing comes off the page. But after a while, still not understanding what it's about, it starts to take on a music. It's already in there somewhere: for example [*snaps fingers*] "blah, blah, blah . . . she opens her eyes." In *Eh Joe,* let me say the four syllables, "men-tal thug-gee." I may not end up saying it like that, but that's how I'm going to start out. There is usually a word that gives a clue, that must be emphasized, that becomes a key. I will be flat at first and then it will take shape. Just working with Beckett at the PLM hotel, even for half an hour, it was starting to begin.

LB: Does Beckett often give you phrases to help you capture the character?

BW: When I was preparing *All That Fall* for a recent radio broadcast, he used the phrase "explosive constipation" to think about Maddy Rooney. She's terribly constipated; she has all these feelings, and wants to explode, to release them, but she can't. She just tries to hang on in there. Hang on, hang on, it will be all right in the end, we hope, god knows.

LB: Do you find the other Beckett women equally brave?

BW: Yes. Winnie is terribly brave, terribly courageous. She is marvelous; she hangs on and hopes things will be better. She is slipping down, slithering down, yet holding on by her eyelashes. She has the self-discipline to get on with her day. Who's to say just sitting and opening

your bag and taking out your lipstick and this and that isn't courageous—perhaps the most courageous thing one can do. I can admire
that spirit. I know I have days when I can't do anything. I think, this
day I am going to tear out of the calendar, this day has not existed.

LB: How did you see the woman in *Rockaby*?

BW: Terribly lonely. I don't know why—maybe because I was doing
it in America—but I thought of the loneliness of apartment dwellers,
the desperate loneliness of New York, people sitting at their windows. I
wrote on the margin of my copy of the play the words *solitary, monoto-
nous, lullaby.* She is again a disembodied voice. There I was working for
a certain inflexion, a certain pitch in order to get that "no color." Different shades of grey.

LB: Are there other writers who require the same concentration, the
same approach?

BW: Well, with certain other plays, I've been around long enough; I
have a rough idea of how to get it, and I could possibly bullshit my way

Billie Whitelaw in *Rockaby*

through a scene. I won't, but I could juggle my way through it. But you can't do that with Beckett. You actually have to *be* these women, and that is what I think is so difficult and also so great about these plays. Getting back to *Not I*, a lot of people thought that I was pacing up and down, that the mouth was moving. It's like looking at a star: after a while it seems to be moving about. A couple of actor friends of mine, I was furious, they thought I put it all on tape. I told them, "No it is not on tape, unfortunately. Each night I have to go through this torture, although sometimes I had the feeling I can't go on, I can't go on."

I experience pain in all these roles. With *Footfalls*, it was physically excruciating to maintain the posture required for the part. As one gets lower and lower, to stand in that position becomes almost intolerable; it is almost as if one is curling round slowly within, into oneself, until finally one disappears, spiraling inward, inward. I said to Sam that as the light goes he should have only a little pile of fuller's earth. There is nothing left. Recently, in Australia, touring with *Footfalls*, I developed shin splints. I had to go every day to get the bone put back onto the marrow or whatever.

LB: Which play did you find the most painful to perform?

BW: *Not I*. Oh boy, very painful, very painful. I felt as if I had an opened wound, and every night I went on in all that pain. You are not even allowed to move your head a fraction of an inch one way or another, so all that energy, which makes the top of your head want to explode, goes inward.

I remember, when I was doing *Not I*, I was rehearsing a Michael Frayn play directed by Michael Rudman. By three o'clock in the afternoon I was spiritually leaving my body; I was honing in to *Not I*. I was not a very popular lady with my leading man, I'm here to tell you.

Footfalls was also difficult in another sense. Just before I did it, my niece committed suicide. I remember seeing her just before; I was the last one to speak to her. And her voice, it was without color, as if she had already done it. She had already left us and was just waiting to commit the act. You see, all that is in Beckett. He is writing about me.

In ... *but the clouds* ... , for instance, I had to keep my eyes open without blinking. Now I have weak eyes. Those hellish lights. It was terrible. I admire actors who don't need to blink; I can't do that.

LB: Does he make his men go through the same sort of physical agony?

BW: Of course. Beckett demands such physical extremes of his male actors too. In *Waiting for Godot*, the German version he directed, there was that physical precision. And when David Warrilow played in *A Piece of Monologue*, oh god, my heart bled for him standing absolutely still.

LB: Moving to another subject, why do you think Beckett has so many women on the stage in the later works?

BW: I'm throwing a guess, I'm just throwing a guess. There were what I call the Beckett triplets: two actors and an actress, of which I was the actress. Jackie MacGowran and Patrick Magee he adored, and they are gone. And I'm left. And based on nothing at all, I wonder if perhaps at times he writes with a voice in his head. Now I'm just guessing.

LB: I know you have been giving lectures to students on acting Beckett parts. In what ways do you see the actor supplementing critical discussions of Beckett's works?

BW: I think you can touch an emotional center. My lectures aren't lectures as such. I leap about and keep on spouting lines. I don't know what happens with lectures—I am not an academic—but I know for a lot of students, they had never seen Beckett before. My leaping up—going through *Rockaby,* back and forth, and from side to side—actually had meaning to them as opposed to an academic taking you through the text of Shakespeare, for instance. I'm sure analysis has to be done, but as an actor I don't do that.

LB: Of course, since you have worked with Beckett, you could offer an ongoing example of how these works should be done.

BW: I think Sam would like that, but I'm not a teacher or an academic. I would do with students what Beckett has done with me, after they are prepared. We would concentrate on the actual process of getting there, which consists of starting from zero and not acting it out, letting it grow. It will be different for everyone who does it—it all has to be different—but *Not I* grew, *Happy Days* was in the process of being born, when it had to come off. I would discuss the courage it takes to go slow, not afraid of being achingly boring, reciting like a metronome, if need be.

LB: If you were asked to sum up the qualities of the women you have played, what might you say?

BW: We have a private joke; it wouldn't mean a damn thing to any one else. I think it's in *Footfalls*. May, or is it Amy, suddenly says she is dreadfully un . . . and she can't finish the word—dot dot dot. It has become a personal private joke between Sam and myself. I will tell him, "I'm dreadfully un . . . this morning, dreadfully un . . . " Maybe you could say all Beckett's women are dreadfully un. . . .

Dame Peggy Ashcroft

INTERVIEWED BY KATHARINE WORTH

My interview with Peggy Ashcroft took place in her delightful house in Hampstead over tea, to which she had invited me when arranging our meeting. She poured tea, we talked, she inquired about Beckett's health, not having seen him for some time, and commented on the closeness of their ages (her eightieth birthday is being celebrated only about a year after his). The interview rapidly turned into a conversation, of a very relaxed and agreeable kind. It seemed appropriate to record this easy flow by letting Peggy Ashcroft speak for herself, merely indicating from time to time the questions I offered for her consideration.

Peggy Ashcroft: Have I enjoyed performing and reading from Beckett's work? Oh yes, it has been a very great experience to be involved with writing of such quality. I respond very strongly to the rhythm (perhaps playing Shakespeare for many years before encountering Beckett has something to do with this), and I love the humor. It is mixed up with so many different feelings and some are bleak, but it always seems to survive.

Playing Winnie in *Happy Days* was a major event for me. I had always wanted to play the part; in fact, I was slightly miffed that George Devine didn't ask me to do it when he directed.the play at the Royal Court Theatre, the first British production. I learned later that he had thought I wouldn't want to. Joan Plowright was to have done it, but she withdrew when she became pregnant, and Brenda Bruce was the first English Winnie, at very short notice (two weeks' rehearsal, terrifying). I was happy when the opportunity came my way some years later, with Peter Hall's production at the National Theatre. Winnie is one of those parts, I believe, that actresses will want to play in the way that actors aim at Hamlet—a "summit" part.

Beckett himself took an interest in the production. He came over from Paris to see the rehearsals and stayed two weeks. I suppose he must have been reasonably pleased with what we were doing: he left it to us in the end. We didn't make any changes. He had the idea of making a major change, cutting the parasol episode, a whole two pages. Peter Hall persuaded him not to, and I'm sure he was right. It would have been a terrible loss, not just to Winnie's part (though I would certainly have been sad to lose it) but to the whole play. It's such a wonderful moment of theater when the parasol catches fire and burns up, so unexpected and comical. The audience loved the little shock; maybe they sensed that it was a technical hazard (quite a bothersome one actually) and enjoyed it all the more for that. Yet Winnie takes it in her stride, just noting that it must have happened before, a nice theater joke. That was an aspect of her personality I particularly enjoyed.

I'm not sure if Beckett would have altogether approved of my interpretation. He might have thought it was too "humanized," I don't know. When he directed Billie Whitelaw in the part, he gave the rhythmic structure priority; I couldn't have worked on the 'metronome' principle—though of course Billie achieved wonders. She did ring me once during rehearsals in despair, however! I was always very conscious of the rhythm and let it carry me along to some extent. But I felt a need to work in terms of character: *why* did Winnie use certain rhythms, what did it tell about her? Beckett would answer questions like "Why does she gabble as she does at a certain point?" by saying "Because it has to go fast there." The emphasis was really musical in his approach, though obviously he has created characters which have an extraordinarily strong life of their own.

The Irish accent I used for Winnie? That was my idea. An actress has to find a "voice" for a role and I heard this one quite distinctly. I told Beckett:

I know what Winnie's voice sounds like.
Oh, how?
Like you.
Oh, I don't know about that.

You know his tone of voice, so you can imagine how he sounded when he said that—a little dry and completely Irish. I went ahead with it and found there were all sorts of little turns of speech which seemed to come more easily in an Irish rhythm.

Some people have been critical of Winnie, I know, because she keeps on chattering and counting her blessings in that awful situation, sinking further into the earth. I think she is very aware of the horrors, but she

Dame Peggy Ashcroft in *Happy Days*

doesn't give in to them. I felt I was combatting them, working to fill in the spaces, working in a way against Willie. He was the negative: I was reacting all the time to his negativism. Did I feel resentful of Willie? Not really, but I had to counter him, make up for his lack; I was almost driven by him to be more positive. When I played the part in Canada with John Neville, there was a more tense relationship with Willie. John made him powerful; there was the feeling that he might break out some-how and the move toward the revolver at the end was really threatening. What do I think is about to happen then? Perhaps he is going to kill her and then himself—that always seemed a possibility. Incidentally, there was a frightful moment in the Canadian production when I cut five pages and had to find my way back; not easy, with so much repetition in the text. I knew I had to get to the revolver, establish its presence: some-how I managed it and was able to go on. So the revolver was my lifeline on that occasion!

The sensation of being enclosed in earth was very real for me. It was definitely earth—not sand, as it has sometimes been described. Peter Hall once made a little slip and referred to the mound of sand when he was giving a talk in front of the curtain to a matinee audience. I was standing in the wings and hissed at him, "Earth!" Madeleine Renaud really did go for sand: it was the seaside for her, with sand castles. She is still playing Winnie after so many years. Theater is her life; she gives everything to it in a way that wouldn't be possible for all actors, how-ever devoted they are to their profession. Life keeps pushing in, after all, with other interests—family and so forth. I couldn't play *Happy Days* again. But it is one of my most intense theater memories. Ah, those days! There'll never be such pleasure again—or such agonies.

Yes, I remain fascinated by Beckett's writings. I've greatly enjoyed reading from his work—the poems and fiction as well as the plays: I think the last program of that kind was at the University of Reading, in honor of Beckett's eightieth birthday. There's no doubt that Beckett has a strong appeal for actors, if once they sense the style, the tune of his writing.

Would I like to perform another Beckett role? Ah, if there were only the right one! There aren't parts for older women, except in the late plays, and those are really Billie's; I couldn't play them. So it would have to be something different. Now the part I rather fancy is Mrs. Gorman. . . .

Madeleine Renaud

INTERVIEWED BY PIERRE CHABERT

My tale with *Les beaux jours* that I've been playing for about twenty years, I believe, and with Samuel Beckett—it all seems quite simple.

Roger [Blin], one day, gave me a manuscript, saying: "I want you to tell me what you think of this. Tomorrow I'll come talk to you about it." I read the manuscript. I found myself carried away with its admirable lines, and the next day I did give it back to Roger and I said to him, "I think there isn't anything finer." That was in 1963. I got busy learning it and working on it.

I met Beckett, whom I didn't know, I don't think, and I said to him: "I am ready to play it when you wish." It was decided right away. I didn't hesitate at all; I wasn't frightened by the character or by her inability to move, for there is nothing more worthy, more human, than these lines, I repeat.

I began making it mine and learning it. I went to play at the Ridotto, a tiny little theater in Venice, as a part of the Festival. Jean-Louis wasn't there; on the phone, I said to him: "You don't need to be afraid. We will play it at the Odéon."

Yes! I thought right away that Winnie was a role for me, that there wasn't any finer role. And besides, it's right there, on my table, my little copy; it never leaves me. It's more or less in tatters, but it's still the same.

Sam and Roger—the two together—made me work on it. It was difficult, very difficult, but wonderful. What struck me? Beckett's attention to detail, and the state of mind of the character, for I always keep coming back to that. There was never any argument, never any disagreement among us.

Once I'd learned my lines by rote, just as I always do, and dispatched with that sort of mental gymnastics, I let myself go with the role, or rather I let it take hold of me.

I can see Beckett at the first rehearsals, sitting opposite me at a table. He had chosen all the things for the play with attention to the most

Madeleine Renaud in *Happy Days*

minute detail. I had to come up with several types of glasses, for these have a lot of importance. Not only the pair of glasses, but the glasses' case. It could be neither too old, too new, nor too gaudy. Still it must be consistent with the character who, in spite of everything, according to Beckett's design, is attached irrevocably to her past. She still has a little string of pearls around her neck, for example.

With Beckett we took each item separately: the magnifying glass, the little mirror, the nail file, the gun—all these objects which serve to punctuate the rhythm of the phrase and which accompany her gestures and complement her thoughts. What there is that is touching is that Winnie's very first gesture—once she had stretched and said her prayer—was to dig around in her purse and pull out a toothbrush and the tube of toothpaste. There is so much meaning in the items she takes out of her purse and scatters about her on the mound! When it's the end of the day, she puts them back, little by little, mechanically, in her purse. It's the end of the day and the end of the evocation of her past.

The least little gesture with those objects, and with the text, for example, all that was methodically worked out by Beckett. Each item was supposed to have its place. When he was ready to try a few rehearsals again, to bring the play back, he changed the tiniest details about the placement of the objects. No one, not even the most ardent fan of Beckett or of *Les beaux jours,* would have caught the change.

One day I said to Beckett: "But really, it's silly, I'm being indiscrete. . . . How is it that you are so utterly aware of the importance a woman attaches to her purse?" He didn't answer me, as I recall.

But the lines are so fine, so suggestive, that I don't worry about the gestures when I'm acting, or about the objects, or the position of my arms—don't I turn my neck a little too much to the right, a little too much to the left—or about my eyes closing . . . I just don't get excited about it. I am calm. For the only thing to do is to let Beckett speak.

I worked on these lines, refining and purifying them. I make no distinction between the words, the gestures, the objects . . . For me it's a whole; it's the inner state that counts. And what reigns over all is joy, a total gift of self.

Delphine Seyrig

INTERVIEWED BY PIERRE CHABERT

Pierre Chabert: You have worked under the direction of Samuel Beckett on two occasions... in 1978 for the French staging of *Pas*, but first in 1964 when *Comédie* was being readied.

Delphine Seyrig: It was Jean-Marie Serreau who was directing, but Sam was very much present. He had asked us, for example, to listen to a tape of the play as staged earlier in England. He was very satisfied with this recording and gave it to us as if to give us some sort of bearing. And this tape really did help us to understand what he wanted of us; nevertheless, the directing was Jean-Marie Serreau's.

PC: I heard a slightly different rendition of the tale by another *Comédie* actor, Michael Lonsdale, who told me that it was Beckett who made the actors conform entirely to the wishes of the director, Jean-Marie Serreau.

DS: That is true, but it's still quite different to be dealing with Beckett as an author who has precise ideas about the way he wishes to be interpreted and to be dealing with that author as a director. For *Pas*, Beckett was the director; we were alone with him. It's both overwhelming and reassuring to be alone with the author-director.

PC: With you there was also Madeleine Renaud, who played the mother, a role people tend to forget because she's not visible on stage.

DS: Of course there was Madeleine Renaud, who, by the way, played *Pas moi* in the first part of the show.

I played *Comédie* in 1964 and *Pas* in 1978; *Comédie*, it seems to me, was an easier play to do, and the text less remote than *Pas*, easier to understand. At one and the same time there are all the elements of the most classic and the most casual theater, as if put through a food mill by Beckett.

Pas is a piece which seems to me more difficult to play, perhaps because there's one person on stage and one person in the wings. Likely, musicians would find it difficult to play a sonata in a concert where the

Delphine Seyrig in *Footfalls*

violinist would be on stage and the pianist in the wings or vice versa. Whatever the reason, I feel that I lacked confidence in *Pas*.

PC: You stress the difficulty of *Pas* and the fact that you weren't able to achieve what you really wanted to do . . .

DS: There is real virtuosity in Beckett's texts, and I am no virtuoso. I was never able to summon the right precision for the role. It was almost as if the instrument itself were insufficient.

PC: What was he asking of you, exactly? What was lacking in the instrument you speak of?

DS: To play Beckett you have to have a real capacity for precision in delivery. You have to know how to talk and to act mechanically and precisely as if for a Bach partita. Enough talk of being supple and inventing all that you will from within. As for me, I have a fluid, undefined, imprecise elocution, which isn't exactly bothersome in playing Turgenev, but which is troublesome in Beckett.

PC: You speak of Paganini, of Bach . . . of precision. Did Beckett make you work musically? On notes, on rhythms? Of course the play is based on the rhythm of steps, the coming and going of feet . . . but also in the manner of speaking the lines?

DS: Definitely. He is like an orchestra conductor: he sets the tempo. Actors, it seems to me, are ever less inclined, or no longer inclined at all, to respect rhythms, and French actors no longer take into account the metrical structure as they used to. When you work with Beckett, you find yourself regretting not having this almost musical education. It's a concrete, real kind of work that is quite distinct from the question of interpretation.

PC: It's curious that you would use the term *concrete*. Usually we hear instead that Sam's work is *abstract* because it is *musical* and that it removes us from the usual sort of theater with its human dullness . . . psychological, etc.

DS: Maybe what is musical is abstract for listeners, but for musicians music is a discipline both concrete and physical. When someone tells us, "There, you have to go *Pam Pam Pam Pam*," that's concrete. Psychology, state of mind, emotions—for me, that's the abstract part of Beckett's music and theater. Sam doesn't try to explain what the play means—the invisible part of the play. He says you have to do that and that, you have to do it with your body, your voice, your lips. That's what I mean by *concrete,* but perhaps I have transposed the sense of the words.

PC: No, I wanted you to define it. On the contrary, I am very happy that you speak of *concrete* in connection with this work. . . . Did he then never speak to you about the play? Never say a thing about the role, the persona whose role you were assuming?

DS: I should have taken notes, but I do remember especially the idea of concrete work. Besides, I have noticed that great artists only say small, very concrete things and not great sweeping generalities.

PC: So you had never worked in this manner. . . . For you, does Sam have a very marked "style" of directing? And do you think that this *concrete* work would apply to other roles . . . or to theater in general?

DS: For me, Beckett was an author who wanted step by step to create images for what he had written on paper—to create a whole, casting the object in its entirety, rather than just describing it. He is not just any director; he is an author who shows what he writes.

PC: In your view, his manner of directing comes entirely from his work as an author . . . and isn't particularly valid for other plays?

DS: In the case of Beckett and Duras, writing is really staging within oneself, and then comes in the imagery. . . . In the context of my work with Sam Beckett, I was strongly affected: I didn't achieve everything I would have wished; I don't have the feeling of having reached the outer limit of everything he might have expected of me. That gives me the feeling of wanting to try again and to do better the next time.

[*Pas* is the French version of *Footfalls; Comedie,* the French version of *Play.*

The interviews with Madeleine Renaud and Delphine Seyrig originally appeared in a special issue of *Révue d'Esthétique,* numero hors-serie, 1986. They are reprinted here with their permission and were translated into English by Elizabeth Berwanger, French Department, Colorado State University. My thanks as well to Pierre Chabert for allowing the reprints and for supplying the photographs that accompany the interviews.—Ed.]

Eva Katharina Schultz

RECOLLECTIONS OF THE REHEARSALS FOR *HAPPY DAYS* WITH SAMUEL BECKETT

There were only thirty rehearsal days. In twenty-one of those days I had to play five main characters in other plays. It's easy to see how little time I had to work on the role of Winnie. But still, Beckett was my calm anchoring point. He never lost patience. He was always prepared down to the last detail. For his own use he had written down the entire piece in German (in several notebooks). On the first day of rehearsal he gave me the key to my role: "Don't ask why—this is how it is!"

Further remarks—those most important to me:

Emphasize humor wherever possible . . .
Don't play Winnie's psychology . . .
Separate phrase and gesture . . .
Unusual nervousness, hands should be in constant motion . . .
Affected friendliness, vindictiveness, cunning . . .
Speak normally, but be curiously uninvolved, impersonal . . .
Rapid changes between aggression, tranquillity, helplessness . . .
Always a little astonished . . .
Flowing passages in motion and text, absolute calm . . .

I remember once, when I was very desperate, he read to me the entire play in German. He was the best Winnie ever.

I thank my lucky stars for having had the chance to work with him. I am grateful for this challenge.

The opening night was in Berlin on September 17, 1979. In November '71 we played in Israel: six shows in Haifa, Tel Aviv, and Jerusalem. All in all we put on the play fifty-nine times. Fifty-nine Happy Days.

Samuel Beckett directing Eva Katharina Schultz in *Happy Days*

Eva Katharina Schultz in *Happy Days*

Nancy Illig

I met Samuel Beckett for the first time when we premiered his *Play* at the Ulm Theater (Ulm, Donau, June 13, 1963). I played the role of Woman I. The stage director was Deryk Mendel, a friend of Beckett's. I think we were at first very apprehensive, the three of us, the actors of the "urn play." Beckett had already become world-famous, and we struggled with his texts, which we weren't able to understand.

The actor of the Man desperately threw this question out into the darkness of the auditorium: "Why am I dead?" The author seemed startled. He made various suggestions. Maybe because of a traffic accident? Or suicide? But mightn't he have died a natural death in bed? Obviously this question was not a relevant one for Beckett. When the actor insisted on knowing, Beckett said to Mendel with a smirk: *"The Absolute Camel."* This referred to a joke both were familiar with which goes something like this: If an Englishman writes about a camel, he will use the title *The Camel;* a Frenchman will call it *The Camel and Love;* and a German, *The Absolute Camel.* The only thing important to Beckett was the situation: we were all three dead.

It was then that I understood something essential. Beckett gives a basic situation which is the starting point for the actor and which he must accept in order to play his role. This situation is part of the composition and, above all, part of the character, who cannot be imagined without it.

One year later, when I played Winnie in *Happy Days,* it was not so important for me any longer to know why Winnie had no legs and was stuck in the sand hill. By the way, Winnie never asks herself this question either. It seems that she is at home in her *as it is,* that she prefers leaving it to us—the actors and listeners—to puzzle over her condition and to ask in her stead, *Why is it like this?* She keeps to her bag, which contains whatever she needs to subsist, and she keeps to her survival rituals. Lipstick, toothbrush, and comb are her weapons, as well as her

Nancy Illig in *Happy Days*

wonderful eloquence. She juxtaposes an incomprehensible universe to a bunch of banalities, left-over information, bits of mutilated memories. She is as courageous and ignorant as only a human being can be who perseveres in the face of such an abstruse situation. It is a matter of personal decision whether one will call this behaviour heroic or ridiculous. I find it human. No heroine, no Phaedra, no extraordinary character, no great destiny. A human. A woman. She is as archetypal as her basic situation.

It was a problem for me to play a role, reduced so much by the author on the one hand and so richly endowed at the same time. Deryk Mendel taught me how important the author's staging directions are—every gesture, every look, every compression of the lips, and every pause. In recreating the gestures and pauses I could suddenly feel the breath of the character. I discovered that Winnie sees the pauses as threatening. What does she swallow there? were my thoughts when she pressed her lips together, and What luck! when the words came back or, as in the end, the song is heard. I had a similar experience in 1966 when

I worked on the *Eh Joe* (Radio Stuttgart) with Sam Beckett as director and Deryk Mendel as Joe. At the beginning of the rehearsals Beckett was still in London, where he was directing the English version for BBC. Therefore Mendel and I started rehearsing on our own. This woman's voice is not real. She exists only in Joe's head. She holds an internal interrogation with him—asks, dictates, and tortures. When Beckett arrived, he was at once concerned that the voice could be mistaken for that of a living woman who is in an adjacent room or in the bathroom. We had been concerned about this also and had therefore had the idea of whispering the part. Beckett was thrilled. I tried at first to make the whisper alive by shading, characterizing, and letting personal feelings show through. Beckett let me indulge in these psychological detours. We worked in complete isolation and wonderful harmony, even though our experiments were often watched skeptically and without comprehension on the monitors. But Beckett did not let himself get annoyed by this. One morning he came in and said, "Now we'll make it all dead," and this is how by progressive reduction we ended up with the hammering staccato of a ghost's voice.

Later I had further opportunities to watch Beckett at work. When he directed in Berlin, I went to visit him for a few days. We walked, almost ran, through Tiergarten or through the Avenues and talked about his rehearsals, about his work—each time it was to be his last. He would be ahead by half a step with his long strides; bent over in his long, fluttering coat; hunted by, and at the same time hunting for, his characters, who seemed to live their own life within him. We had kept up a special communion, formed in the days of *Eh Joe,* which expressed itself in the mutual wish to work together once again. The ideal project would have been Winnie, but Beckett could not persuade Barlog in Berlin, and he did not want to come to Düsseldorf. Having had ties with the Schiller Theater for many years, he would certainly have thought it a breech of faith to direct *Happy Days* at the theater in Düsseldorf.

His delicacy, his friendliness, and his shyness were personal requirements against which he was incapable of sinning. I have always considered him an extraordinary personality. In his gentle and unyielding, completely concentrated and collected way he keeps trying again and again to penetrate the cosmos he himself has created in his writing.

P.S. *Come and Go:* I do no longer have the text and cannot retrace which woman's role I played. It is a very short work.

Gudrun Genest

MEMORIES OF SAMUEL BECKETT IN THE REHEARSALS FOR *ENDGAME*, 1967

What an experience to work with Samuel Beckett! His German is fluent. He knows his play *Endgame* by heart in German. He handles the actors with delicacy and treats me, the only woman, with special courtesy. His eyes always look at me attentively, and he regrets not having seen me when there have been a few days without rehearsals. "We have missed you, the female element." Who is likely to say such things nowadays?

Gudren Genest as Nell, with Werner Stock as Nagg, in *Endgame*

Each pause is planned. You can feel the need for it. Nothing is explained. "I cannot explain my plays. Each must find out for himself what is meant."

Beckett remains modestly in the background but is unrelenting in what he wants from us. He did not attend opening night but had a beer next door. He only once took his bows, in Berlin, at his *Waiting for Godot*.

Endgame was a wonderful success. We played it more than 200 times, and in many other cities also, among them London in 1971.

A high point in my career in the theater!

[The responses by Eva Katharina Schultz, Nancy Illig, and Gudren Genest were translated from German by Barbara Thiem, Department of Music, Colorado State University. I thank Dr. Gottfried Büttner, who contacted the German actors, arranged for their essays, and was so supportive of this project.—Ed.]

Shivaun O'Casey

INTERVIEWED BY ROSETTE LAMONT

Shivaun O'Casey belongs to a rare breed, women directors who have tackled a Beckett script. Although Beckett has written some of the juiciest parts for women in twentieth-century theater, few women have undertaken to direct him. Part of the answer may lie in the paucity of women directors, but this is hardly the only reason. Perhaps women are intimidated by the austerity and rigor of the Beckett text. I believe the best approach to understanding why Shivaun O'Casey undertook this arduous and exciting task is to inquire into her own background. She grew up with theater, as the daughter of one of the great playwrights of the century and of an actress. She knew quite early that she wanted to act. Let us begin by exploring her relationship to theater.

Shivaun O'Casey: Gordon Craig was my idol when I was very young. He's a wonderful visionary. I read everything about him. In a sense he was a minimalist before the term was ever used.

RL: How did you first hear about Gordon Craig?

SO'C: Through Shaw. My father also admired him.

RL: Somehow one does not associate the kind of theater your father wrote with Craig's vision.

SO'C: That's because most people see my father's plays as realism, whereas he's a poet of the stage. There is a great deal of abstraction in his plays. That's the way they ought to be staged, and I hope to do this at some time in the near future. My father and I talked a great deal about this. For example, he did not wish *The Silver Tassie* to be done in a realistic style, not even *Juno and the Paycock*. All of these are bigger than life. He loved the abstract sets that Augustus John painted for *The Silver Tassie* in England. His later plays are even more difficult to do, but they have to be approached in that way. In this sense, Sean was a profoundly modern writer, one of international stature. He must not be reduced to Irish realism. So you see, he is not far removed from Beckett.

RL: I would like to ask you whether, as the daughter of Sean O'Casey and a reader of Irish literature, you have staged a very Irish Beckett.

SO'C: I did not set out to do so, consciously. But I believe that my production is unavoidably Irish. After all, I grew up on Sean's work. I also read Yeats, Lady Gregory, Synge, Shaw. I read Beckett's work in that same context. My father and Beckett both grew up in Dublin. In Dublin, even if you come from very different social classes, there is always something in common. Perhaps it is a feeling of not being frightened at the beauty of words, of being at ease in language. When you visit Ireland, you become aware at once of this rich language. I myself don't have it. I speak as an English person. But Aideen O'Kelly has that quality. Beckett doesn't have that working-class ability to relax and project, but he has an acute awareness of language, and that's typically Irish. Sean was very inquisitive; he always made people talk, but he was basically a lonely man, as is Beckett.

RL: Is there something in the Irish temperament that you feel your father and Beckett may have in common?

SO'C: Perhaps the complete lack of interest in material things—no money sense. The Irish are much like the old Russians in the Chekhov plays with their utter lack of self-interest, their inability to be calculating. Of course it is part of their charm.

RL: Do you feel that, having had Aideen O'Kelly play Winnie, your *Happy Days* acquired an Irish flavor?

SO'C: Certainly. Aideen was born in Dalkey; that's near Foxrock, where Beckett comes from. She knows his area and also comes from the middle class. For me, Winnie is almost a caricature of the genteel Dublin lady. Aideen was tempted to play her in that kind of accent . . . you know, lips pursed, butter would not melt in her mouth. We both held back from going all the way in this direction.

RL: There have been great Irish actors of Beckett, isn't that so?

SO'C: Yes, Jackie MacGowran and Patrick Magee. They immediately understand the Irishness of Beckett's language. In Ireland, you have a sense of going back to the past. It has something to do with the harshness of life. It's always rainy and cold. You come in from the cold and steam near the fire. The weather is awful and yet there is always this human warmth, this sense of home. So this Irish harshness is enlivened by warmth, wit, and language. You can laugh off some of the difficulties. There's a mixture of austerity and humor, a sadness in humor and wit in the tragic.

RL: Was the blend of the tragic and the comic one of the tasks you set for yourself in this production?

SO'C: Very much so. We did not have much time, unfortunately. We rehearsed for four weeks. But there were improvements made during the run. Every movement began to be bigger than life. Just getting the words under your belt is already a mammoth task.

RL: Why did you chose this particular Beckett play?

SO'C: I've always loved *Happy Days* because of its delicacy. Originally I was going to do a series of one-act plays: Beckett's *Footfalls* and my father's *The End of the Beginning,* the latter a feminist text, the former all about women alone, the relationship between women.

RL: Your father was a feminist, wasn't he?

SO'C: Sean always said that presidents should be women and then there would be no wars because women know what it means to lose a son.

RL: Why did you want to juxtapose your father's work and that of Beckett?

SO'C: I wanted to show the similarities and the differences. I thought it would make a very interesting evening. But two sets proved expensive, and I had to give up my initial idea until some later time perhaps. I knew Aideen. We talked about what we could do, and so we settled on *Happy Days.* She trusted me as a director, although I had never done directing before. She even let me guide her about the color of her hair. We decided to make it baby blond, taking a cue from the Mildred story. Her frock was also white, almost like a little girl's dress. Of course, at the end, we do not see the frock, we simply remember it, but when Willie crawls in, it's like their wedding day all over again. I enjoyed working with beautiful language and beautiful images. Also we decided to keep many of the passages Beckett cut from the final published text. Some very interesting passages have been cut out and we decided to restore them. We asked his permission, of course.

RL: Did you ever see Beckett direct one of his plays?

SO'C: Yes, I did. He will say a line and then ask the actor or actress to repeat it. He works with rhythm, almost as though he were conducting a musical composition.

RL: How did you work on the text?

SO'C: I examined the text very closely and I broke it into parts. I followed a kind of Stanislavski method. He spoke of main beats and little beats. That's what I did also for this text. Also I was able to consult Beckett's published production notebook, James Knowlson's book. It became my bible. We went over to Paris to see Beckett and he gave me this book. I discussed some of the changes I wanted to make—putting in an extra mound and moving Winnie's mound off-center. He wasn't too happy about the extra mound, but he finally let me have it when I explained that I had to create perspective on a tiny stage. We also made a change having to do with Winnie's parasol. It is supposed at one point to ignite and burn. We just had it smoldering—nothing too abrupt, too dramatic. On the other hand, the sound of the bell in our production was extremely sharp, really a kind of assault on the senses and the spirit. Also, with Winnie's mound slightly to one side, one tends to pay more attention to Willie when he sits up and we see him reading his paper or looking at his dirty postcards. He becomes much more of a partner, a presence to reckon with. It made the play more of a duet instead of a solo. Actually, Beckett said that at the Royal Court the mound had also been placed to one side, for this very reason. From that meeting with Sam we got quite a few leads. For example, Beckett said that Aideen was giving an impression of self-confidence whereas Winnie has none. He described her as "precarious," like a bird that can't fly, a bird with a broken wing. She's unaware, on the verge of madness and yet not mad. Martha Fehsenfeld also noted these observations. I thought of my own mother when I was directing Aideen, and I know that Aideen brought something of her mother to the part. Winnie has a kind of profound frivolity; she's a child-woman. Musically, Beckett thinks of the second act as an andante; I thought of it as a fugue.

RL: What kind of interplay did you try to create between husband and wife?

SO'C: I think they're very cruel with one another. That's what I was striving for. We worked a great deal on the subtext to reach for the real meaning below the lines. A director is a kind of translator. Aideen and I tried to discover what every sentence meant. There are lots of images which are never shown on the stage and yet the words suggest them. For example, when Willie is sunning himself behind the mound, we don't get to see him, but we visualize him from what Winnie is saying. She tells him to rub some stuff into his body. It's some kind of oil so he won't get burned. Where is he rubbing it . . . on his balls. That's quite clear. Winnie may not be sexually active, but she still directs him to protect himself, to take care of his body and that part in particular. Aideen thought that Winnie is frightened of sex, like so many Irish women. We played it to suggest this possibility.

RL: You and Aideen worked very well together. Perhaps because you are friends, and two women, a particular relationship was created.

SO'C: This may be so. I think what we achieved was this process of translation. We worked principally on the subtext.

RL: Do you think there's a great deal of difference between the two acts?

SO'C: The second act is a condensation of Act I. Most of the things which are said in the first act are touched upon in the second. There's more needling and cutting as the play progresses. It's more to the point. In the second act Winnie gets out all the agony she was repressing in the first.

RL: Speaking of agony, I feel that Aideen was particularly wonderful, particularly funny, in the scene she recounts of the couple that comes to stand before her, contemplates her predicament, but does nothing to help her. She used a very special accent as well for them, so that the whole episode became a little play within the play.

SO'C: We decided to give them a cockney accent. It's not unlike the Irish accent, by the way.

RL: It is a cruel story, isn't it, that of the couple passing by, looking down at her, wondering why her husband does not dig her out of the mound, and yet doing nothing about it?

SO'C: It's obvious that Willie will do nothing to assist her. Perhaps the couple is another image of Winnie and Willie, or at least a way of attracting our attention to Willie's unwillingness to change the situation. Yes, there's a lot of cruelty in this little play. People are cruel to one another—husband to wife, wife to husband, the two strangers to the wife and by implication to Willie, the husband. There is also the boundless metaphysical cruelty of life itself—the process of aging, of decay, and the gradual dying. Although there is none of Artaud's violence in Beckett's discreet text, it is still, in a way, "theatre of cruelty."

RL: Since you have had the chance to meet with Mr. Beckett in Paris and consult with him on this production, what is the most salient thing he said to you, the one you retained and which guided you in your work?

SO'C: It is about Winnie being pulled apart. She is drawn down into the earth, which is imprisoning her, and yet she also feels that she is being sucked up. This double pull is simultaneous. The forceps of the gravedigger, as Beckett writes in *Godot,* are opposed by the pull of the beyond, the heavens. Winnie is not a spiritual person and yet she does wonder.

RL: Did you enjoy your work as director?

SO'C: I worked under ideal conditions, with a close friend. I'm only sorry we did not have more time to rehearse, but we went on working throughout the performance. I was there every night; I never wearied of the play. It was so wonderful to delve deeply into Beckett.

RL: Now that this is over, where do you go on from here?

SO'C: I am writing a book about my father, and that will take a good deal of time and energy, but I would also like to stage some of his plays. I feel that working on Beckett helped me understand my father's theater much better, just as Sean's plays also assisted me in understanding Beckett. Both are rooted in classical theater; both are great modern classics.

Shivaun O'Casey on the set of *Happy Days*

Aideen O'Kelly

INTERVIEWED BY ROSETTE LAMONT

Aideen O'Kelly began her acting career at the Abbey Theatre, Dublin, at the age of seventeen. During her long association there, she starred in a wide range of roles, particularly in the plays of Sean O'Casey. Since 1979, she has resided in the United States and has appeared on Broadway in Hugh Leonard's *A Life* and in *Othello,* playing Emilia, opposite Christopher Plummer with James Earl Jones as Othello.

Rosette Lamont: How did you happen to play *Happy Days?*

Aideen O'Kelly: It all happened in my friend Shivaun O'Casey's apartment on Riverside Drive. She said, "Aideen, would you like to play *Happy Days* for me?" I said, "Sure!" I thought we'd just do this in her living room. Suddenly I realized she was planning a production. A little theater downtown expressed interest. I had not read it in years. I remembered seeing a production of it at the Abbey, many, many years ago. Marie Kean played Winnie. When I saw it, in the late sixties, it didn't mean a damn thing to me. I was in my prime, full of piss and vinegar. When I read it again, I was shattered. What really stunned me was that so much of it was my mother. I couldn't get over the childlike quality of this woman.

RL: Do you believe that as people age they recapture something of their childhood or of their child-like nature?

AO'K: I see this more in women. My mum is eighty-six now. She sits in front of the television, and when she likes something, she rubs her feet together and she emits this funny little sound of delight: "Ou! Ou!" It's that kind of quality in Winnie which made me cry when I read the play after Shivaun and I started planning. My mother had a very hard, unsatisfied life. She had a lot of talent, for theater perhaps. Women of her generation did not do anything about this. She was the traditional wife, very subservient to my father, who had a strong personality. He died quite a long time ago, and yet he was much younger than my mother. Strangely enough, although she missed him dreadfully, she blossomed. She could take on the world now which she couldn't do before. But to get back to our Winnie, the more I read [*Happy Days*] the more I realized things in my own life. I thought of the fantasies we create just to keep going. That's what Winnie's doing much of the time. I went through a time when I felt there was nothing to get up for in the morning, about a year of that awful feeling. It goes on all day, and finally in the evening you pull yourself together. This is what Winnie is carefully covering up. In the early stages of the production, I failed to do this, as a matter of fact, but gradually it developed. Some of the more intelligent critics wrote that I let too much out too soon. Probably it was so. Of course I was trying to follow what Beckett said to me.

RL: What was that?

AO'K: First let me describe the experience of meeting him. On the day of our appointment I saw this incredible man walking in our direction, immensely tall and thin, with these amazing eyes. He just takes over a room without even intending to. He was so charming, such a gentle, sweet person. I said to him, "I'll sit behind you, Mr. Beckett. I cannot stand to watch you." "Why?" said he, surprised. I insisted, "No, I'll sit right here." We had to show him the video we had made of an unrehearsed reading of the play, just to get his impression. I swear I'll never do this again. In spite of the fact that we explained what it was, I couldn't help feel that we would be judged by this work. He didn't say much; he just asked, "Aideen, would you read with me?" I almost threw up. That was the last thing I wanted to do. But we sat facing one another, closer than you are to me now. He picked a piece out of the second act, and he started reading in his Foxrock accent, so funny.

RL: What kind of accent is it?

AO'K: Upper class. He never pronounces *d*s and *t*s, which is Irish upper class, a kind of "ish" instead of "it." He read very slowly, so slowly that it struck me as funny. I couldn't help myself, I cracked up. Then I looked into his eyes and saw there was a twinkle. So I roared. He stopped and inquired, "What's the matter?" "You're so funny," I said. He thought about it for a moment, then he began to roar with laughter himself. That was that. He clapped me on the knee, and we began to talk about Foxrock, about my part of Dublin. Then he mentioned the Forty-Foot, a bathing place where ladies were not allowed.

RL: Why this name?

AO'K: Because of the height of the diving board. Beckett told me he never made it to the top. He said he missed the mountains. Then, all of a sudden, he stopped reminiscing and said: "Aideen, you're very capable, perhaps too capable. Winnie, she's precarious, precarious. She's floating,

floating between realities. Of course it's in the text of the play. Winnie keeps on feeling she might float up into the sky, be 'sucked up.'" Beckett is very naughty with language in an Irish, or even Shakespearian, way. So many lines can be interpreted in two ways and sometimes the meaning changes in mid-sentence.

RL: Does this present a problem for the actors?

AO'K: You've got to keep thinking. You can't let the text carry you. It's all a matter of rhythm. At first I found the *voix blanche* very difficult, but then I got it through the music of the language. Beckett thinks in musical terms. I'll never forget when he told me as I was working on a passage, "Aideen, this is andante." Then he added, speaking of Winnie in Act II: "Remember she can no longer wave. She's almost dead." Then I realized that the *voix blanche* was something like the Queen of Night in *The Magic Flute*—a pure, cold voice. I worked very hard on that because I wanted to do what he wanted. Gradually, I modulated it a bit. I even told him, "I won't subjugate myself." "I don't think you will," he said. I didn't want to be a puppet. Winnie is very much her own self.

RL: What is your sense of Winnie? Where does she come from? What would be her social background?

AO'K: I think she's very much a middle-class to upper-class house-wife. She's aware of her social standing, of what she wears. She keeps herself looking nice, even under these weird circumstances. She's shocked by Willie's sloppiness. Respectability at all cost. I could hear my mother saying some of the things she says. There's also a denial in her-self of her real feelings and her longings.

RL: Is she a sexual being?

AO'K: In her mind she certainly is. Did Charlie ever exist remains an unanswered question. Perhaps she only uses this reminiscence to tease her husband, as women often do. But there is all this talk about the tool shed. Whether she fantasized this or not, it is about a roll in the hay, or in the tool shed. Beckett knows that words are never innocent. When he speaks of the tool shed, he must be having a bit of a laugh at the hus-band's expense. Willie's a washout. He has no tool shed because he has no tool, meaning dick. And when Winnie speaks of not being able to conceive, we remember that she does not seem to have had any children. We must listen to Beckett with both ears and perhaps with another sense as well.

RL: Do you play Winnie for humor?

AO'K: Definitely. She's very funny. There's her wonderful descrip-tion of the couple walking by. They look at her plight, discuss her as though she were nothing but a mound. They speak in a cockney accent. The rhythm from the British vaudeville is unmistakably in the text. Then there's the joke she shares—or does she?—with her husband about "for-mication" and "fornication." One evening, a woman walked out of the theater when I reached this part. Winnie really loves to be shocked by her husband. When Willie is caught by her, looking at his collection of French postcards, she has a good look herself. She pretends to be horri-fied, but she makes sure to check them out and note what's going on in every one of them. So, to answer your question, yes she's a sexual woman even though she may never have used her sexuality. Beckett must mean something by having her buried in sand from her waist down. She has rarefied her sexual instincts—not an unusual situation among the Irish upper classes. There is this emphasis on respectability, and of course the influence of the church. She does not let herself have any feelings in the lower parts of her being.

RL: What about the story Winnie is writing in the second half of the play, the one about a little girl?

AO'K: The little girl is herself. She's writing the story to keep herself alive. She also keeps herself alive by holding on to her classics, but she

Aideen O'Kelly as Winnie, with John Leighton as Willie, in *Happy Days*

doesn't really remember the lines, even the one she calls "that unforgettable line." That's hilarious!

RL: Isn't there something also disquieting about the little-girl story?

AO'K: Yes, all that business about the mouse running up her leg. I don't think it's a mouse at all. It's just the most terrible thing that happened to her when she was a child. I use something from my life for this scene. When I was nine years old I was left home alone—my parents had gone out to the movies—with my uncle. He raped me. Then he made me promise I would never tell. Said he'd kill me if I did. That's what I use when I play this scene.

RL: How about the discomfort of playing without being able to move?

AO'K: That's really hard. You can't even move a knee, because it would show immediately in the neck or face. Also one night a fly got into the mound. I couldn't do a thing about it.

RL: In conclusion, let's discuss how you worked with your director, Shivaun O'Casey. Did it help you to work with a woman, since *Happy Days* is a play about a woman.

AO'K: Not necessarily, but what I discovered is how Beckett understands the mind of a woman, how he can see into our little foibles, our fears of growing old, our anguish at the thought of upsetting the man in our life, our panic at the realization of our inner strength.

RL: Did you two discuss the ambiguous end of the play, when Willie crawls out from behind the mound, dressed in his cut-away?

AO'K: Shivaun and I talked about this a great deal. We decided it was more likely the gun he's reaching for. He wants to put an end to it all because it is the end, the end of life, the end of the play. Beckett writes in his stage directions that Willie "is dressed to kill." All of Beckett's words are charged with meaning, as we said before. Yes, Willie is dressed as he was on his wedding day, but also as he will be when they lay him out in his coffin. Perhaps love and death come together at the end. Winnie must be aware of it. At first she is delighted to see her husband, and she takes it to be a gallant call, but then her joy must give way to apprehension.

RL: What about the waltz from *The Merry Widow?* Is this an ironic touch?

AO'K: I think so. It is so nostalgic. Winnie is like all these Irish women who are widows even before their husbands' death. They live side by side but in solitude. Look at Willie; he lives in some hole at the foot of the mound, in the back where Winnie can't see him. He occupies himself by reading his paper or picking his nose. He seems to be listening to her chatter, but one can't be sure. Basically she's alone and very brave. *Happy Days* is a tribute to womanhood. As Martha Fehsenfeld wrote in her notes to her own interpretation of the same role: "Winnie is an organized mess. Her strength is through unawareness." It is no easy task for an actress to make herself aware of this unawareness, to communicate it to her audience. It is the most difficult role I've ever had to do because of the absolute discipline required, the precision in terms of rhythm. The whole play is like a musical score. In fact, when I met Mr. Beckett, one of the first things he said to me was, "Aideen, sing the song." He meant the song from the end of the play, but the whole play is a song.

[My thanks to Rosette Lamont, who arranged for both interviews and for the photographs.—Ed.]

Hanna Marron

INTERVIEWED BY LINDA BEN-ZVI

Hanna Marron, Israel's leading stage actress, was born in Berlin, where, at the age of four, she acted on stage and in films with Max Reinhardt, Emil Jannings, and Peter Lorre. She came to Palestine in 1933, joined the British army at the outbreak of World War II, and entertained Holocaust survivors in Europe. A co-founder of Israel's Cameri Theater, she acted with them for thirty-five years, playing over sixty roles, ranging from *Medea* to *Hello Dolly*. In February 1970, en route to London to audition for a part, she was wounded in a terrorist attack at the Munich airport, and she lost her leg. One year later she returned to the stage. I interviewed her twice, in the summer of 1985 after her successful performance in *Happy Days* and two years later, both times at her home in suburban Tel Aviv.

Hanna Marron: My reaction to *Happy Days*? That depends. I read it many, many times over many years before I finally played it. I remember reading it as a young actress and being terribly excited about the play. It was during the time when I discovered Beckett and other writers of that era. At that time I thought, "Will I ever be good enough to get this part?" Later it was suggested that I do it, but I was afraid. I got cold feet. As the years went by it became more and more of a gigantic task.

My love affair with *Happy Days* was always connected to things in my life. First in my professional life. I was a member of the Cameri Theatre and everything was going very comfortably—a little too comfortably—and four years ago I suddenly decided to leave this permanent company and become freelance. In the beginning it was difficult, and the parts I was offered in other companies weren't very exciting. Strangely enough, it was the Cameri Theatre which offered me *Happy Days*. This time I said, "Okay, I'll do it. What can happen? I mean, I'll dare it." I wanted very much to do the play justice. I really still think it is a masterpiece; there are very few plays like this and very few writers like Beckett.

The play had first been done in Israel twenty-five years ago by a German actress in a shoestring production, and it had made a great impression. Then Madeleine Renaud came to Israel and presented *Happy Days* in French. Somehow I wanted my production to be different from these. I knew I wanted to bring *Happy Days* nearer to audiences nowadays, to get young people to come, not to play only to the bourgeoisie.

It was important to find a director sensitive both to Beckett's text and to the needs of the audience. Michal Govrin, a young woman from a religious background, a professor of literature, became the director. She had earlier done a production of Beckett's *Mercier and Camier* at the Khan Theatre in Jerusalem. I thought, This has to be a special combination: me, Beckett, and a religious director!

We prepared for this part differently than I usually prepare. First of all we talked a lot. Maybe this was wrong. We did not approach it as any other play; both of us were reverential. Then I had a problem with the sheer amount of the text; I had never worked on this kind of text. Even when I played in Pinter's *Landscape* and *Silence*—plays that in some ways are similar to Beckett—I did not have this problem of building a whole subtext in order to get the logic of what I am saying.

Then there was the problem of getting the movements correct. In most plays when the author writes, "She gets up and is furious," so you decide how to show this. It is your way of doing it. Beckett does not work like this. When he says, "Looks up, takes out toothbrush," well, she has to look up and take out the toothbrush. It is part of the words and the play.

I am not ashamed to admit that I found it very, very difficult to memorize and to learn the role. I was in despair. I prepared a whole subtext to parallel the text of Beckett. When, for instance, I say, "What are you doing, Willie?" I thought, "Oh my god, he is coming out."

Michal wanted to portray her in a completely unnatural way—almost a puppet-like way. At the beginning I was willing to try anything. It was a physical way of expressing it. Together with Beckett's interruptions and descriptions of what to do, we added completely puppetlike gestures. I worked very hard on artificial body movements, which were very difficult since I could only move my upper part; but we tried it, we worked. I spent mornings and evenings with the text and during the day these convulsions.

Our original idea was to get closer to the public, so we imagined Winnie and Willie as people of the fifties, immigrants who came to Israel from Poland, especially, with—as Winnie says in the play—"the old style," their way of culture, their way of living. This I accepted, but it didn't work with the puppet gestures. There was a complete breakdown between the two styles.

Another mistake which we never corrected concerned the mound, which was made of a tough, scratchy plastic into which were embedded items that these immigrants would have brought with them to such a desert-like place. I had to fight against this plastic thing. If Beckett wrote "earth," it should have been earth. I felt I wanted to put my nails into this earth, the feeling of it coming up over me. This we never changed.

I didn't know what to do; I was very unhappy. I had a complete feeling of failure. When you feel that you are going to be a failure, you don't work well anymore. I couldn't learn the text; I couldn't go on with the studies. We rehearsed eight weeks, which saved us. At the beginning we had planned to rehearse only four weeks, but I felt we had to have more time and to start from scratch.

This time I began to think of Winnie as a woman, and since I retained the idea that she sprung from fifties, and I related the play so

Hanna Marron in *Happy Days*

closely to my own life, I began to think of my mother, who had come to Israel from Germany and who till her death was not happy in this country. She never learned the language; she was always in the life she had before, in her memories, which made my life very difficult at the time. I suddenly felt this was it; never mind the puppets. *This is a woman.* Beckett wrote a real person. The situation is a strange one, maybe, but don't we all have in our lives these situations where we feel we are stuck, and even the way I had worked on the play and had become stuck, and not knowing how to go on, rooted somehow. I knew that this was how I was going to play Winnie. So it became a kind of mixture of my mother—the way she had reacted to a new life, even her relations with my father—and my professional struggles with freelancing and with this play; then I knew I was on the right track.

Of course, I also added my own experience with my leg, the way I find it difficult to move. Somehow the play is also about me. I had long felt that Beckett had also written my story. I thought, How did he know? Every day having to start from the beginning, to remind myself of my situation—the loss of my leg, of having to get going, of continuing.

Finally, I thought about this country. We too are sinking in the sand but we go on. That insistence on survival is also a part of Winnie, and Beckett understands this quality. All this together, this mixture, became Winnie.

I want to make it perfectly clear that I did not alter Beckett's play. All the little instructions—I did not lose them; I was very strict with every look and every gesture as it was written; I did not run away from any of the text. But I think you do not have to play a puppet, because Beckett has it; it is there—the strangeness, yes, but also the real emotion, the real woman. This is the way I did it, and I felt good about it.

It was still difficult. With *Happy Days* from the morning I was preparing myself. I think it was the force of Beckett, of his way. Every sentence, every little pause, every change of mood was so full of meaning. And then it was all I had gone through; I had put so much of myself into it.

Yet, despite all the difficulties of playing the role and of the situation of Winnie herself, I always felt that the play was optimistic. I understood Winnie. All the *tsuris* that people go through, I understood, just as Winnie does. Life consists of pain and joy. If you feel pain, you are living also. This woman is stuck with this husband, with this life, with these memories, and yet she still wishes for love; she still can say "oh happy days," no matter what happens, and in the last moments she still sings. *She sings!* If that is not optimism, I don't know what is. In answer to those who call Winnie stupid because of this optimism, I say she is not a stupid woman. She has her limitations; she is a small woman, she is not a queen. She is one of those simple, very positive persons, in spite of everything. That's how I felt about it.

I have never been the same since I played the role. I recently watched the video of the role and I thought I should maybe . . . I should do it again. I won't, I won't, but theoretically there were things there which I should have done differently. Because of its greatness, it is the kind of play where you are never satisfied; you always want to correct something. I don't feel this with other parts; *c'est passé* and that's it and it's gone. But this play, no. It is somewhere inside me—still there, still there. In a way I feel, if I were a painter, this would be the painting I would never finish. Maybe it is not good to put the last little dot. It was like climbing the Everest and trying to put your little flag up there with all the rest.

Regarding the meaning of the play. It *is* important what it means, but it can mean so many things. At a certain stage it means to every actress something else. You can take it for the whole of humanity, which is also Winnie and Willie. You can consider her a nation. We as a nation are stuck; we are sinking in the sand. That is what the director wanted. But you cannot act that; you have to act the concrete. And if you act the concrete, you have to act what you feel. After a certain moment I decided that the philosophy should come from the audience. If they get all sorts of associations, fine.

For example, the story about the mouse. There is such a wealth of memories that everybody can have: as a child, as a woman, or even erotic associations—your first encounter with a man or the fear of becoming a woman—it's a world of associations. Then the couple, Shower and Cooker. Although it is a sort of a humorous interlude, you can also think of them as the audience, and you can think of them as people you have met during your life who were staring and looking at you, and again with my own experience, with my leg. In the first few years it was very difficult to have people say hello, and then the eyes would go down; I could always feel their eyes on my back—that sort of thing. I suppose every actress has her own things like that.

On the language of the play. We re-translated *Happy Days* especially for this performance. We worked with the French and English. When we began, and looked for Israeli expressions, we were a little afraid, because maybe we would be changing the text. But then when we saw how Beckett himself changed his play from English to French, taking into account the special rhythm and idiom of each language, we were not afraid anymore.

On Beckett's attitude toward women. Beckett has a great feeling for womanhood. He understands women, I think. Very often in other plays over the last thirty years, you feel that the author's heart is with the male character. For example, Arthur Miller. I like him very much; I played Kate in *All My Sons* when he was in Israel. He writes wonderful parts for women, but he writes the parts because he has to have a counterpart for the main actor, who is male. The woman is there only to provide a focus for the man. But not with Beckett. He writes a woman and it *is* a woman. If you look at the male parts—for example, in *Krapp's Last Tape*—it is meant to be a man, and he doesn't need a woman to develop the character.

On other Beckett roles. I did one Beckett play on radio, *All That Fall,* but many years ago. I loved it, but it was much easier. She's a wonderful character; he writes wonderful characters. I also did a little part of *Footfalls,* at a lecture for an international congress of psychiatrists. The voice of the mother; we all have our mothers inside us, whether we like it or not.

Irena Jun

INTERVIEWED BY ANTONI LIBERA

Antoni Libera: Many consider you to be a Beckett actress. Over a four-year period you appeared in seven of his plays. In the theater you played Woman 2 in *Play*, Mouth in *Not I*, May in *Footfalls*, Woman in *Rockaby*, and Nell in *Endgame*. Quite recently you took part in TV productions of *Eh Joe*, *Ghost Trio* (Woman's Voice) and . . . *but the clouds* . . . (Woman's Face). We know that you are also planning to play Winnie in *Happy Days* and Mrs. Rooney in *All That Fall*. Can you tell us about your fascination with Beckett?

Irena Jun: I owe it to Antoni Libera, the translator of Beckett's work into Polish, who also directed all these productions. It was he who taught me to love this writer. Of course, I knew Beckett's plays earlier and I liked them, though I had never realized how deep and beautiful they were. Probably it was due to the fact that the Polish translations that existed before Antoni translated all the plays anew were not accurate. Also the productions I had seen were not particularly good. Today, after I have experienced playing in so many Beckett's plays, I know that there are certain rules one has to observe while playing and directing Beckett.

AL: What are these rules?

IJ: Playing Beckett requires a very special attitude. It cannot be really explained; one has to experience it. First of all, one has to understand that Beckett's plays are in fact simple and clear. It is the simplicity of great masterpieces. When one starts to work on a production, it is no use looking for a "deep meaning." Instead, one has to concentrate on the meaning and sense of the basic situations. What is *Footfalls* about? If one started to work on it with a philosophical conception in mind, one would risk a failure. What one has to do is to realize certain very simple facts, such as May's craving to speak to somebody or that her slowing down is a sign of growing old. Only in this way can one obtain an image that will provoke some philosophical reflections.

Another matter is the question of form. Beckett's works resemble musical compositions. Words, punctuation, moments of silence are justified not only by the situation and stylistics. They become sounds, musical phrases, melodies. An actor therefore has to know and understand the work's musical structure. It even seems to me that quite often it is the way the text sounds that is more important than what it actually says or means.

Finally, there is the question of the acting technique—basically the technique of speaking but also of movement and gesture. Beckett should not be approached psychologically. He should be performed quite formally. In others words, the actor is not expected to *feel* what he plays but to perform very accurately what he is supposed to do. When we were rehearsing *Footfalls,* Antoni acted as if he were a sculptor. When he had finally shaped my body—found the right position of my head, hands, and even fingers—my task was to memorize it, to remember exactly the tension of every muscle. As far as the text is concerned, I learned it as a melody, with recurring phrases that I had to pronounce exactly the same way, as if they were a refrain. Altogether, I found it really difficult. Another problem was to find the right tone for the story about Mrs. W. and Amy, which is supposed to be improvised.

AL: The reviewers wrote about the precision of your acting. Did you not feel restricted as an actress?

IJ: I do not consider the actor's freedom to be of paramount importance in our profession. For me, the most important thing is to be able to carry out one's task. In the case of Beckett's plays this task is a real challenge. This was what I had been waiting for during the thirty years of my career. (In fact, I came across similar methods as a very young actress when I worked with Jerzy Grotowski; however, Grotowski went in a different direction.) In other words, the task that one is confronted with in Beckett's plays requires maximum concentration and absolute control of one's body and voice. Rehearsing and playing Beckett gives an actor the opportunity to master his own body and to turn it into a perfect instrument.

AL: Was it only the technical aspect that interested you in the parts you played?

IJ: Of course not! If they were only breakneck etudes (like, for instance, Brahm's piano exercises) I would not find them exciting. The thing that fascinated me in the first place was their profound and deeply human message. To explain it, I shall give you another musical example. They make me think of Chopin's etudes, which, while being exercises aimed at improving the pianist's technique, are among the greatest achievements of human spirit.

Irena Jun in *Footfalls*

AL: What do you mean by saying "profound and deeply human message?"

IJ: Two things at least. First of all that they apply to the deepest and most universal human problems, such as solitude, suffering, and hope of salvation. Secondly, that certain aspects of womanhood have been raised as problems applying to all human beings. I am not sure whether it is quite clear... What I mean is that in many cases Beckett has chosen Woman as his medium to express the essence of Human Being. If it were not so, he would replace women figures by men. Why is it that *That Time* or *A Piece of Monologue* is played by men, and *Not I* or *Footfalls* by women? The answer is not easy. One can imagine an old woman in a dark room saying to herself "birth was a death of HER" and thinking obsessively about various sources of light—the sun, flames of matches, lamps. Or a man walking up and down a room and improvising a story in form of a dialogue. It is all possible. But those situations would strike you as false. What follows is that some aspects of human condition can only be expressed by the image (medium) of a female figure.

AL: What does playing Beckett mean for you as an actress?

IJ: Undoubtedly it has been the most important stage in my acting career. Regardless of what I am still going to play, the parts of Mouth and May will always remain in my repertoire.

UNITED STATES

Brenda Bynum

INTERVIEWED BY LOIS OVERBECK

[Brenda Bynum, an actress and director, lives in Atlanta. She has directed Beckett's *Come and Go* for the Beckett/Atlanta Festival in 1987 and starred in *Not I* during the same festival. In 1987 she also appeared as Winnie in *Happy Days* at Theatre Emory in Atlanta. She was interviewed by Lois Overbeck.—Ed.]

Lois Overbeck: Discuss how you did *Come and Go*.

Brenda Bynum: I tried to be as faithful as I could to the script. But not being a scholar, I knew that my initial response, and my strongest response, would be an emotional one. That's really the point of departure for me: how did it make me feel and what did that lead me to do. It was the first time I had to deal with Beckett's requirements to be exact, which for your average theater person is a red flag: they think, "How can I adjust it, how I fit *me* into the part to make it a little different?" When I actually brought the women together, I found that there was in fact freedom. I found myself as director watching these women, seeing a kind of graceful dance which seemed to me to be there. To use another image, they seemed almost like three bells standing in a row that you would lift and ring from moment to moment. It was as if Beckett were celebrating this mysterious aspect of woman and almost admitting that he didn't understand it. The questions the play raises are unanswered. We know that no one will come along and say, "This is what was wrong with her; this is why she seems melancholy." It is the very mystery that Beckett is showing us which cannot be explained. Nothing concrete, just feelings, responding. For me, the more I worked with that feeling the more magical the play became. I didn't know exactly what I wanted the actresses to do, but I knew that hands had to be a certain way. I couldn't say it, but I would know when they did it the wrong way. I wanted intellectually to do what Beckett wanted, but really I was trying to attach my spirit to the work, to feel it and see it.

LO: Were you conscious of building the visual and verbal images?

BB: Yes, the visual images are overwhelming . . . absolute purity, not a syllable that wasn't essential. It seemed almost mathematical, a certain number of required syllables. Yet the emotions are in the spaces between. In all of Beckett, we have to fight our natural instincts to want to explain and to make connections, to clearly illustrate getting from here to there, cause and effect. All of which you have to let go of when you do Beckett.

When you see *Come and Go,* it seems that not much happens, but there are so many moves and sounds and so many opportunities to compromise on moments. Just a change in the angle of a hand can change things. Once you enter into Beckett and learn the rules and accept what he wants, it is wonderful what happens.

LO: Is there room for the actress to interpret, to be herself in the text?

BB: There is room if you submit to the discipline. A Beckett play in many ways is like haiku or a sonnet. The rules give you the freedom. In the most restricted circumstance, if you accept those restrictions, it is like a world in a grain of sand; you get inside those parameters and you find so much, a new universe. I know that his work for me is extremely affirmative, life affirming.

LO: Could *Come and Go* be played by men?

BB: The layers of interaction and the social connections seem clearly to be those of women.

LO: What is feminine about the play? The intimacy?

BB: The delicacy of it, the acceptance, the kind of memories they seem to share, the earlier intimacy, which has a different quality. Athol Fugard in *Road to Mecca* speaks of entering uncharted territory by putting women on the stage. Suddenly after so many years of presenting mainly men, he felt as if he were handling Dresden china, and he was terrified the whole time, handling something that could break. That feeling of fragility is in *Come and Go.* You can see, watching it, a spell is being cast, and it can be broken. If Beckett is saying something, he seems to be celebrating the mystery he feels. He may be sharing with Fugard the feeling of the mystery of life, which women often hold for men. Perhaps it comes from the fact that women can give birth.

LO: Yet there is that sense of loss in the play, that the women will never regain the intimacy they once had together.

BB: Why does it have to be that *they* have lost something, why can it not be Beckett's longing for intimacy that they can have and he can't? Something available that he can't have, or many of us can't have.

LO: In *Happy Days* you are away from a female community. Part of Winnie is being a couple, Winnie and Willie, Winnie and her bag, Winnie and herself.

BB: When the lights went up and play began, I had the feeling that her situation was absolutely normal. How real it seemed. Once you accept the parameters, all seems normal. Neither Winnie nor I seemed to question the situation. Beckett puts you in a strait jacket as he does with the text. He makes your body and your senses cut off; whether it's your legs or eyes, physically he takes things away from you and puts you in an impossible situation, and yet you must go on.

LO: How did you gradually unfold the character?

BB: In the first two weeks of rehearsal we tried to make things make sense, and of course that was wrong. You must work on letting go of things. Beckett seems to see Winnie close to a certain kind of precariousness, as he told Aideen O'Kelly. I think it is crucial that at any moment she could disappear, go up in smoke, or lose control completely. That very precariousness is so much of what the play is about. Willie is the audience, the ear into which her lines are poured. We must all be heard by someone.

Winnie's picking up of things reminded me of how my mother acted when my father died. She kept dealing with physical activities; that was what kept her grounded. When she couldn't bear to think of what lay ahead, she dealt moment to moment.

LO: Living in the moment seems a crucial point. In the Lacanian understanding of femininity, it is the male prerogative to tell a story, to build a continuity, and what is particularly feminine is the ability to be there in the moment. Beckett is constantly disengaging us from the throughline. The reality is moment by moment.

BB: This living in the moment allows audiences a kind of freedom, since a storyline is omitted. They can interpret the play differently, depending upon where they are in their own lives. This seems to be the opposite of a playwright such as Arthur Miller, who wants to make absolutely sure that we know what he wants us to think. He doesn't want to be ambiguous. If it were left up to me, I would develop a point of view and tailor everything I did to serve that point of view, and it would come out making a statement. All our training tells us to do that; with good old-fashioned plays we have to do that. But not with Beckett. You play the text and what you can do physically. You learn from each play.

LO: What did you learn from *Not I*?

BB: I learned to be strong. I am glad I did *Not I* before *Happy Days* because I had already gotten through so much. The life of the woman in

Not I is full of pain, loss of intimacy, as in the other plays. Again the affirmative part was her will. Language keeps her going on, if nothing else. I saw Joe Chaikin the other night. He said that the words are so hard for him, so hard to come by because of his aphasia, that each one is a jewel. I think the same situation exists in Beckett. In *Happy Days,* at certain times, she pours them out in a torrent, and at other times they are like jewels: here and here.

Brenda Bynum in *Happy Days*

Martha Fehsenfeld

Playing *Happy Days,* I soon discovered, was very different from research-ing and studying it. When I examined the play critically, I found that the themes of expansion and contraction appeared to predominate. The familiar first-act specification "Expanse of scorched grass," the second-act "Scene as before, and Winnie embedded up to her neck" testify to this, as does the list of properties in Beckett's rehearsal notebook, encompassing both exaggeration and collapse. The accompanying re-minder, "Gen. principle: hypertrophy secondary, atrophy primary," could be a description of the play itself.

But all that was when I was outside the text looking in. Afterwards, when I began to change perspective and to work on Winnie from the *inside,* I had to start from cause rather than effect. Beckett suggested that I "think of her as a bird with oil on her feathers," and this became the central image of the part for me—physical, external, and very playable. It is her home where she is comfortable, her element. She yearns for the air, but she is imprisoned in the earth, pulled down further and further into its trap. She has her song. That is what she waits for every day—"time for my song"—the announcement of night's beginning. In a re-hearsal account of *Happy Days* (*Glückliche Tage*) by Alfred Hübner, Beckett is quoted as saying, "Winnie is a bird, Willie a turtle." A turtle belongs to the earth as a bird to the sky. The line "Or were we perhaps diverted by two quite different things?" took on special meaning here—the need expressed plus the inevitable separation. In the 1979 London rehearsals with Billie Whitelaw, Beckett told her to "give a kind of peck-ing quality" to the way she picked out her props one by one from the bag. "What a graceful manipulator she is," he said admiringly, as if de-scribing an actual person. I carefully studied the movements of birds—particularly those of the head and eye, those nervous sudden quick changes from one second to the next. And I remembered Beckett insist-ing to Billie that "a clue of the play is interruption. Something begins, something else begins. Winnie is constantly being interrupted or inter-rupting herself. She is an interrupted being." This "bird" characteriza-tion also determined my posture and voice quality, and both became infused with an energy that pulled me up, in contrast to the downward thrust of her immobility.

I talked to Alan Schneider, who had directed the first Winnie (Ruth White) in New York in September 1961. We discussed the problems of the set, and he told me not to worry: "Just make it as comfortable for her as possible. God knows she's uncomfortable enough as it is." This advice was a great help. Given this condition of discomfort, I tried to find a level of comfort and relaxation within it, as I imagine Winnie would have done. This was very useful, particularly in Act II. I did not suffer the agonies of neck spasms, as other Winnies had, because the base of my skull was supported by a padded head rest invisible to the audience, and I could concentrate all my energies on this desperately inward second act without external distraction.

I soon discovered that you don't play a Beckett character but that a Beckett character plays through you—a you that is the barest bones of

Martha Fehsenfeld in *Happy Days*

your own existence. So you must start with your own truth. I found idiosyncrasies in myself I could use. For example, I (like Winnie) talked to myself a lot when I was lonely and wanted company. "Remember, she's not speaking to anyone. She's completely alone," Beckett had warned Billie. The truth of my life—with its falseness, traps, concealments, fears—all resonated from Winnie's truths.

I have since tried to describe playing a part in a Beckett play to others by saying, "He takes you from safe places to unsafe places." And for me this is true. And this is to me what acting is all about—to risk one's vulnerability to the ultimate. But I came to trust Beckett's text to support me. And I dared to venture further and further away from the "safe" places as I became increasingly confident that the text would sustain me wherever I went, as long as I remained absolutely faithful to it.

As I discovered the Winnie in myself and in other women I have known—my grandmother, mother, aunt among them—I realized that Winnie is in all of us. She is whatever survival is. She is a survivor above all and in spite of all. Like the healthy heart of a decayed body that refuses to stop beating, she goes on past the time of longing to die. As Beckett has said, she has no idea of what is happening to her; she has no control over it. Like the bird with damaged feathers, hers is a survival under the most difficult circumstances and in spite of impossible conditions. She keeps up a struggle unaware that it is a struggle—and one that she is doomed to lose. It is neither intentional nor preferable. It just *is*. She is the epitome of Beckett's "on" in the face of every possible enemy that denies and defies her to continue.

Some time after playing in *Happy Days*, I came upon some notes made by a critical scholar during a meeting with Beckett in 1962. He quoted him on the subject of the play. Anyone who plays Winnie in the future cannot help but be enriched by what Beckett said: "Yes, saying 'yes' to this atrocious affair of life, like the 'oui' in *Ulysses*. I hope this comes through in *Happy Days*."

As a scholar I have been involved in trying to discover insights into Beckett's patterns—his textual style, his sculptural silence, the contrapuntal relationship between Winnie and Willie's actions, his repetition of prevailing themes, use of props, separation of word and movement. I've been concerned with the ambiguity that is a continuous thread in the play, as it is in all of Beckett's work, with the patterns of hand gestures, with the Dantean allusions—all theoretical elements. I tried to explore the various references to time in an attempt to get to the essence of the play in terms of Beckett's statement in his *Regiebuch*: "Relate frequency of broken speech and action to discontinuity of time . . . time experience incomprehensible transport from one inextricable present to the next. Those past unremembered, those to come inconceivable."

As an actress I am part of these patterns. Sometimes I am creator of them as I invent games to pass the time. The silences are moments of doubt, confusion, or transitional space between changes of thought. Sometimes they are threats of ultimate stillness. I use the props: they are my only friends, the bag that holds them is my only escape—my way out, along with my stories. The "inextricable present" is where I am, to be repeated over and over. And each present is different and the same. It is no longer theoretical, but practical. I am engaged in the experience itself, with the emotional and immediate life of the character.

I am aware of these patterns because I've researched them. I'm not concerned so much with *how* the props are used as with *using* them. But as the actress I don't discount what the scholar has discovered. I am informed by the scholar. I use the patterns as a frame and as a discipline to channel and focus my energies, to make them specific, to regulate the rhythms of my song. The patterns do not impose; they are the frame that determines and allows her being. It is a totality—all one piece, the-oretical and practical together. I realize that this is what Beckett's theater is about. It is always the thing itself, but it is also always the form or the shape of the thing itself—both objective and subjective. And in the com-ing together of these two seemingly disparate elements is a synthesis which may be close to what Beckett is attempting to do within the lim-itations and possibilities of the theater.

PART TWO

Re-Acting to Beckett's Women

Patterns of Rejection
Sex and Love in Beckett's Universe

MARTIN ESSLIN

Un seul être vous manque et tout est dépeuplé.
Lamartine, "L'Isolement"

... the loved one, who could not love and will not come back.
Beckett, *"The Calmative"*

But there it is, either you love or you don't.
Beckett, *"First Love"*

WORDS:—to wit this love what is this love that more than all the cursed deadly or any other of its great movers so moves the soul and soul what is this soul that more than by any of its great movers is by love so moved. [Clears throat. Prosaic] Love of woman, I mean, if that is what my Lord means.
CROAK: Alas!

Beckett, *Words and Music*

Love of woman—alas! Ever since he emerged into maturity in the persona of Murphy, the Beckettian (male) hero has been in full flight from that prime mover of the soul: Murphy himself from Celia; Victor from his clinging fiancée in *Eleuthéria;* Krapp, who rejected the love of the girl in the punt; Hamm, who denied Mother Pegg oil for her lamp so that she died "of darkness," although "she was bonny once, like a flower of the field"; M in *Play*, who, torn between two women, sought refuge in death; and Joe, who drove one of the women who loved him to suicide.

Always it is the man who rejects the love of woman, woman who yearns for the love of man: Maddy Rooney, loveless and childless— "Love, that is all I asked, a little love, daily, twice daily, fifty years of twice daily love like a Paris horsebutcher's regular";[1] childless Winnie, who can hardly elicit a grunt from Willie; May of *Footfalls* and the Mouth of *Not I*, who have no sense of self because they lack an "Other"; the old lady in *Rockaby*, who has been searching through a long life for someone "a little like" herself; the narrator of *Enough* who was once simply told to leave the man she had so long served and loved.

The perhaps most paradigmatic of these male Beckett heroes, the narrator of *First Love,* clearly explains what it is that makes the men dread the onset of "love." It threatens them with loss of autonomy:

> What mattered to me in my dispeopled kingdom, that in regard to which the disposition of my carcass was the merest and most futile of accidents, was supineness in the mind, the dulling of the self and of that residue of execrable frippery known as the non-self and even the world, for short. But man is still today, at the age of twenty-five, at the mercy of an erection, physically too, from time to time, it's the common lot, even I was not immune, if that may be called an erection. It did not escape her naturally, women smell a rigid phallus ten miles away and wonder, How on earth did he spot me from there? One is no longer oneself, on such occasions, and it is painful to be no longer oneself, even more painful if possible than when one is. For when one is one knows what to do to be less so, whereas when one is not one is any old one irredeemably. What goes by the name of love is banishment, with now and then a postcard from the homeland, such is my considered opinion, this evening."[2]

There is a comic reversal of traditional clichés in this view: If it is generally assumed that to be in love makes a man feel "more alive," more "in the world," then a man subscribing to Beckett's view that to be alive is the source of all suffering and hence striving to feel as little alive, as much out of the world as possible, infinitely preferable, clearly must regard falling in love and being in love as the worst possible thing that could happen to him.

Another source for the incongruities of black comedy lies in the imprecise way in which the term *love* crops up in human discourse. Is *love* a physical act—the "act of love"— or is it a sublime romantic feeling? The narrator of *First Love* makes much of this confusion: "Yes, I loved her, it's the name I gave, still give alas, to what I was doing then. I had nothing to go by, never having loved before, but of course had heard of the thing, at home, at school, in brothel and at church, and read romances, in prose and verse, under the guidance of my tutor, in six or seven languages, both dead and living, in which it was handled at length."[3]

Here the suggestion that he had been a frequenter of brothels focuses the mystery onto the romantic side of love. And the woman in the case—although, like Celia, a prostitute—also clearly separates the physical side from the romantic one. When asked by the narrator to sing him a song, she offers him one of the most romantic love songs in world literature: "I did not know the song, I had never heard it before and shall never hear it again. It had something to do with lemon trees, or orange trees, I forget, that is all I remember and for me that is no mean feat."[4] This, unmistakably, is Mignon's song from Goethe's *Wilhelm Meister:*

> Kennst du das Land wo die Zitronen blühn,
> Im dunkeln Laub die Gold-Orangen glühn...
> ... Dahin! Dahin
> Möcht ich mit dir, o mein Geliebter, ziehn!
>
> [Do you know the land where the lemons bloom
> in the dark foliage gold-oranges glow...
> ... There! There
> I wish to go with you, O you, my love!]

It is from the contrast between such high romance—Mignon is the waif who accompanies an old blind itinerant harpist, very much like the female narrator of *Enough* who is so callously dismissed by her mentor (the ghost of Goethe strides through that story too!)—that the sardonic comedy of *First Love* springs.

When the narrator moves in with his lover and is—in typically sexist manner—shocked to find that she takes money from men, this avatar of Goethe's Mignon is brutally down-to-earth: "So you live by prostitution, I said. We live by prostitution, she said."[5] It is the grotesque linkage between the sordid mechanics of sex and the "higher" feelings of "love," the inexplicable way in which the physical leads to the "spiritual," and vice versa, which underlies much of Beckett's treatment of the relationship between men and women.

What is love? The male protagonists ask again and again. And when they have encountered it: was *that* love?

> It was she made me acquainted with love. She went by the peaceful name of Ruth I think, but I can't say for certain. Perhaps the name was Edith. She had a hole between her legs, oh not the bunghole I had always imagined, but a slit, and in this I put, or rather she put, my so-called virile member, not without difficulty and I toiled and moiled until I discharged or gave up trying or was begged by her to stop. A mug's game in my opinion and tiring on top of that, in the long run. But I lent myself to it with a good enough grace, knowing it was love, for she had told me so. She bent over the couch because of her rheumatism, and in I went from behind. It was the only position she could bear, because of her lumbago. It seemed all right to me, for I had seen dogs, and I was astonished when she confided that you could go about it differently. I wonder what she meant exactly. Perhaps after all she put me in her rectum. A matter of complete indifference to me, I needn't tell you. But is it true love, in the rectum? That's what bothers me sometimes. Have I never known true love after all?[6]

So negligible as well as disgusting is the physical act to these Beckettian heroes that even the actual sex of the person whose orifices are involved becomes a matter of indifference. "Perhaps she too was a man?"
asks Molloy, as ever uncertain about the accuracy of his memory as he
recalls his experience of "love." What, after all, does it matter as long as
the skin rubs against mucous membrane.

In *Enough,* for one, the sex of the narrator is left uncertain to the very
last line of the story. The sex acts that occur between the old tramp and
the narrator might equally well be heterosexual or homosexual: "When
he told me to lick his penis I hastened to do so. I drew satisfaction from
it. We must have had the same satisfactions. The same needs and the
same satisfactions."[7] That the narrator of the story is a woman is only
disclosed in the final sentence: "Enough my old breasts feel his old
hand." (Assez mes vieux seins sentent sa vielle main.)[8]

The old tramp in *Enough* rejects the woman who provides such comforts. The narrator of *First Love* bolts as the cries of his newborn baby
echo down the street. The rejection of physical "love" is also a rejection
of the procreation of life itself—reasonable enough in a view of the
world that regards, in the words of the great choral ode of *Oedipus at
Colonus*—not being born as the greatest possible good: Μὴ φῦναι τὸν
ἄπαντα νικα λόγον."

Here, in a very Irish way, Beckett joins forces with George Bernard
Shaw, who regarded women as the instruments of the Life Force's will,
capturing the best possible men to drive evolution forward, except that
he inverts the valuation put by Shaw on the upward drive of Life. His
men are the philosophical executors of the opposite drive, the creation
of a utopian universe cleansed of life and the suffering it entails. It is
when the last of the seekers in *The Lost Ones (Le dépeupleur)* have given
up their quest that the ceaseless fluctuation of light and dark, hot and
cold, the whole infernal mechanism of endlessly repetitious Time will
come to a final, redemptive, halt.

And yet, beyond and outside the toiling and moiling of skins on mucous membranes there is another *love* that transcends those feeble transports through complete stillness: "on the stone together in the sun on
the stone at the edge of the little wood and as far as eye could see the
wheat turning yellow vowing every now and then you loved each other
just a murmur not touching or anything of that nature you one end of
the stone she the other. . . ."[9]

There is a similar moment of stillness in Krapp's recollection of a
supreme moment of fulfillment: "upper lake, with the punt, bathed off
the bank, then pushed out into the stream and drifted. She lay stretched
out on the floorboards with her hands under her head and her eyes

closed. Sun blazing down, bit of a breeze, water nice and lively. . . . I lay down across her with my face in her breasts and my hand on her. We lay there without moving. But under us all moved, and moved us, gently, up and down, and from side to side."[10]

Yet it is during this very episode of ultimate fulfillment that Krapp rejects that love: "I said again I thought it was hopeless and no good going on and she agreed, without opening her eyes. . . . "[11] Indeed, the approximation of fulfillment in such a moment of quiet union of bodies and "souls" itself underlines the impossibility of going on, simply because, as Beckett pointed out as early as his essay on Proust: "When it is a case of human intercourse, we are faced by the problem of an object whose mobility is not merely a function of the subject's, but independent and personal: two separate and immanent dynamisms related by no system of synchronisation. So that whatever the object, our thirst for possession is, by definition, insatiable. . . . The tragedy of the Marcel-Albertine liaison is the type-tragedy of the human relationship whose failure is preordained."[12] It is because its failure is pre-ordained that the male Beckettian heroes flee the inevitable deterioration, trivialisation, and domestication of the relationship that produced such sublime moments of near-synchronicity.

The tragedy here is that, having done so, they tend, for ever after, to seek to recall and to re-live those sublime moments. Krapp lingers over replays of his account of that episode. Croak in *Words and Music* finally succeeds in evoking the "face" as "words," the poet within him, offers him the poem about old age:

> . . . She comes in the ashes
> Who loved could not be won
> Or won not loved
> Or some other trouble
> Comes in the ashes
> Like in that old light
> The face in the ashes
> That old starlight
> On the earth again
>
> [*Long pause*]
> CROAK: The face.[13]

It is the face that the old man in . . . *but the clouds* . . . strives so desperately to evoke. In one of his rare moments of fulfillment the old man in *Ohio Impromptu* has "seen the dear face and heard the unspoken word"; it is, no doubt, that face the bent figure in *Ghost Trio* tries to conjure up but merely succeeds in evoking the ghost of the perhaps-unborn child of that relationship.

The "face" is precious, but even more precious to these recollectors of supreme moments within the face are the eyes—the eyes that opened for a moment for Krapp, the eyes that are the true entrance to the soul: "the eyes ... open ... Then down a little way ...

> Then down a little way
> Through the trash
> Towards where
> All dark no begging
> No giving no words
> No sense no need
> Through the scum
> Down a little way
> To whence one glimpse
> Of that wellhead.[14]

One glimpse of that wellhead of another being's inmost Being, down there beyond the opened eyes—that is the most these Beckettian heroes can ever gain and, having gained, forever try to recapture. Re-capture, not by conscious effort but through the epiphany of involuntary memory—the only way, as Beckett pointed out when discussing Proust, through which past time can become, for a brief moment, fully reconstituted, fully present again.

Why should it always be men who are shown by Beckett as caught in this inexorable process of loving, rejection, and endless quest for re-call? Surely, merely because Beckett must always draw on his experience, and his experience is that of a man.

Beckett's women are by no means passive objects; on the contrary, like Shaw's executrices of Nature's will, they take an active part in arousing men's desire, in drawing them reluctantly into the experience of Eros. Yet perhaps because they are seen as desirous to nurture a new generation, they are less repelled by the routine and domesticity of a relationship that is no longer at its lone, momentary climax of almost complete union. Like Winnie these women are seen as gamely trying to make the best of the trivia of mundane everyday existence, trying to persuade themselves that these routines constitute series of "happy days."

At a deeper level love loses its ties to anatomical sex. As Malone muses, "Perhaps I shall put the man and the woman in the same story, there is so little difference between a man and a woman, between mine I mean."[15] The little figures moving through the mire in *How It Is,* the hooded shapes hurrying along their pre-ordained paths in *Quadrat 1 + 2* are clearly engaged in a quest for an Other, yet they are not differentiated by their sex: the little creatures of *How It Is,* indeed, in trying to communicate with those they encounter on their course, alternately play the active and the passive role in those contacts on their way. And the center that the hooded wanderers have so fearfully to avoid is obviously the point at which real communication, a real "encounter," would be potentially possible but inevitably proves—by the very nature of existence itself—impossible. If sex is physical desire, the relentless striving of the Life Force, the unending pressure of the Schopenhauerian "Will," paradoxically, those moments when desire has been stilled and two beings glimpse that wellhead deep down through the windows of the eyes, those moments when Time stops and the "Will" is overcome, also are, ultimately, the products of that same sordid and disgusting quest that Baron Corvo punningly termed "the desire and pursuit of the whole."

That is the basic paradox of Beckett's universe: that the sublime moments of mystical (almost, but never quite, achieved) insight spring from the "soul," that mysterious entity—"what is this soul that more than by any of its movers is by love so moved?"—which by some gigantic practical joke of nature is linked to and carried by that grotesque and sordid apparatus of skins and mucous membranes, the human body. Beckett does not moralize about it: he merely puts it before us in concise, compressed, spare images that endlessly ring the changes of his basic perception of the tragi-comic essence of human existence. The part love and sex play in it is by no means central to him; and yet sublimated love, stilled of desire, seems among the few fulfillments that existence can bring—however brief those moments must prove, however long, thereafter, the pain and longing to re-capture them.

NOTES

1. In *All That Fall*, in *Shorter Collected Plays* (London: Faber & Faber, 1984), 17.

2. *First Love*, in *Shorter Collected Prose 1945–1980* (London: Calder, 1984), 6.

3. Ibid., 8.

4. Ibid., 11.

5. Ibid., 17.

6. *Molloy*, in *Three Novels* (New York: Grove Press, 1965), 56.

7. *Enough*, in *Shorter Collected Prose*, 139.

8. Ibid., 144; French version from *Assez* (Paris: Les Editions de Minuit, 1966), 29.

9. *That Time*, in *Collected Shorter Plays*, 228.

10. *Krapp's Last Tape*, in *Shorter Collected Plays*, 61.

11. Ibid.

12. Samuel Beckett, *Proust* (New York: Grove Press, 1970), 6–7.

13. *Words and Music*, in *Collected Shorter Plays*, 131.

14. Ibid., 133–34.

15. *Malone Dies*, in *Three Novels* (New York: Grove, 1965), 181.

FICTION

Beckett and the Heresy of Love

JAMES ACHESON

In *Samuel Beckett: A Biography* Deirdre Bair tells how, one night in a pub during the late fifties, Beckett remarked to some friends: "'This thing called love, there's none of it, you know, it's only fucking. That's all there is—just fucking.' 'Oh, come now Sam, you can't mean this,' they cried in unison, in disbelief. 'I do indeed,' he repeated, 'there's only fucking.'" Bair comments that Beckett's attitude toward women had for many years "ranged from careless indifference to basic distrust and irritated dislike. He gave the impression that women were necessary inconveniences, and in an attitude that his French friends found 'very Irish' professed to find true happiness only in . . . good male companionship late at night in a pub."[1]

Since Beckett's works are often partly autobiographical, it is perhaps unsurprising that the fiction contains only a few female characters and that these few generally serve as sexual partners for his male characters, who share their creator's "very Irish" attitude to women. Yet in much of the fiction and drama spanning the thirty-year period from his first short story, "Assumption," published in 1929, to *Krapp's Last Tape,* written at about the same time as his remark about love being "only fucking,"[2] it is clear that these male characters are also influenced by Beckett's interest in such novelists and philosophers as Joyce, Lawrence, Proust, Spinoza, and Schopenhauer. In many of his works of this period, Beckett's men devote themselves to private religions of art or self that derive from these writers, while his women act either as destructive temptresses or as exponents of what might be termed the heresy of love.

Beckett's first short story, "Assumption," is clearly influenced by his interest in Joyce.[3] Its nameless main character is an artist who, like Stephen Dedalus in *A Portrait of the Artist as a Young Man,* has adopted a strategy of silence, exile, and cunning in order to defend himself against a largely philistine society. He spends much of his time sitting silently in a café frequented by members of "the unread intelligentsia" ("Assumption" 268). Rather than join in their conversation, he remains in self-imposed exile a few tables away, but from time to time, in an exercise of cunning, succeeds in "whispering the turmoil down" (268).

"He could have shouted," says Beckett in the story's opening sentence, "and could not. The buffoon in the loft swung steadily on his stick and the organist sat dreaming with his hands in his pockets" (268). To shout would be to give expression to his imagination: in this context, we must remember that it is Stephen Dedalus's "heart's cry" that gives rise to the villanelle in *A Portrait of the Artist as a Young Man*.[4] But although the "buffoon in the loft"—the metaphorical "conductor" within himself—swings his baton, the "organist"—the part of himself capable of answering the conductor's gesture with a creative act—fails to respond.[5] Though subject to an inner "obligation to express," Beckett's artist/character has found that he has "nothing to express,"[6] for he is inhibited by the awareness that "the highest art" requires "bombshell perfection" (269)—perfection he may not be capable of producing. Stopping conversations—bringing people "within the wide orbit of his control" (269)—is a game he plays in compensation for the fact that he lacks the omnipotence of an artistic god of creation.

In time the urge to shout takes on a life of its own, warring within him against the urge to remain silent. "Its struggle for divinity was as real as his own," we are told, "and as futile" (269). Beckett's character "struggle[s] for divinity" in that he aspires to artistic godhead; the "rebellious surge" (269) within him—the urge to shout, rather than to shape his "heart's cry" into a finely-crafted work of art—aspires to dominance and is in this sense a satanic rival. In order to defeat the rebel angel within, the artist ceases even to whisper; he finds, however, that "by damming the stream of whispers he had raised the level of the flood, and he knew the day would come when it could no longer be denied" (270).

It is at this point that "the Woman" (the use of a capital *W* suggests that she stands for all women) enters his life. Because her arrival is compared to an "irruption of demons" (270), she seems in some way allied to the inner satanic element that threatens the artist with destruction. In spite of himself, the artist finds her attractive: he is especially drawn to her eyes, which seem to him to be "pools of obscurity" (270). This phrase is the first of a number of hints to the reader that what the Woman is offering the character is a heresy of love to rival his own religion of art. For Beckett's description of her eyes recalls not only "the dead, bottomless pools of [Minette's] eyes" in Lawrence's *Women in Love* but also the ultimately destructive heresy practised by some of that nov-el's characters.[7] One such character, Hermione Roddice, who is de-scribed both as a "priestess" and as a "demoniacal ecstatic," tries to kill Birkin, the man she loves; another character, Gerald Crich, reflects to himself that it would be "a perfect voluptuous fulfilment" to murder his mistress Gudrun.[8]

When Beckett's artist enters into an affair with the Woman in "As-sumption," he initially finds that each of her visits "loosen[s] yet another stone in the clumsy dam [of whispers] set up and sustained by him frightened and corruptible" (271). He is aware of having been cor-rupted by the heresy she practises, and he fears for his safety. Later, however, in a complete reversal of his expectations, she releases him (as he thinks) from the power of the satanic element within himself, so that he becomes at one with "the blue flower, Vega, GOD" (271).[9] Since the mystical experience of union with God is often described in sexual terms,[10] it might appear that the artist's experiences of "ecstasy" with the Woman—experiences in which he "die[s] and [is] God" (271)—are meant to be spiritual. However, in context it seems more probable that Beckett is describing his character's experience of sexual union in mysti-cal terms for the sake of suggesting that in making love to the Woman he has abandoned his religion of art in favour of her heresy of love. The artist believes he has experienced the sexual equivalent of the Virgin Mary's Assumption into heaven (the "Assumption" of the story's title), but the heaven on earth to which he is transported has nothing to do with art. "In the virgin womb of [his] imagination" the word is not, as in Stephen Dedalus's imagination, "made flesh."[11] The Woman distracts him from the act of creation, and the level of the reservoir of whispers within himself rises and threatens to burst the dam he has constructed to hold them back. That the Woman acts in effect as an ally to the artist's inner satanic element, and ultimately contributes to his destruction, is clear from the ending of the story. Here, while "contemplating the face that she had overlaid with death," the Woman is "swept aside by a great storm of sound" (271) as the whispers break their dam and take the form of an horrendous shriek, the artist's final utterance before dying. His deviance from his private religion of art in favor of the Woman's heresy of love has proved fatal.

Murphy is the next of Beckett's works to feature a male character who has devised a special religion for himself, as well as a female character who tries to dissuade him from practising it.[12] The male character, Mur-phy, is a former theology student who becomes romantically involved with, then engaged to, a prostitute named Celia. Unfortunately for Celia, the love of women and, indeed, of all worldly things runs counter to Murphy's uniquely personal religion of self.

From his study of Spinoza and Schopenhauer, Murphy has concluded that absolute freedom of will can be attained through the transcendence of worldly desire. Spinoza holds self-transcendence to be a supreme good; for once an individual has renounced the world, he is able to make his volitions conform to divine reason and thereby experience the "intellectual love of God."[13] Spinoza distinguishes the love of God clearly from self-love, which he believes to be the root of all moral evil. Murphy, however, either is unaware of this position or has dismissed it from mind on the basis that God does not exist. For, as Beckett's parody of Spinoza in the epigraph to chapter six indicates, Murphy's behavior is based not on the intellectual love of God but on the love of himself.[14]

The self he loves is, in Schopenhauerian terms, his will-less self: Murphy believes that by loving it he can attain to complete freedom from deterministic influence. According to Schopenhauer we are all subject to an inner striving force, "the will to live," which drives us unceasingly towards the gratification of physical and psychological needs.[15] As will-motivated (or "willing") subjects we consistently treat people as the means to our own well-being. We are all basically selfish.

Yet it is open to us to deny our selfishness. In search of a better life, Schopenhauer notes, the mystic (of whatever persuasion) traditionally dedicates himself to voluntary chastity, renounces all worldly goods, and learns to welcome every "injury, ignominy and insult" (*World* 1:493) the world has to offer. As a result of his deliberate denial of the will to live, the mystic's willing self languishes and his latent will-less self—the part of himself that is free from desire—comes to the fore. When this happens, he finds himself completely free from selfish desire and totally indifferent to the world at large—which for him fades into "Nothing" (*World* 1:532).

Murphy eventually experiences "Nothing." But in a succession of episodes Beckett demonstrates satirically that the path he follows in pursuit of freedom is one of imperfect asceticism and also that his assumption that freedom *from* will is equivalent to freedom *of* will is mistaken. Early in the novel Murphy is revealed as too weak to undertake voluntary chastity: though his will-less self wants to deny Celia, his willing self craves her, and it is in answer to this craving that he temporarily subscribes to the heresy of love and has sexual relations with her. For the sake of avoiding this heresy and devoting himself exclusively to his religion of self, he leaves Celia and takes a job in a nearby mental hospital. Here, through his association with one of the patients, Mr. Endon, he attains to "Nothing"; however, because he reaches it by the wrong route—by way of dedication to self rather than to selflessness—his experience of it is accompanied by an unprecedented "torment of mind" (*Murphy* 168) and is followed by a series of events beyond his control (events demonstrating that he is not free), leading ultimately to his death.[16]

Significantly, it is Murphy's adherence to his religion of self rather than to the heresy of love that brings about his downfall. Celia is not an agent of destruction like the Woman in "Assumption"; for that reason, and because she is ultimately less selfish than Murphy, she is presented more sympathetically than either of these characters. In the last chapter of *Murphy* there is a particularly poignant scene in which she helps her grandfather, Mr. Kelly, fly his kite in the park. Beckett hints that Mr. Kelly's "tired heart" (192) will probably fail him in the not-too-distant future and that with his death Celia will be left alone. If she had married Murphy and been permitted to leave her sordid profession, she might have found comfort in a child—a child, perhaps, who enjoyed flying kites. Unfortunately, however, she has been unable to control the course of events, and Beckett's description of her in the novel's closing sentences, wheeling Mr. Kelly out of the park at the command of the attendants, emphasizes how little life has in store for her now. "Celia toiled along the narrow path into the teeth of the wind, then faced north up the wide hill. There was no shorter way home. The yellow hair fell across her face. . . . She closed her eyes. *All out*" (192). Celia's case is pathetic, because she can do nothing to prevent the death of her grandfather and lacks the financial and educational resources to start a new life for herself in any but a futureless job. Beckett ends the novel as a lament—a personal and sincere, rather than ironic, lament—for her inability to determine her own happiness and her impotence in the face of death.

Like Murphy, the first-person narrator of Beckett's four *nouvelles* is well-educated: he mentions his university tutor twice and alludes in various places to Wordsworth, Heraclitus, and Dante; and, again like Murphy, he has made a private religion of spurning the pleasures of the world in order to achieve the mystical experience of "Nothing."[17] "What mattered to me in my dispeopled kingdom," he says in *First Love* "was supineness in the mind, the dulling of the self and of that residue of execrable frippery known as the non-self and even the world, for short" (*Prose* 6). Because this "dulling of the world" is something the narrator experiences in all four *nouvelles,* all four have a curiously dreamlike atmosphere. In *The Expelled* the narrator comments, indeed, that his everyday experience is "most dreamlike" (*Prose* 22), while in *The Calma-*

tive he speaks of moving along "in a dream" (*Prose* 35) and at one point asks rhetorically, "Into what nightmare thingness am I fallen?" (*Prose* 42). Throughout the *nouvelles* he describes the world about him in the vaguest of terms, hinting that the action takes place in either Ireland or France but offering no very definite evidence as to which.[18]

The dreamlike quality of *First Love* suggests that its title may derive from a case Freud discusses in *The Interpretations of Dreams*. In the case in question, the subject is a physician who tells Freud that he dreamed of having a " 'primary syphilitic affection' " on his left forefinger. "If one takes the trouble to make an analysis," Freud comments, "one learns that 'primary affection' reduces itself to 'prima affectio' (first love), and that the repulsive sore, in the words of [the physician], proves to be 'the representative of wish-fulfilments charged with intense emotion.' "[19] In other words, the physician would like to experience his first love affair but fears the consequences, both emotional and physical. Similarly, though in *First Love* the narrator finds that he has fallen in love with a woman he initially calls Lulu, then Anna, he is unhappy at the thought that she has lured him away from a life of ascetic self-denial.[20] "What goes by the name of love," he says, "is banishment" (*Prose* 6)—banishment from a life that might have led to the mystic's experience of "Nothing."

He is embittered by his first direct experience of love, finding it an intrusive distraction from solitary self communion. Aware that we may find him inexperienced and naive, he deliberately seeks to either shock or insult us. "Would I," he asks at one point, "have been tracing [Lulu/Anna's] name in old cowshit if my love had been pure and disinterested? And with my devil's finger into the bargain, which I then sucked. Come now!" (*Prose* 9). The impatient "Come now!" with which this passage ends finds an even more aggressive counterpart in another passage, in which he starts to explain why he behaved as he did, then breaks off abruptly with the comment that he had "other reasons [too,] better not wasted on cunts like you" (*Prose* 8). Here the narrator dismisses us harshly because he is all too aware (but does not wish to admit to us) that his banishment from the mystical experience of "Nothing" is self-imposed.

For in spite of his wish to avoid worldly pleasure, the narrator finds himself (like Murphy before him) at the mercy of his sexual cravings. Though he would like to spurn Lulu/Anna, his body yearns for her, and it is because of this yearning that he allows himself to suppress some of his misgivings about love. When he discovers that she is a prostitute, he is untroubled by the thought that she might infect him with some form of venereal disease. What bothers him is that involvement with her will

oblige him to forego the life of introspective self-denial he has relished
in the past. As soon as Lulu/Anna gives birth to a baby, the narrator
leaves her, because the prospect of having to love both mother and child
would make greater demands on his life than he is prepared to accept.
His devotion to a private religion of self precludes anything more than a
brief dalliance with the heresy of love.

Like the main character in "Assumption," Krapp in *Krapp's Last Tape*
is devoted to a self-styled religion of art, though it is a religion that
derives from Proust rather than Joyce.[21] On tape at the age of thirty-
nine he speaks of "that memorable night in March . . . when suddenly I
saw the whole thing. The vision at last" (*Krapp* 15–16). The vision he
describes has an important counterpart in a passage at the end of *Le
temps retrouvé,* where Proust's narrator too sees "the whole thing"—
sees, that is, how the novel we know as *A la recherche du temps perdu*
should be written.[22]

That novel is to derive, as Beckett tells us in his 1931 essay on Proust,
from the narrator's successive experiences of the "miracle" of involuntary
memory.[23] Proust's narrator ultimately dedicates himself to a religion of
art—to the "vocation" of writing; he envisions the task before him as
being so demanding as to become "the harshest school of life and the
true last judgment" (*recherche* 3:880). Similarly, Krapp undertakes the
task of translating *his* vision into a work of literature in a spirit of determined self-sacrifice: the taped memory of his excitement over that
"memorable night in March" (*Krapp* 15) will, he thinks, sustain him
against the trials and privations to come.

Foremost amongst these privations is the sacrifice of love and friendship. Proust's narrator speaks for the artist's need to isolate himself from
the rest of society: he holds love to be a waste of intellectual energy—
the hopeless pursuit of a constantly changing object of desire by a
constantly changing subject—and considers friendship to be a cowardly retreat from the difficult, essentially solitary task of artistic
creation.[24] Nevertheless, friendship has a part to play in an artist's
life, and he speaks of his need as an artist to venture occasionally into
society.

Krapp takes a more extreme view of artistic self-isolation than Proust.
Rather than permit himself even the occasional dalliance with "des jeunes
filles en fleurs," he breaks off with a woman he deeply loves shortly
after his vision and therefore limits his sexual life to masturbation and
casual encounters with prostitutes. Why he does this is implicit in his
description of the vision: "What I suddenly saw then was this, that the
belief that I had been going on all my life, namely—[KRAPP *switches off*

impatiently, winds tape forward, switches on again]—great granite rocks the foam flying up in the light of the lighthouse and the wind-gauge spinning like a propeller, clear to me at last that the dark I have always struggled to keep under is in reality my most—[KRAPP *curses, switches off, winds tape forward, switches on again*]—unshatterable association until my dissolution of storm and night with the light of the understanding and the fire" (16).

As James Knowlson has shown, "the dark" Krapp had always struggled to keep under prior to his vision is the irrational, unconscious part of his mind, whereas "the light" represents his intellect.[25] What the vision has revealed to him is that the unconscious is a rich source of material for art and that artistic creation is (as for Proust) a matter of the intellect's translating this material into language. Where Proust believed love to be a waste of the intellectual energy that could be applied to artistic creation, Krapp holds both love and friendship to be a waste of that energy and an unjustifiable dissipation of the dark, the material from which art is made. Krapp rejects love and friendship more firmly than Proust, regarding them as heretical departures from his own private religion of art.

Knowlson points out that Krapp's behavior has a counterpart in the practice of an early group of Christian heretics, the Manicheans, who dedicated themselves to "the light"—the intellect—and sought to suppress "the dark"—passion and sensuality. "Krapp," says Knowlson, "has equated woman with darkness and the irrational";[26] in his "Farewell to Love" Krapp recalls that "I said again I thought it was hopeless and no good going on and she agreed, without opening her eyes. [*Pause.*] I asked her to look at me and after a few moments—[*pause*]—after a few moments she did, but the eyes just slits, because of the glare. I bent over her to get them in the shadow and they opened. [*Pause. Low.*] Let me in" (16–17). The reason Krapp asks the woman to look at him (and shades her eyes in order that she might) is to gauge her reaction to his proposal that they end their relationship. She has said that she agrees it is "hopeless" going on, but Krapp is not satisfied: only by looking into her eyes—traditionally the windows of the soul—will he know how she really feels. As the stage directions indicate, he is deeply moved to discover that she is willing to open them and "let [him] in"—that is, welcome the continuance of his love.[27] But although the sensual part of himself, represented by the shadow, wishes to maintain the relationship, the passion he feels cannot survive the harsh glare of his intellectual decision to devote himself exclusively to art. In this passage, as in the play as a whole, there is a strong sense of regret: Krapp at thirty-nine is obviously sorry to break with the woman and at sixty-nine regrets having sacrificed so much for the sake of an "opus magnum" that, unlike Proust's great novel, is a colossal failure.[28]

At sixty-nine, only a year short of the traditional three score and ten, Krapp is approaching the ultimate darkness, death. His mother and father are both dead, and the woman in the punt is present only on tape. Intensely lonely, Krapp finds solace partly in memories, partly in drink, and partly in visits from Fanny, that "bony old ghost of a whore" (18). Though his ability to laugh sardonically at himself has not left him, he recognizes clearly that his "best years are gone. When there was a chance of happiness" (20). Krapp would like to think that it has all been worth it, for the sake of his art; however, he gives himself away when he reveals that he now spends much of his time rereading Theodor Fontane's sentimental novel, *Effi Briest*, weeping as he reflects on Effi's failed love affair and as he reflects, too, on what his own life might have been like.

The hopelessness and pathos of Krapp's situation arise from his having taken too seriously Proust's call for the artist to isolate himself from the rest of the world. The narrator's willingness even to dally with "des jeunes filles en fleurs" is in Krapp's view heresy; once we recognise this, we can see why Beckett incorporated the Manichean dichotomy of light and dark into the play. Krapp is Beckett's portrait of the artist as an old solitary—a solitary all too aware of the folly of his devotion to an unnecessarily ascetic religion of art.

The implicit alternatives to bidding farewell to love are of considerably greater interest in *Krapp's Last Tape* and *Murphy* than they are in "Assumption" and *First Love*. While it is not clear that refusing to become involved with the Woman would have made a difference to the artistic endeavours of the main character of "Assumption," or that staying with Lulu/Anna would have prevented the narrator of *First Love* from achieving the mystic's experience of "Nothing," the wistfulness of Krapp's description of breaking off with the woman in the punt suggests that he would have done better to have devoted himself to her rather than to his art. Similarly, in revealing in the last chapter of *Murphy* that Celia has devoted herself to the care of her aging uncle, Mr. Kelly, Beckett is inviting us to reflect on how much better her life and Murphy's might have been if Murphy had married her instead of adhering to his private religion of self.

Though to friends in a pub Beckett might say that love is "only fucking," the fact that love features so prominently in "Assumption," *First Love, Murphy,* and *Krapp's Last Tape* suggests that it is more important to him that he might care to admit. His male characters may regard love as heresy, but in *Murphy* and *Krapp's Last Tape* in particular we can see that love's absence has a significant influence on the course of either their lives or the lives of the women they have loved. While the absence of love makes for misery, in its presence there is, as Krapp says, "a chance of happiness."

NOTES

1. Deirdre Bair, *Samuel Beckett: A Biography* (London: Jonathan Cape, 1978), 481.

2. Beckett's remark about love appears in chapter 20 of Bair's biography, which is concerned with the years 1955–57. In *The Samuel Beckett Manuscripts: A Study* (Boston: G. K. Hall, 1979), 61, Richard L. Admussen reveals that Beckett began work on the first manuscript of *Krapp's Last Tape* on 20 February 1958.

3. "Assumption" was first published in *transition* 16–17 (June 1929), 268–71; page numbers are given in the text. "Assumption" contains a number of minor typographical errors which I have corrected silently.

4. James Joyce, *A Portrait of the Artist as a Young Man* (1916; rpt. Harmondsworth, Middlesex: Penguin, 1973), 218.

5. In *The Development of Samuel Beckett's Fiction* (Urbana: University of Illinois Press, 1984), 16, Rubin Rabinovitz identifies the "buffoon in the loft" as a conductor and comments that "the conductor and organist are metaphorical representations of pyschological impulses: one demands an utterance; the other, capable of producing it, does not."

6. These phrases are, of course, from Samuel Beckett's "Three Dialogues," first published in 1949. See *Proust/Three Dialogues: Samuel Beckett and Georges Duthuit* (London: John Calder, 1965), 103.

7. D. H. Lawrence, *Women in Love* (1921; rpt. Harmondsworth, Middlesex: Penguin, 1973), 88.

8. Ibid., 101, 23, 518. Lawrence's chief exponent of orthodoxy in *Women in Love* is the largely autobiographical Birkin, who speaks at one point to Ursula of the mystic union he wants to achieve with her: " 'What I want is a strange conjunction with you—' he said quietly; '—not meeting and mingling;—you are quite right:—but an equilibrium, a pure balance of two single beings:—as the stars balance each other' " (164). Further evidence of Beckett's interest in Lawrence is to be found in Beckett's unpublished first novel, *Dream of Fair to Middling Women*, 63, where the main character, Belacqua Shuah, says in a poem to a woman called the Smeraldina-Rima that he wishes to be "irrevocably" at one with her, and at one

> . . . with the birdless, cloudless, colourless skies
> One with the bright purity of the fire
> [O]f which we are and for which we must die
> A rapturous strange death and be entire.
> Like syzegetic stars, supernly bright,
> Conjoined in One and in the Infinite!

Interestingly, the artist in "Assumption" also wishes to be at "one with the birdless, cloudless colourless skies, in infinite fulfilment" (271)—the fulfilment, as we shall see, of love for the nameless woman who enters his life.

9. The blue flower derives from Novalis's unfinished novel, *Heinrich von Ofterdingen*, published posthumously in 1802. In it the main character, Heinrich, dreams a dream in which a blue flower figures importantly. This blue flower, a symbol in the novel of Heinrich's love for the character Mathilde, was destined to become the widely recognized symbol of all Romantic longing. See Henry and Mary Garland, "Heinrich von Ofterdingen," in *The Oxford Companion to German Literature* (Oxford: Clarendon Press, 1976), 366. Vega in the Lyre is the constellation Bloom and Stephen observe in the "Ithaca" section of *Ulysses* when they come together in a moment of spiritual union. See James Joyce, *Ulysses* (1922; rpt. Harmondsworth, Middlesex: Penguin, 1968), 624. Beckett mentions Vega again in his unpublished novel, *Dream of Fair to Middling Women* (completed 1932), 63 and passim, where the Smeraldina is described as his "douce Vega."

10. See, for example, St. John of the Cross's poem, "Stanzas of the Soul," in which union with God is described as follows: "Oh, night that joined Beloved with lover, Lover transformed in the Beloved!/Upon my flowery breast, Kept wholly for himself alone,/There he stayed sleeping, and I caressed him, And the fanning of the cedars made a breeze," quoted from *The Complete Works of St. John of the Cross*, trans. E. Allison Peers, 3 vols. (London: Burns, Oates & Washbourne, 1953), 1:326.

11. *A Portrait of the Artist as a Young Man*, 217.

12 *Murphy* was first published by George Routledge & Sons Ltd. (London, 1938). All quotations are from the Calder reprint (London, 1970); page numbers are given in the text.

13. See S. V. Keeling, *Descartes* (London: Oxford University Press, 1968), 234, for a helpful commentary on Spinoza's concept of the intellectual love of God.

14. The epigraph, "Amor intellectualis quo Murphy se ipsum amat" ["The intellectual love with which Murphy loves himself," 76], is a parody of Spinoza's well-known proposition "Deus se ipsum amore intellectuali infinito amat" ["God loves himself with an infinite intellectual love"], Book V, Prop 35 of *Ethica Ordine Geometrico Demonstrata*.

15. Arthur Schopenhauer, *The World as Will and Idea*, trans. R. B. Haldane and J. Kemp, 3 vols. (London: Routledge & Kegan Paul, 1948), 1:141–43. All quotations from *The World as Will and Idea* are from this edition; page numbers are given in the text, preceded by *World*.

16. For a fuller discussion of Murphy's experience of "Nothing," see my "*Murphy's* Metaphysics," *Journal of Beckett Studies* 5 (Autumn 1979), 9–23.

17. All quotations from *First Love, The Expelled, The Calmative,* and *The End* are from Samuel Beckett, *Collected Shorter Prose, 1945–80* (London: John Calder, 1984). Page numbers are given in the text, preceded by *Prose*. This essay's one quotation from *Premier Amour* (in note 18) is from the Minuit edition (Paris 1970). All quotations from *L'Expulsé, Le Clamant,* and *La Fin* are from *Nouvelles*

et Textes pour rien (Paris: Minuit, 1955); page numbers are given in the text.

The narrator mentions his tutor in *First Love* and *The End* (*Prose*, 9, 62); he alludes to Wordsworth in *The Expelled*: "Recollecting these emotions, with the celebrated advantage of tranquillity . . . " (*Prose* 31–32); he mentions Heraclitus by name in the same *nouvelle* (*Prose* 26) and alludes to Dante both in *The Calmative*, where he mentions "the wood that darkens the mouth of hell" (*Prose* 40), and in *First Love*, where he mentions "Giudecca" (*Prose* 17), the last of the four divisions of Circle IX of Hell (see *Inferno* xxxiv.117).

18. When the narrator says in *First Love* that "what constitutes the charm of our country, apart of course from its scant population, and this without help of the meanest contraceptive, is that all is derelict, with the sole exception of history's ancient faeces" (*Prose* 8), he seems to be hinting that the story is set in Ireland. But in the original French *Premier Amour*, 17, when he says of Lulu, "N'étant pas française elle disait, Loulou. Moi aussi, n'étant pas français non plus, je disais Loulou comme elle," it appears that the setting is France and that Lulu and the narrator are expatriates—possibly Irish expatriates. In *The Expelled*, the narrator says he is in a capital city (*Prose* 27), which may be either Dublin or Paris but could well be some other capital. Amounts of money are given in sterling in *The Calmative*, and these appear in the same form (not in the equivalent French amounts) in the *Le Calmant*. Thus "a penny," for example, in *The Calmative* (*Prose* 40) appears as "un penny" in *Le Calmant* (53), and "One and six" (*Prose* 46) as "Un shilling . . . six pence" in *Le Calmant* (68). Similarly, in *The End*, "A penny . . . tuppence" (*Prose* 65) is given as "Un penny, deux pence" in *La Fin* (*Prose* 112). This suggests that the setting in each case is Ireland (or possibly Britain); however, there is no explicit confirmation of this in either nouvelle.

19. Sigmund Freud, "The Interpretation of Dreams," in *The Basic Writings of Sigmund Freud*, trans. A. A. Brill (New York: Modern Library, 1938), 234.

20. I am indebted to Peter Falkenberg, a colleague in the University of Canterbury German Department, for suggesting to me that the name "Lulu" is taken from Frank Wedekind's two plays about a character named Lulu, a woman of loose morals. See Frank Wedekind, *Five Tragedies of Sex*, trans. Frances Fawcett and Stephen Spender (London: Vision Press, 1952). Mr. Falkenberg has also suggested that the name "Anna" may derive from the work of the Dadaist writer Kurt Schwitters, who wrote extensively about a fictional character named Anna Blume.

21. All quotations from *Krapp's Last Tape* are from Samuel Beckett, *Collected Shorter Plays* (London: Faber, 1984); page numbers are given in the text, preceded by *Krapp*.

22. *A la recherche du temps perdu*, 3 vols. (Paris, Gallimard, 1954), 3:899. All quotations are from this edition; page numbers are given in the text. Beckett's debt to Proust in *Krapp's Last Tape* has been commented on by various critics, though most fully by Arthur K. Oberg in "*Krapp's Last Tape* and the Proustian Vision," *Modern Drama* 9 (Dec. 1966), 33–38 (rpt. in *Theatre Workbook 1: Samuel Beckett*, Krapp's Last Tape, ed. James Knowlson (London: Brutus Books, 1980), 151–57; and by Rosette Lamont in "Krapp, un Anti-Proust," in

Beckett, ed. Tom Bishop and Raymond Federman (Paris: L'Herne, 1976), 295–305 (trans. Helen Wehringer as "Krapp, and anti-Proust" and published in *Theatre Workbook 1: Samuel Beckett,* Krapp's Last Tape, 158–73). Oberg and Lamont reach conclusions quite different from mine.

23. *Proust,* in *Proust/Three Dialogues,* 34. *Proust* was first published by Chatto & Windus (London, 1931), as the seventh volume in the Dolphin Books Series. All quotations are from the Calder edition; page numbers are given in the text, preceded by "Proust."

24. See *recherche* 2:93, and 3:100, for comments to this effect about love; and 2:394, for comments about friendship. Beckett either alludes to or quotes from these passages in *Proust,* 63, 58, and 64–65, respectively. As I have shown in "Beckett, Proust and Schopenhauer," *Contemporary Literature* 19 (Spring 1978), 178–79, Beckett distorts Proust's view of friendship, *Proust,* 64–65.

25. James Knowlson, "*Krapp's Last Tape:* The Evolution of a Play, 1958–75," *Journal of Beckett Studies* 1 (Winter 1976), 60–61.

26. Knowlson, 62.

27. This is even clearer in Beckett's French translation of the play, where "Let me in" appears as "M'ont laissé entrer" (see *La dernière bande, suivi de Cendres* [Paris: Minuit, 1959], 25.

28. "Seventeen copies sold," confesses Krapp, "of which eleven at trade price to free circulating libraries beyond the seas" (*Krapp* 18).

FICTION

"Meet in Paradize"
Beckett's Shavian Women

KRISTIN MORRISON

The allusion to Hesione Hushabye in "A Wet Night" is one of the few
Shavian references in all of Beckett's work. Dante, Shakespeare, Mat-
thew, Mark, Luke and John, major poets, minor poets, philosophers,
mathematicians: writers of various kinds are pressed into frequent service; but Bernard Shaw, rarely.[1]

In this fourth story of *More Pricks Than Kicks,* as guests arrive at the
Fricas' party, the elder Frica responds fondly to P. B.'s greeting with
" 'Too good of you to come,' she hushabied, 'too good of you.' "[2] She,
like Hesione Hushabye of *Heartbreak House,* is hostess at a motley gathering of eccentrics. Her welcome soothes, hushes, the Polar Bear's
"squalled . . . 'God *wat* a night!' " And her unspoken view of him as a
child or a poppet—"She wished she could dandle him on her knee"—
reproduces Hesione's maternal attitude toward all men, of whatever age
or station.[3]

The allusion consists of one adapted word, a little joke is made for
those who happen to notice, connection with *Heartbreak House* ends
there, and the narrative moves on. Then, in a later story in the same
collection, a character is introduced who seems like a grotesque version
of Hesione: she has a "sound-alike" name, Hermione; she is "powerfully
built" (just as Hesione is "statuesque," with "nobly modelled neck" and
"magnificent black hair"[4]); she wears black and mauve (like Hesione's
"rich robe of black pile"); without her crutches she is as "unsupported"
as Hesione without her corset; both women cast enchantment on men
with whom they associate; and while Hesione's own "missing sexual
hemisphere" (her husband, Hector) merely wanders away occasionally,
Hermione has never been "rounded off" and continues in nymphoma-
nia. Finally, just as Hesione Hushabye presides over a vital alliance, a
spiritual marriage between Ellie Dunn and Captain Shotover, Hermione
Näutzsche, her grotesque counterpart, officially witnesses Belacqua's passive nuptuals in "What a Misfortune."[5]

Whether this particular extended parallel between a Beckettian character and a Shavian one was deliberate is not the issue here. That Hesione Hushabye was somewhere in Beckett's mind as he wrote *More Pricks Than Kicks* is clear enough from that earlier explicit reference in "A Wet Night."

That Beckett would at all draw on Shaw's work raises the inevitable question of other possible points of similarity, intended or not. And once such a question is raised, some interesting parallels begin to present themselves. Most striking of all is the attitude toward women which many of Beckett's earlier male characters share with many of Shaw's. For Belacqua, for Murphy, for Krapp, for the narrator of *First Love,* as for Captain Shotover, Hector Hushabye, and Jack Tanner, woman is the enslaving seductress who deflects man from his proper work, his proper self. Murphy's terse complaint that women "can't love for five minutes without wanting it abolished in brats and house bloody wifery"[6] is matched by Jack Tanner's more elaborate argument that "vitality in a woman is a blind fury of creation" which sacrifices man as a mere "instrument of that purpose" and makes him her slave.[7] Thus in Shaw's view enmity is set up between the man with a sense of individual purpose and woman in the grip of Creative Evolution: "Of all human struggles there is none so treacherous and remorseless as the struggle between the artist man and the mother woman. Which shall use up the other? that is the issue between them. And it is all the deadlier because, in your romanticist cant [Tanner says to infatuated Octavius], they love one another"(49). Certain that he is not the slave of love nor its dupe, Tanner advises Tavy to learn wisdom from the bee: "If women could do without our work, and we ate their children's bread instead of making it, they would kill us as the spider kills her mate or as the bees kill the drone"(75).

The fact that Beckett's "heroes" are not men of genius who must flee women in order to realize their individual gifts does not invalidate the Shavian parallel: it simply makes it the more ironic. Artists manqué, they are also husbands and fathers manqué.

In *More Pricks Than Kicks,* Belacqua's history is a series of half-hearted encounters with and escapes from a variety of women. Even at his most willing—which is not very—Belacqua sees marriage and sexual alliance as a form of self-destruction. In his escapade with ITless Ruby the substitution of sex for suicide seems reasonable since *"l'Amour et la Mort—* caesura—*n'est qu'une mesme chose"* (100); later the happiness of his short marriage with the maimed Lucy seems to depend on a kind of rapport with her great physical suffering; then finally, in the only conjunction where the details of the marriage arrangements are described, the wedding announcement is likened to an epitaph (122). Though Belacqua perceives the nuptial sacrament itself with doctrinal accuracy as "an outward and visible sign," his sense of being "cauterized" (rather than, as the theologians have it, "marked") with this sign indicates both the pain and the mutilation he fears from Holy Matrimony (140). Later, after the ceremony itself, in flight with his bride Thelma nee bboggs, when Belacqua decides " 'it is right that they who are loved should live,' " the narrator comments, "It was from this moment that he used to date in after years his crucial loss of interest in himself, as in a grape beyond his grasp" (150). Thus Belacqua on his way to the Bower of Bliss finds himself once again in Melancholy's Shrine: straining to burst one grape he loses the other that is himself. Marriage, sexual alliance with a woman, has thrust him into "life," ordinary conventional life, and thus barred him from his real work, his real self. That he seems not to know what this real work is, what his real self is, simply intensifies the sense of mutilation and loss associated with these intrusive women.

Even Belacqua's actual death is connected with women and with the state of marriage. Throughout "Yellow," that fatal penultimate story, Belacqua comments on the persistent presence of women attendants in the hospital, all *doing something* to him: "Now two further women, there was no end to them" (172). Then the operation itself is associated with a nuptial ceremony: "He bounced up on the table like a bridegroom" (174). The surgeon, fresh from serving as best man at an actual wedding, becomes Belacqua's "best man," quite literally and carelessly giving him away to death.

Murphy's experience, of course, is similar. In loving Celia he is bound to the world, rather than to the chair of his deliverance from that world. In this novel, too, there continues the association of love and marriage with death: "those sanguine days when as a theological student he had used to lie awake night after night with Bishop Bouvier's *Supplementum ad Tractatum de Matrimonio* under his pillow. What a work that was to be sure! A Ciné Bleu scenario in goatish Latin. Or pondering Christ's parthian shaft: *It is finished*" (71–72). Even that frequent allusion to the horse leech's daughter couples love and death, sex and destruction,[8] as do various other elements in the novel such as the story of Cooper's two loves (206), the wordy aphorism that women "never quite kill the thing they think they love, lest their instinct for artificial respiration should go abegging" (202–3), and indeed the very "climax" of the novel, in which Murphy's desire to return to Celia and sex coincides with his explosion into the superfine chaos of his death, orgasm and annihilation serving as mutual metaphors.

The comic tone of Jack Tanner's "boa constrictor,"[9] Hector Hush-abye's "vampire women, demon women,"[10] and the various verbal jabs at women in *More Pricks Than Kicks* and *Murphy* are not really so different from each other; in each case the narrating voice or the dramatic situation suggests that the male speaker is both justified in his perception and ludicrous in his response to women. These females *are* disruptive; they *are* dangerous; and indeed these men *do* lose themselves because of them. But in Shaw's work such individual loss is Creative Evolution's gain, and thus the comedy of man domesticated by woman in her search for a father for the Superman is basically genial in tone, optimistic in intention. For Beckett, however, the situation is grimmer. Sexuality is not positive in its procreative activity; eros is both maimed and maiming.[11] In *More Pricks Than Kicks* and *Murphy,* the central male characters die either at the hands of the woman or, in imagination, in the arms of a woman; and both works sardonically conclude with the hero's most recent woman alive and doing well for herself: Smeraldina hooks a new lover and Celia efficiently resumes her career and her familial relationship with Mr. Kelly. The final quip, "So it goes in the world," gives *More Pricks* a sprightlier end than *Murphy,* with its rather melancholy *"All Out,"* but in both works it is clear that, in relation to the central male character, women are the successful survivors.

One mechanism which contributes to female success in both Beckett's early work and Shaw's plays is the fact that the women, unlike the central male character, are not burdened by thought. "The normal woman of sense asks 'what?' in preference to 'why?'" the narrator of "Love and Lethe" asserts (adding parenthetically that "this is very deep"), while the hero is swamped by "the usual pale cast."[12] The naturally happy-go-lucky Smeraldina, widow to the prophetically souled Belacqua, despite a momentary sense of her own mortality ("She had died in part," 187), readily resumes Everyday Inauthentic Existence: "The Smeraldina, far far away with the corpse and her own spiritual equivalent in the bone-yard by the sea, was dwelling at length on how she would shortly gratify the former, even as it, while still unfinished, had that of Lucy, and blot the latter for ever from her memory" (190). The narrating voice denies in a footnote that Belacqua while still living (i.e., "unfinished") rationalized his remarriage as a way of "gratifying" the corpse of Lucy, though clearly this is what Smerry does as she accepts Hairy: "Perhaps after all . . . this is what darling Bel would wish" (190). But her ploy is a double one: she must rationalize her remarriage, her own pursuit of life, and she must also refuse to acknowledge her inevitable death, blot forever from her memory that earlier sense of her own potential for corpsehood.

All the women in *More Pricks* pursue life with energy. Alba takes home whom she will when she will; Ruby, though her IT has run dry, seduces Belacqua; maimed Lucy gets her man; even the embarrassing derelict sells Bel seats in Heaven against his will. And Smeraldina, despite her brief realization of mortality, remains "a fine strapping lump of a girl or woman, theatre nurse in "Yellow" from the neck down, bursting with Lebensgeist at every suture, itching to be taken at her—very much so to speak—face value, and by force for preference" (188). Like Shaw's Ann Whitefield, Smeraldina can be taken "by force" only when she, as the stronger, makes it happen.

In *First Love* the reluctant male "lover" does finally succeed in escaping the predatory female but only after fulfilling her purpose. In this piece, too, marriage and death are juxtaposed, right from the opening sentence: "I associate, rightly or wrongly, my marriage with the death of my father, in time. That other links exist, on other planes, between these two affairs, is not impossible."[13] This narrator thinks "women smell a rigid phallus ten miles away" (18) and feels himself at the mercy of and betrayed by his own erection. The Lulu, or Anna (name he says doesn't matter) who pursues him does so with an ingenuity and vigor worthy of Shaw's Ann Whitefield, though the scene Beckett presents is more physically sexual than any of Shaw's: "I woke next morning quite spent, my clothes in disorder, the blanket likewise, and Anna beside me, naked naturally. One shudders to think of her exertions. . . . I looked at my member. If only it could have spoken! Enough about that. It was my night of love" (31). Like Ann pursuing Jack Tanner in *Man and Superman,* she has had her way with him; and he (despite the shield of a well-placed stewpan) like Jack has not been able to resist the assault. Indeed, his passivity and concomitant mental blanking out of sexual response, though different in mode from Jack's behavior, is explained in terms Tanner understands: "One is no longer oneself, on such occasions, and it is painful to be no longer oneself. . . . What goes by the name of love is banishment, with now and then a postcard from the homeland. . . . When she had finished and my self been resumed, mine own, the mitigable, with the help of a brief torpor, it was alone" (18). This ecstasy, this orgasm, has taken him away from himself in a way that he resents. Only when alone is "it," his self, present to him, a sentiment shared with Belacqua and Murphy, and one the independent Jack Tanner and Don Juan also experience in their own ways.

Struggling to hold this woman at a distance, the narrator of *First Love* recounts arguments and strategies which are also found in *Man and Superman.* Beckett writes: "So you don't want me to come any more, she said. It's incredible the way they repeat what you've just said to them, as if they risked faggot and fire in believing their ears. I told her to come just the odd time" (19) and then a page later, "Next of course she desired to know what I meant by the odd time, that's what you get for opening your mouth. Once a week? Once in ten days? Once a fortnight? I replied less often . . . to the point of no more. . . . And the next day . . . I abandoned the bench" (20–21). Similarly Shaw's Don Juan complains that after a woman has been won "she always said, first, 'At last, the barriers are down,' and second, 'When will you come again?' "[14] She becomes "bent wholly on making sure of her prey," and he becomes "famous for running away" (128). Beckett's narrator runs away when Anna, refusing to abort their child at his urging, gives birth and he finds he cannot bear the infant's cries.

Much of what Shaw has written in his Epistle Dedicatory to *Man and Superman* might well serve as comment on *First Love*: "It does not occur to [persons who are shocked by "the tragi-comic love chase of the man by the woman"] that if women were as fastidious as men, morally or physically, there would be an end of the race" (11). "There are no limits to male hypocrisy in this matter. No doubt there are moments when man's sexual immunities are made acutely humiliating to him. When the terrible moment of birth arrives, its supreme importance and its superhuman effort and peril, in which the father has no part, dwarf him into the meanest insignificance: he slinks out of the way . . . " (11). In similar fashion, Beckett's narrator's grotesque passivity also has a certain hypocrisy about it (he may be at the mercy of his erection, but it is, after all, *his*); and his flight from the birth cries is indeed an expression of his sense of "acute humiliation" and "insignificance." His revulsion indicates rejection of both pain and basic human states (childhood and parenthood) in which he cannot participate autonomously, solipsistically.

The flaccid narrator of *First Love* flees to vague isolation and passivity in some unidentified elsewhere. One of Beckett's better known and more feisty characters poses his life choice in terms even closer to the ones Shaw actually uses. Krapp is Beckett's "artist man" and he, like Tanner and Don Juan, rejects bondage to a woman for the sake of his magnum opus. But successful resolve for a "less . . . engrossing sexual life" in his youth leads to a bitter old age in which it is clear that what he regrets most is, in fact, lost love.[15]

This sense that marriage, or sexual conjunction with a woman, is damaging to a man's peculiar genius, imperiling his individuality, his selfhood, is a notion shared by characters in both Shaw's work and Beckett's. And while there is a tragi-comic irony in the fact that Beckett's characters are *not* bubbling gene pools of extraordinary accomplishment and vitality (no temptation at all to Hesione Hushabye or Ann Whitefield), nonetheless male Beckettians may not be entirely alien to Shaw's world. Oddly enough, because of the very fact that they have no Shavian vision of a better future peopled by superior beings, their very resistance to conjugal enslavement makes them heroes of a sort, successfully defending their negative philosophy against the predatory women who pursue them: Hesione may *want* to dandle Polar Bear on her knee, but she does not succeed; Belacqua, Murphy, Krapp, and the narrator of *First Love* all eventually make their escapes, one way or another. If there is on the one hand no Superman to be engendered, nor on the other any great individual art to be produced, Beckett's men will still, with Shavian determination, shield their bodies against female exploitation and defend their own personal rights to misery and oddity.

Or so they say. But they are interestingly and revealingly conflicted: although the mothering Hesiones and manipulative Rubys, Lucys, and Annas are resisted, desire for union with a woman of a different kind haunts Beckett's work. Krapp's case is instructive: as an old man he is as much at the mercy of his erection as is the younger Belacqua and dallies willingly with Fanny, that "bony old ghost of a whore."[16] Thus "mere sex" is not the problem, but emotion, as his poignant last moment on stage illustrates. He clasps the tape recorder in surrogate embrace as it recites the words which enshrine his loving union with a woman many years before: his assertion that he would not want those years, that intense emotion, back again is pure bravado, belied by his replaying the passage and by his grief-stricken final posture. This artist-man knows all too well that he made an irrevocable and deadly mistake in sacrificing love to work, turning in to his "talent" rather than out to that idyllic woman.

Murphy, too, though earlier hating the part of himself that craved for Celia, after being lessoned by his experience with psychotic patients, did, in fact, intend to return to her: his "escape" is purely accidental, a comic consumation he did not at the end devoutly wish. To the extent that Celia herself may be seen as the central character in *Murphy* (not only the most sympathetic but also the only one who does not *seem* a puppet, the narrator's editorial remarks notwithstanding), to that extent Murphy's desire to return to her, to be united with her suggests desire on his part for another kind of self. It is, after all, not Celia herself who kills Murphy, despite his fears, but Murphy's own oddity which destroys him, choosing the garret, the gas fire, the chair rather than the conjugal bed.

Even Belacqua, despite his worry that conventional marriage destroys his "self," betrays a very interesting affinity with a particular woman at the opening of *More Pricks Than Kicks*—an affinity which his subsequent reluctant erotic career may be simply an attempt to deny. Studying the

Paradiso, he finds Beatrice's explanation of the spots on the moon rough going and is eager to move on, as the narrator puts it "impatient to get on to Piccarda" (9). The fact that Dante's Belacqua's namesake is "impatient" to progress seems a contradiction in terms; this original personification of sloth was only too willing to loiter among the late repentant of the Antepurgatory.[17] Beckett's Belacqua, however, is introduced in the first paragraph of *More Pricks Than Kicks* as being interested in Dante's Belacqua's celestial counterpart, Piccarda. Yes, it is true that the verses about her in any case follow those taxing ones about the moonspots; but Beckett as author could have chosen the subsequent lines about "Lorenzo in su la grada" as an object of Belacqua's pressing interest, St. Lawrence's torture being so appropriately "Beckettian."[18] The gentle ex-nun warrants a closer look precisely because she seems an odd goal for the usually unenthusiastic Bel.

Piccarda is Belacqua's counterpart in more ways than one. Just as, in Dante's poem, Balacqua is "content" to wait in Antepurgatory because his will had not been firmly set on repentance when he was alive, so Piccarda in the *Paradiso* is "content" to abide forever in the circle of the moon among those inconstant saints whose will was not set firmly enough on the good while they were alive. His sullen sloth in the *Purgatorio* is matched by her more positive joyous peace in the *Paradiso*.[19] With Beckett's Bel she has an additional bond. Piccarda's specific inconstancy had been her failure to maintain her vow to a heavenly spouse to lead a "higher life"; after being torn unwillingly and by violence from her convent, she was married and succumbed to ordinary life in "the world." Such conflict between spiritual marriage and carnal marriage is one Beckett's Belacqua can appreciate, torn as he is between the passions of his body and his desire to lead a quiet life. He is continually and against his will being ripped from the sweet cloister of himself, by his physical attraction to the Alba and others; and, like Piccarda, he succumbs to the ordinary formal relationships of ordinary people, a series of affairs and marriages. Like Piccarda, he has been unfaithful to a choice, a "vow," but unlike her he finds little peace. If Bel, studying the *Divine Comedy,* is "impatient to get on to Piccarda," it is not only to escape from ponderous medieval science. He actually has much in common with her and seems to realize that she constitutes his goal, belies his cynicism, and reveals what his real desire is: to be peacefully fixed in paradise rather than sullenly killing time in purgatory.

Piccarda—or someone like her, calm and contemplative—could possibly have supplied Belacqua with suitable model and mate. Certainly he has spent his life looking for some satisfactory alliance, only to go from disappointment to disappointment, like all of Beckett's male characters, finding sex and marriage personally disruptive rather than peacefully self-fulfilling. In *Heartbreak House,* Shaw presented a paradoxical alliance of the kind Belacqua never knew but could have appreciated: when Ellie Dunn announces that she has become Captain Shotover's wife "in heaven, where all true marriages are made" (148), she proclaims a sexless union of vital partners, one strong of soul, the other wise, and both quite peacefully linked in an idyllic night which bombers enliven but do not destroy. This conjugal union brings not death but "life with a blessing" (149). Unlike Murphy, unlike Belacqua, the benedict of this spiritual marriage survives explosion.

Such consummation is not to be granted, however, in Beckett's work. The consolation offered Smeraldina by the parson in the final story of *More Pricks Than Kicks* is perfunctory, comic, and of use only to a successful survivor: "Meet in Paradize [*sic*]" he advises (179), leaving the corpse of Belacqua to the grave and the lively widow to another suiter. For the defunct there is no Dantean apotheosis, no Piccarda, no Paradise: "Belacqua had often looked forward to meeting the girls, Lucy especially, hallowed and transfigured beyond the veil. What a hope! Death had already cured him of that naïveté" (181). Smerry, however, blotting such thoughts of death forever from her mind, lives (like Shaw's women of the Life Force) vigorously and triumphantly in the present, bursting, as Beckett says, with Lebensgeist.

NOTES

1. Inspection of the indices of books about Beckett tends to reveal either no listing of Shaw's name or else a single reference to Beckett's own frequently quoted refusal to endorse a tribute to Shaw in honor of the centenary of his birth on the grounds that Beckett would "give the whole unupsettable applecart for a sup of the Hawk's Well or the Saints', or a whiff of Juno, to go no further." Eoin O'Brien, in a recent book on Beckett, states there are only two references to Shaw in all of Beckett's writing: the quotation just cited and Belacqua's quip about "George Bernard Pygmalion" in *Dream of Fair to Middling Women,* unpublished manuscript, MS 1227/7/16/9, Beckett archives, University of Reading. See O'Brien, *The Beckett Country: Ireland in the Literature of Samuel Beckett* (London: Faber & Faber, 1986), 276f.

2. Samuel Beckett, "A Wet Night," in *More Pricks Than Kicks* (New York: Grove Press, 1972), 63.

3. Hesione calls Boss Mangan "Little Alf" (113); she considers her husband, Hector, "a baby" (110), and says openly, "It matters very little which of you [men] governs the country so long as we [lovely women] govern you" (146). George Bernard Shaw, *Heartbreak House,* rev. standard ed. (London: Penguin, 1964).

4. *Heartbreak House,* 58.

5. Samuel Beckett, "What a Misfortune," in *More Pricks Than Kicks,* 138.

6. Samuel Beckett, *Murphy* (New York: Grove Press, 1957), 36–37.

7. George Bernard Shaw, *Man and Superman* (New York: Bantam, 1967), 48–49.

8. If the reference is taken to be to Proverbs 30:15f, that passage contains as one of its illustrative examples of "things [that] say not, It is enough:/the grave; and the barren womb."

9. *Man and Superman,* 62.

10. *Heartbreak House,* 88.

11. See my article "Defeated Sexuality in the Plays and Novels of Samuel Beckett," *Comparative Drama* 14 (Spring 1980), 18–34, reprinted in *Drama in the Twentieth Century: Comparative and Critical Essays,* ed. Clifford Davidson et al. (New York: AMS Press, 1984), 223–39.

12. Samuel Beckett, "Love and Lethe," in *More Pricks Than Kicks,* 89, 95.

13. *"First Love" and Other Shorts* (New York: Grove Press, 1974), 11.

14. *Man and Superman,* 127.

15. For detailed analysis of this play see my *Canters and Chronicles: The Use of Narrative in the Plays of Samuel Beckett and Harold Pinter* (Chicago: University of Chicago Press, 1983), 54–65.

16. *Krapp's Last Tape, and Other Dramatic Pieces* (New York: Grove Press, 1960), 25.

17. Dante, *Purgatorio,* Canto IV, ll. 98–135.

18. *Paradiso,* Canto IV, ll. 83.

19. "Frate [she says to Dante], la nostra volontà quïeta/virtù di carità, che fa volerne/sol quel ch'avemo, e di'altro non ci asseta" [Brother, the power of charity quiets our will and makes us wish only what we have and thirst for nothing less] (III, 70–72), and, of course, the famous explanation "e la sua volontate è nostra pace" [and in His will is our peace] (III, 85).

FICTION

Clods, Whores, and Bitches
Misogyny in Beckett's Early Fiction

SUSAN BRIENZA

> I didn't understand women at that period. I still
> don't for that matter. Nor men either.
>
> *First Love*

If we change our perspective and visual fields, we change what we see: Beckett scholars working on the early fiction have for years focused on the style of *More Pricks Than Kicks*, the humor of *Murphy*, and the structure of *Watt*; as a result they have overlooked serious implications of the collective characterization of women in these novels. The re-focusing presented here exemplifies one tenet of feminist criticism: "Feminist thinking is really *re*thinking, an examination of the way certain assumptions enter into the fundamental assumptions that organize all our thinking." (Jehlen 69). One of Samuel Beckett's first male protagonists proclaims of women: "They were all the same when it came to the pinch—clods." A concentrated reading of the early fiction reveals a disturbing negative depiction of female characters: coupled with a pervasive disgust, cruel humor, and Swiftian revilement toward her physicality is the idea that woman as a clod of earth impedes intellectual man. Obviously woman as body versus man as mind is not a contrast new to Western literature, but the overwhelming mean-spirited tone of Beckett's male narrators compel the female reader to reassess the early fiction.

In general, Beckett's characterization of women alternates between stereotypes of femininity and bizarre reversals of the stereotypes. Whether paragon or parody, the woman here is limited to the body and to the emotions. She is either too sensuous and too concerned with matters of appearance or totally unattractive—indeed, a grotesque victim of severe physical deformities. The sensuous woman persona suggests once again the Mary/Eve polarity and the mythic Eve/Lilith tension, as Elizabeth Janeway argues: "Within Eve, there can exist only unresolved ambiguity, dread and desire in the same figure" (15). For Beckett's early fiction (though the image shifts in the plays and late fiction), if women are ugly they are shunned and ridiculed; if they are attractive they are dreaded and feared—and therefore ridiculed. Either way, as the dark side of humanity, the realm of physicality and feeling, they hinder the male's intellectual pursuits in *More Pricks, Murphy,* and *Watt.*

While the early Beckett hero needs women sexually at times, he bitterly resents this need in himself; for preference, he seeks to escape the corporeal world and live in his mind. Cartesian creatures, Beckett's males uphold the axiom of a definite and desired mind/body dichotomy. As opposed to the Romantic quest, transports of physical pleasure here seldom if ever promise emotional or spiritual elevation. Consequently, romantic love (even when it appears in non-parodied form) provides no philosophical enlightenment; instead, it thwarts the hero's transcendence. True escape and fulfillment come through death (in "Assumption," *More Pricks than Kicks,* and *Murphy*) or madness (*Murphy* and *Watt*) or in the peace achieved—paradoxically—when the male protagonist abandons the search for knowledge (in *Watt* and later *The Lost Ones*). In the meantime, women associated with degraded physicality (Thelma *bboggs* in *More Pricks,* bogs and "clods" of earth) weigh down the would-be mental travellers.

When analyzing the misogynist rhetoric here, the female critic must be careful: saying that the early narrators degrade or diminish women is not necessarily to say that Samuel Beckett does. The issue of sliding relationships among author, narrating consciousness, and character of course has occupied many studies on narrative technique, on irony, and on persona. With Beckett heroes, the author/narrator problem is an especially vexing and paradoxical one: while some of the male characters, languid and reluctant Romeos, recall Beckett himself as young and lazy lover (as described by Peggy Guggenheim), no neat equation operates. On the one hand the author expressly differentiates himself from his narrator-protagonist by making cameo appearances (à la Alfred Hitchcock in his movies), and yet on the other hand Samuel Beckett does reveal his sympathies for his male heroes. In *Watt* one of the main characters is named Sam, and in the unpublished first novel *Dream of Fair to Middling Women* and its published brother, *More Pricks Than Kicks,* a Mr. Beckett arrives.[1] In these works and in *Murphy,* as John Fletcher argues, the author, despite his apparent detachment, privileges the male hero by protecting him from the scathing humor that surrounds every other character (28); conversely, women receive the most consistent and vehement satire.

In *More Pricks Than Kicks* many of the women associated with sexuality are reduced, demeaned, and objectified through the use of the definite article, never applied to males: the Frica, the Alba ("Belacqua's current and one and only"), and "the Venerilla [that is, little venery], his friend and bawd to be." In the course of his adventures Belacqua marries three times, always reluctantly (perhaps the Beckett male's only viable reconciliation between indolence and sexual need); and his women, wives or not, are often aggressive and carnal. Likened to a randy animal in heat, Frica appears as a "martyress in rut" (61). Other women are depicted as ripe for rape—for example, Ruby Tough, with her "taut Sabine coiffure."

In the story "Love and Lethe," Ruby—a woman again more concerned with things of the body than with matters of the brain—foils Belacqua's well-considered plan for a double suicide by causing it to degenerate into the farce of sex. Ruby becomes increasingly festive, drinks too much; and when the fateful gun accidentally discharges in mid-air, the two lovers suddenly feel very much alive; and their only "death" is the sexual one. It is the woman's fault that the afternoon's pursuits descend from metaphysical to physical.

Ruby Tough's own father terms her "a slut" [she *does* have a wonderful name for a prostitute], and whores are everywhere in Samuel Beckett's early fiction. Another *More Pricks* story, "A Wet Night," introduces a woman with the sentence "Behold the Frica, she visits talent in the Service Flats. In she lands, singing Havelock Ellis [a pioneer in sexual psychology] in a deep voice, frankly itching to work that which is not seemly" (50).

The image of prostitution is also seen in *Murphy*. Murphy's room had been previously occupied by "a harlot, long past her best, which had been scarlet" (7). Celia, first and last, walks the streets—an occupation she insistently threatens to resume if Murphy does not get her a decent job. Both Murphy and Mr. Kelly compliment Celia on her talent and success in her profession, and Murphy terms his praise "the highest tribute that a man can pay a woman."

Prostitution, in fact, seems to be a major source of income for women in Beckett's early fiction; in sum, they earn their livelihood not with their minds but with their bodies. Curiously, for the lower classes in Victorian England, this picture would approximate reality as far back as 1850: a study of England and Scotland in that era estimated 50,000 prostitutes "known to the police." But one could indicate—as Beckett's narrators do not—that women chose or were forced into this career, called "the best paid industry," because of work restrictions and pitifully low wages in other sectors (Walkowitz 147). For non-economic reasons, though, prostitution is a popular career for women in Beckett. In *Watt* there is a minor character aptly called Penny-a-hoist-Pim, and we can also imagine what sort of streetwalking occupies another great walker, Lady McCann, on her day trips: the narrator assures us that "few women had a more extensive experience of the public road than Lady McCann." After the heroine in *First Love* takes in the hero and supports them both, the protagonist/narrator slowly determines how she earns her livelihood because of the periodic male moans and groans in the adjoining room, and he notes that one of her favorite pastimes is disrobing.

Throughout most of the early fiction, Beckett depicts women as swayed more by eros than by agape or cupid; romantic love suffers death by absurdity. Overturning the literary convention of celebrating the lover's beauty, the narrator of *More Pricks Than Kicks* delights in degrading and debasing his paramours. When Belacqua reads a newspaper ad for corsets, for example, even while the reader laughs at the heightened parodied magazine language, she notes that the premise here is that women's figures desperately need to be lifted or bound—and that these mashings "thrill" the male: " 'A woman' he read with a thrill 'is either: a short-below-the-waist, a big-hip, a sway-back, a big-abdomen or an average. If the bust be too cogently controlled, then shall fat roll from scapula to scapula. If it be made passable and slight, then shall the diaphragm bulge and be unsightly' " (52). Belacqua, in particular, fears that his lover's scarlet gown will be backless: "Was she a short-below or a sway-back?"—he wonders—"She had no waist, nor did she deign to sway. She was not to be classified" [implying that women are categorized by body type]. And of course the gown's red color links Alba with the scarlet woman image and thus back to whores.

Women's faces fare no better than their figures when deformed and defamed by the narrator of *More Pricks*. He occasionally descends to a totally gratuitous and therefore especially hostile disparagement of a woman's looks, as in the following simile: "six hours were allotted to him in which to make up his mind, as a pretty drab her face for an enemy" [that is, just as she needs six hours for cosmetics] (160). Earlier, Belacqua envisions "the Frica, looking something horrid":

> Throttled gazelle gives no idea. Her features, as though the hand of an unattractive ravisher were knotted in her chevelure, were set at half-cock and locked in a rictus. She had frowned to pencil her eyebrows, so now she had four. The dazzled iris was domed in a white agony of entreaty, the upper lip writhed back in a snarl to the untented nostrils. . . . It was impossible to set aside the awful suspicion that her flattened mammae, in

sympathy with this tormented eructation of countenance, had put forth cutwaters and were rowelling her corsage. But the face was beyond appeal, a flagrant seat of injury. (61)

Considering the grotesque language here, the female reader wonders if these are solely Belacqua's sentiments or if a more general attitude against women surfaces in the obvious stylistic glee: the overflowing energy and verbal display of the description encourages the male reader to enjoy and share the misogyny.

Equally disturbing to the woman reader is the tone of the entire book. Sometimes the female of the species is not even granted admission to the human race. In frequencies too often to be haphazard, a woman metamorphoses into an animal: one character does not "say," she "whinnied"; and another begins to look "more prognathous than ever," suggesting an ape. Presumbly Woman in battle combines the violent qualities of horse and cat, for "Belacqua, fighting like a woman, kicking, clawing, tearing and biting, put up a gallant resistance" (112). Passive Belacqua can marshall the required force only by imitating the supposed animal aggression of a woman; yet ironically, in the animal world the female will fight viciously only for good reason—when her young are threatened. Elsewhere woman becomes the equivalent of a moustache-twirling melodrama villain: "She reloaded and trained her charms more nicely upon this interesting miscreant, of whom she proposed, her mind full of hands rubbing, to make a most salutary example" (77). In the male characters' views, early Beckett women chase, capture, and metaphorically castrate their prey; as animals they are more hunter than hunted. Still other women are termed "furies" whose pursuits and attacks must be evaded and escaped.

Not a departure from—but the inverse of—the traditional femme fatale pattern, however, is found in Dante's Beatrice, who makes a brief appearance in the first story of *More Pricks* as Belacqua's symbolic spiritual and intellectual guide; later in the story her ideal is embodied in the Italian teacher, Lady Ottolenghi, who literally guides him through the difficult passages in Dante's poem. But the tutor is such a counter-example to Belacqua's stereotypes of women that he relegates her to a different category, almost a different species: "He did not believe it possible for a woman to be more intelligent or better informed than the little Ottolenghi. So he had set her on a pedestal in his mind, apart from other women" (16). Because of this atypical elevation of her intelligence and the governing male convention that women possess either a sharp mind or a good body but not both,[2] Belacqua as a narrator never grants the reader a physical description of the teacher. Instead he supplies a qualified, evasive, much-embedded Jamesian sentence that leaves all details to the imagination and yet allows us to imagine nothing: "There subsisted as much of the Ottolenghi as might be expected to of the person of a lady of a certain age who found being young and beautiful and pure more of a bore than anything else" (18). She rejects her own beauty, and she too is reduced with the definite article "the."

In sum, Beckett's narrator in *More Pricks* seems more misogynist than merely misanthropic. It is not Belacqua or a male character whose language is subjected to the most vicious parody in the book, but rather a ladyfriend, Smeraldina, writing a love letter. Even the nickname given her, Smerry, is loathesome; and her emotions spill over in badly spelled baby talk about Belacqua that moves beyond the boundaries of satire: "When I got in to the bus I got out a little Book and pencil and wrot down 100 times: Bloved Bloved Bloved Bel Bel Bel, I felt as if I never longed so much in my life for the man I love, to be with him, with him. I want you so much in every sence of the word, you and onely you" (153). It is significant that these letters present the only extended prose in the book rendered in a female voice: woman as brainless.

In Beckett's early fiction, as a whole, love seems a "blotch," a disease that threatens destruction: a woman then becomes a disgusting blight or an impediment to peace. For Murphy, like other Beckett heroes, can concentrate either on his body or on his mind but not both together. His astrological chart warns Murphy that "when Sensuality rules there is danger of Fits" (32), and if Miss Counihan is "the one symptom" (59) then love again is disease. Celia is both symptom and cause of Murphy's conflict: in spite of himself, he wants and needs her. This ambivalence merging desire and fear of women is an idea as ancient as early interpretations of Genesis, as Mieke Bal shows: "The split between body and soul was retrospectively projected upon Eve as a character . . . so attractive in body, so corrupt in soul, and hence, dialectically dangerous because of her attractiveness" (320).

While each character in *Murphy* shrinks to a caricature, depicted with a few exaggerated bodily features (Federman 62–64), only Celia is unfairly presented as all figure and no intellect. At the beginning of chapter 2 the narrator depicts Celia geometrically, segmented into several parts, with "Head," the second item listed, described as "small and round." By contrast, the narrator devotes the entirety of chapter 6 to the concept of Murphy's mind, with all three of its complex "zones" analyzed in detail. Later we are told that Celia possessed "not a large brain" (18), yet her *physical* statistics, "vital" and not so vital, are given (e.g., neck, calf, ankle; the narrator stops only at instep, which he comically deems "Unimportant"). This blond-haired, green-eyed Irish male fantasy surpasses the stereotype and is fetching enough to render Neary and

Wylie speechless and her grandfather incestuous. To Murphy, she represents primarily body and the "music" that their two bodies produce together. In his subconscious zone, ideas of Celia surface twice during a long series of distractions, yet in demeaning juxtaposition to the buzzing trivia of the "big world" outside; she, more than anything, gnaws at his peace. When he moves out of the flat and later in his garret rocks to oblivion in his chair, it is only the "musical" aspect of Celia that he misses, and only fleetingly. His job as caretaker in an insane asylum serves to reinforce the mind/body split, not harmonize it. Significantly, during his time as custodian the one creature with whom he truly craves intimacy is Mr. Endon ("endon" meaning "within"), a man with a "tiny body" and a "skull, large for any body, immense for this." In contrast to Celia, he is physically and behaviorally all head rather than, literally and metaphorically, all body. While Mr. Endon represents the extreme of solipcism which Murphy seeks, Celia in her care of Mr. Kelly looks without rather than "within" the self.

Both Murphy and the narrator tend to underestimate Celia at the same time that she is earning the reader's respect. During one fight, Murphy patronizingly finishes Celia's sentences for her and then rephrases a rhetorical question "thereby giving the conversation a twist that brought it within her powers of comment" (35). While this accurately expresses Murphy's consciousness, the narrator can be even more condescending and disparaging. There ensues "a scene" instigated by Murphy in which he attempts all the ploys in the human arsenal in order to avoid work, including playing the martyr and whining, "Why can't you love me as I am?" Yet Celia compels him to take action; her ultimatum of Work-or-I-hit-the-streets does succeed. In actuality Celia easily sees through all his ruses: when Murphy rejects her proposed visit to discuss his finding a job with the excuse, "That is not possible. I expect a friend," Celia cleverly retorts, "You have no friends" (8). Over and again the reader perceives that Celia matches Murphy's wit and could in fact be equally cerebral and pensive, since she takes to pacing, brooding, and rocking after he leaves. Unfortunately, Murphy never sees beyond her body, although his creator does—shown by the fact that Celia is allowed to close the novel with such grace and dignity.

Celia stands in obvious contrast to Miss Dwyer, "the morsel of chaos" who is shunted aside by Neary as soon as he has his way with her, and to Miss Counihan, described as "quite exceptionally anthropoid." Negative type of femininity that she is, Miss Counihan (her name meant to suggest "a cunt") still escapes a worse narrative fate; she is spared other conventional stigmas of women that afflict two minor characters in *Murphy:* smelliness, nosiness, and ugliness. Again, Beckett's women are either stereotypes of "feminine" attractiveness or their reversals and still circumscribed by the body. Miss Carridge—presumably a miscarriage of a human being—bears an elephant-like stench: she "smelt, with a smell that not even her nearest and dearest had ever got used to," thus making her suspect as a genuine female, given that one notion of femininity demands that a lady exude an aroma of lilies and roses. Another minor character, Rosie Dew, despite a lovely and floral name, is no certifiable lady either, but rather more like a fat water animal—suffering as she does from Duck's Disease, "a distressing pathological condition in which the thighs are suppressed and the buttocks spring directly from behind the knees.... Happily its incidence is small and confined ... to the weaker vessel" (97). Happily for whom? we might ask. Denied the "celestial thighs" of Art and of her prayers and dreams, Miss Dew in fact possesses no thighs at all; moreover, in addition to having the body of a "stunted penguin" Rosie has a mind like a woman—that is, like a sexist male depiction of female mentality: full of irrelevant detail, ideas divorced from all logic, and governed exclusively by non sequitur (99). Even Rosie's dog suffers from Murphy's negative stereotyping of the female of the species: "dog or a bitch.... It certainly had the classical bitch's eye, kiss me in the cornea, keep me in the iris and God help you in the pupil" (98). Besides being a witty contraction of the sultry female's ocular expressions and deviousness, this aside, by extension, suggests the image (common among surrealists) of destructive, man-devouring woman; vagina dentitia, a tunnel filled with sharp teeth. In the central core of the eye, or of her being, she is dangerous, so "God help you."

The position of woman falls even lower in *Watt*, whose narrator seems—if you can believe it—more misogynist than *Murphy*'s. Indeed, by contrast to Celia's stabilizing and almost noble presence in *Murphy*, women in *Watt* have virtually vanished—appearing in weird minor characters, and only temporarily. Lady McCann exists primarily to witness Watt, and after she performs this function twice, she is narratively obliterated: she simply and inexplicably has no more dialogue and thus evaporates. The first female character we meet, Mrs. Nixon, appears exclusively in the prologue to the novel, introducing this strange man Watt; and after Mr. Hackett [Mr. Beckett?] bids her goodbye, she never surfaces again. While fictionally alive, she reveals herself to be utterly non-analytical and totally uninterested in the person and purpose of Watt—that is, the obverse of a good reader of this novel: "What does it matter who he is? said Mrs. Nixon.... Or what he does.... Or how he lives. Or where he comes from. Or where he is going to. Or what he looks like. What can it possibly matter, to us?" (23). A stranger to the life of the mind, Mrs. Nixon is remarkable only for her motherhood, her accelerated labor, and no-nonsense birthing techniques; in fact her first name, Tetty, suggests "teats" for nursing. In the middle of a dinner party at which she is, of course, the perfect hostess, even as her unborn baby begins to kick and descend, she absurdly retains her feminine grace: " 'I continued to eat, drink and make light conversation,' said Tetty, 'and Larry to leap, like a salmon' " (13). Like some elemental earth goddess, she gives birth quickly and without assistance, severing the umbilical cord with her teeth. " 'I would have snapped it across my knee, if necessary' " she says (15). In this she becomes a comic dramatization of the icon of primitive woman in labor, similar to the African statue in D. H. Lawrence's *Women in Love,* representing pure physicality. Earlier, Tetty in the "anguish" of labor also comically recalls the archetype of Eve and her curse of painful childbearing: "I went up those stairs, Mr. Hackett, said Tetty, on my hands and knees, wringing the carpetrods. . . . "

Of course the Christian ideal of motherhood, and the obverse of Eve, is Mary, but her namesake in *Watt* is absurdly parodied. That Beckett's Mary is named after the Virgin is clear because she is precisely described as coming after an "Ann," the name of the biblical Mary's mother, as a servant in Knott's [or God's] house (50). Rather than upholding cleanliness, godliness, purity, or spirituality, however, Beckett's Mary embodies the extreme opposite of putative feminine behavior, in particular, dainty and sparse eating. Mary eats constantly—exclusively onions and peppermints (one obstacle to romantic kisses followed by its antidote, perhaps)—in great quantities and in strict alternation, turn and turn about. Indeed she becomes a human or (inhuman) eating machine, her fingers working like pistons up and down between her brim-full pockets and her overflowing mouth, to the point where she is incapable of speech: "Whole days, and even entire weeks, would glide away without Mary's having opened her gob for any purpose other than the reception of her five fingers fastened firmly on a fragment of food, for to the spoon, the knife, and even the fork, considered as aids to ingestion, she had never been able to accustom herself, in spite of excellent references" (52). With his cruel understatement and use of the demeaning term "gob" for "mouth," the narrator ridicules the female body, and her brain is later described as null and void. Mary roams the house in a stupor, and "little by little the reason for her presence in that place faded from her mind" (51). Even though she is named after the Virgin, she more resembles the mythic opposite, Eve, who became by medieval times a warning against female bestiality. "Eve the temptress," writes Janeway, "was pictured not only as impure but as filthy. Her needs were declared to be excessive and disgusting" (5). Beckett's Mary/Eve has intemperate, demanding appetites comparable to those in the legends of the first evil woman—though here they become desires for food, not as symbol for sex (the famous apple) but as replacement. Mary in *Watt* emerges as the most disgusting woman in Beckett's canon, a horrifying reversal of one ideal of feminine beauty (ivory-smooth and thus hairless skin, shining hair, full breasts, and a flat stomach): "her long grey greasy hair framing in its cowl of scrofulous mats a face where pallor, languor, hunger, acne, recent dirt, immemorial chagrin and surplus hair seemed to dispute the mastery. Flitters of perforated starch entwine an ear. Under the rusty cotton frock, plentifully embossed with scabs of slobber, two cuplike depressions mark the place of the bosom and a conical protuberance that of the abdomen" (54–55).

With a similar grotesque appearance, Mrs. Gorman, the fishwoman, is the female character in *Watt* who most closely approximates a love interest, and her relationship to Watt the one closest to a romance. Everything about her compromised love, however, is comically undercut. While the relationship begins optimistically enough, with the sort of requited love missing from *Murphy* (by a "merciful coincidence" Mrs. Gorman "pleases" Watt, and vice versa), their manner of pleasuring each other fits no romantic convention. On Thursdays, her good health allowing, Watt would "lean his head upon her right breast (the left having unhappily been removed in the heat of a surgical operation), and in this position remain, without stirring.... From time to time, hoisting his weary head, from waist to neck his wary hold transferring, Watt would kiss, in a despairing manner, Mrs Gorman on or about the mouth, before crumpling back in his post-crucified position" (140). In this comic distortion of the *Pieta,* neither character appears a fully sexed human being, since Mrs. Gorman resembles an ancient Amazon and Watt (as at the beginning of the novel) a rolled tarpaulin. The goal of their union is never orgasmic passion, but a mother/child calmness and "peace": again the goal for the male character is mental transcendence.

At the very best (probably Celia), Woman in Beckett's early fiction is a desirable and lovable creature who nonetheless deflects the philosophical male hero from his metaphysics and possible Belacqua bliss. At the worst, in *First Love,* the narrator's desire for solitude and quiet leads to a hatred of women that extends outward to the female reader: he abandons his bench, he says, because it was growing chilly outside "and for other reasons better not wasted on cunts like you" (21). If addressed to the male reader, the derision is just as sexist, of course—an Anglicized version of an insult popular in France and parallel to the American slur deriding a man as a "pussy." (And the same usage occurs in *Malone Dies* when the narrator angrily lashes out at the "they" trying to disrupt his "programme" for stories: "Proper cunts whoever they are.") The pervasive pattern of negative and physical imagery associated with counter examples: Lady Ottolenghi, the intellectual Italian teacher, and Celia. The teacher is no more than a plot vehicle, and Celia, for all her love and compassion, fits neatly into yet another stereotypical role—the prostitute with a heart of gold.

Overall, several disturbing generalizations are unavoidable: disparaging depictions of female protagonists often seem gratuitous; attacks on women emerge from cruel physical descriptions; and insistent derogatory remarks about female characters take on the cumulative force of dogma. But dogma of what sort? Not a clear male supremacist one, since Beckett's men suffer physical disease and decay and possess a complex of various faults that leave them scarcely more attractive personalities. Beckett's men, however, transcend their imperfect bodies: as limbs decay and parts descend, the mind grows more alive. The male's impatience with the corporeal is displaced onto the woman as Other and expressed as aversion to or disgust with Woman as body, as clod. While this dichotomy emerges from age-old depictions of women as breasts and holes in Irish art and paradigms in the Irish Catholic culture, it takes on special force and configuration in Beckett. The huge gender difference emerging in Beckett's fiction decrees that it is the male figure, seeking to escape physical reality, who wrestles with philosophical issues, while the woman, delimited by the physical self and of limited mental capacity, becomes an obstacle or a trap. Not quite as reductive or systematic as negative images of women in D. H. Lawrence, Arthur Miller, Norman Mailer, and Sam Shepard, Beckett's depiction of the female in the early fiction is nonetheless dismaying. Their autobiographical origins are yet to be explored.

Since Beckett has been writing fiction for almost sixty years, the reader is compelled to turn to the later stories to see if his image of woman is consistent. Are females still clods and whores? By *Molloy*, two years after *Watt*, romantic love still survives—but only to be comically satirized (Cohn 84); Beckett's trilogy contains some of the funniest anti-erotic and anti-romantic passages in all of Western literature. In *Malone Dies* the negativity continues: Mrs. Saposcat was "always wrong" with any information; and the love interest Moll (like the women in *Pricks*) was "immoderately ill-favored of both face and body" (85). Worse than being disparaged, she is indifferently dismissed on the basis of her gender: "Our concern here is not with Moll, who after all is only a female" (92). Even more sexist is the marriage of the Lamberts: "And even his young wife had abandoned all hope of bringing him to heel, by means of her cunt, that trump card of young wives. For she knew what he

would do to her if she did not open it to him. . . . at the least show of
rebellion on her part he would run to the wash-house and come back
with the beetle and beat her until she came round to a better way of
thinking" (24–25).

By the prose fragment *Imagination Dead Imagine,* from the late
1960s, there remain no recognizably human characters, merely a stylized
male and female fetally curled in an embryonic yet cranial dome. As they
face away from each other, they cannot even make eye contact; and the
real focus here is on the observer's "eye of prey," the reader's imagination. In *The Lost Ones* "husbands and wives" are said to exist, but they
pass each other unrecognizing, each lost one obviously seeking something other than romantic love in this light-baked universe that dries all
mucuous membranes and makes the act of love an act of assault. In *Ping*
of the middle sixties, only the vestiges of a recollection of a woman remain, in the suggestive phrase "black lashes imploring," and soon even
the vision recedes, leaving for the man, utterly alone, "that much memory henceforth never." And by 1982 in *Ill Seen Ill Said* the female protagonist is less character than metacharacter, neither taken by a man nor
overtaken by emotion but grasped by the narrative eye, striving to envision her and then capture an image in writing: "But quick seize her
where she is best to be seized." Not a man possessing a woman here, but
a writer possessing words. Beckett has traveled quite a distance from
More Pricks Than Kicks and *Murphy,* in which love and sex were still
occasionally to be wished and the male protagonists fought against romantic entanglements precisely because they still strongly felt erotic
needs.

If readers jump in fictional time and look at the semi-realistic vi-
gnettes in the autobiographical story *Company* (1980), they will notice
some of the same earlier attitudes towards women. The father in one
reminiscence shuns his wife in labor (as does the male protagonist in
First Love) and hikes in the thickets all day until the screaming at home
stops. In another memory passage, a young man sitting in a summer-
house evades his anxiety about his lover through mathematics and geom-
etry: "She is late. You close your eyes and try to calculate the volume.
Simple sums you find a help in times of trouble. A haven" (40). He
does not realize the woman is pregnant ("late") because he does not
want to realize it. He then fragments his visual field, segments her body,
and thus reaches an unavoidable and unsettling conclusion: "Your gaze
descends to the breasts. You do not remember them so big. To the abdomen. Same impression. Dissolve to your father's straining against the
unbuttoned waistband. Can it be she is with child without your having
asked for as much as her hand? You go back into your mind" (42). Like

a Belacqua afraid of commitments (here striving to explain her swelling stomach as mere asexual overweight), he may not have asked for her hand, but he certainly must have accepted more than that. Unhappily, he retreats from thoughts of the woman's body to return to the shelter of his mental calculations ("You go back into your mind"). Like Dan Rooney, Molloy, Krapp, and many of Beckett's dessicated men, he takes flight in arithmetic.

It is curious, then, to return to *The Lost Ones,* the fiction Beckett had abandoned for three years as "intractable" before he suddenly appended a final section in 1971. In this conclusion it is a woman, specifically the north woman, who has reached the mental stillness and tranquility that the other "searchers" seek, who has achieved peace initially by her calm posture of self-containment. This transcendent creature sits in the same womb-shaped position as Belacqua (both Dante's and Beckett's). Although she is described as a naked woman with red hair and exposed private parts, she is expressly *not* an object of sexual desire. Instead, the north woman serves as guide, as the north pole, because of her "greater fixity"; and she is "the first among the vanquished" ("vanquished" here paradoxically meaning the victorious), presumably both the first creature to attain peace and also the prime model. It is toward *her,* neither a sensual nor a repulsive body but a tranquil mind, that the remaining searcher, the "last of all if a man" travels, there to probe the eyes of this female Mr. Endon: "In those calm wastes he lets his wander till they are the first to close." Since Beckett's characters and themes endlessly recycle, this scene may refer readers to his first story, "Assumption," and the poet's mystical experience with the seductive woman whose eyes are "pools of obscurity" and whose sexuality destroys the male protagonist. One critic notes that the feast of the Assumption (celebrating Christ's mother being assumed into heaven) is called in the Eastern Church "Falling Asleep" to refer to the Virgin Mary's sleeplike death (Rabinovitz 19). This is the same semi-conscious state admired by the searchers and attained by the north woman. The final (male) lost one cannot yet match her vacant gaze, but when ultimately he does, he will earn the name of "sage," gaining his mental peace by ceasing to seek, ironically (considering Beckett's early fiction) finding his spiritual transcendence in the eyes of a woman.

NOTES

1. "Behold, Mr. Beckett," said [Belacqua] whitely, "a dud mystic." He meant *mystique raté,* but shrank always from the *mot juste.*

Guardedly, reservedly, we beheld him. He was hatless, he whistled a scrap of an Irish air, his port and mien were jaunty resignation.

Fletcher supposes that Beckett inserts himself "in order to emphasize the fact that he observes his heroes from a neutral position " (28).

2. This adoration of the female again calls up the Virgin Mary side of woman's assumed binary nature, and becomes the only alternative to female as reflection of male desire. Thus, in order to observe herself correctly, argues Sigrid Weigel, she must practice *de-reflection*: "That this de-reflection also contains *disenchantment* has its roots in the fact that male images of women—in contrast to the social reality of women—not only present woman as an underprivileged sex but also set her on a pedestal, so that the images encompass humiliation and veneration, as well as fear of the supposed omnipotence of woman" (70).

WORKS CITED

Andersen, Jorgen. *The Witch on the Wall: Medieval Erotic Sculpture in the British Isles*. London: George Allen & Unwin, 1977.

Bal, Mieke. "Sexuality, Sin, and Sorrow: The Emergence of Female Character (A reading of Genesis 1–3)." In *The Female Body in Western Culture: Contemporary Perspectives*. Ed. Susan Rublin Suleiman. Cambridge and London: Harvard University Press, 1986, 317–38.

Beckett, Samuel. "Assumption" in *Transition* (Paris), 16–17 (June, 1929), 269–71).

———.*Company*. New York: Grove Press, 1980.

———.*"First Love" and Other Shorts*. New York: Grove Press, 1974.

——— *More Pricks Than Kicks*. 1934; New York: Grove Press, 1972.

——— *Murphy*. 1938; New York: Grove Press, 1957.

———.*Watt*. New York: Grove Press, 1959.

Ben-Zvi, Linda. *Samuel Beckett*. Boston: Twayne Publishers, 1986.

Bullfinch's Mythology. New York: Avenel Books, 1978.

Cohn, Ruby. *Back to Beckett*. Princeton: Princeton University Press, 1976.

Federman, Raymond. *Journey to Chaos: Samuel Beckett's Early Fiction*. Berkeley and Los Angeles: University of California Press, 1965.

Fletcher, John. *The Novels of Samuel Beckett*, 2nd ed. London: Chatto & Windus, 1972.

Hardy, Barbara. "The Dubious Consolations in Beckett's Fiction: Art, Love, and Nature." In *Beckett the Shape Changer: A Symposium*. Ed. Katharine Worth. London and Boston: Routledge and Kegan Paul, 1986.

Harvey, Lawrence. *Samuel Beckett: Poet and Critic*. Princeton: Princeton University Press, 1970.

Janeway, Elizabeth. "Who Is Sylvia? On the Loss of Sexual Paradigms." In *Women—Sex and Sexuality*. Ed. Catharine R. Stimpson and Ethel Spector Person. Chicago: University of Chicago Press, 1980, 4–20.

Jehlen, Myra. "Archimedes and the Paradox of Feminist Criticism." In *The Signs Reader: Women, Gender, & Scholarship*. Ed. Elizabeth Abel and Emily K. Abel. Chicago: University of Chicago Press, 1983, 69–95.

Millett, Kate. *Sexual Politics*. New York: Doubleday, 1970.

Rabinovitz, Rubin. *The Development of Samuel Beckett's Fiction*. Urbana: University of Illinois, 1984.

Walkowitz, Judith. "The Politics of Prostitution." In *Women—Sex and Sexuality*. Ed. Stimpson and Person. 145–57.

Weigel, Sigrid. "Double Focus: On the History of Women's Writing." In *Feminist Aesthetics*. Ed. Gisela Ecker. Boston: Beacon Press, 1985, 59–80.

FICTION

Stereoscopic or Stereotypic: Characterization in Beckett's Fiction

RUBIN RABINOVITZ

Samuel Beckett's characterizations are, to say the least, unconventional. The people depicted in his fiction are at times grotesquely deformed and at times the very opposite: neutral shapes as smooth-featured as Brancusi's. No less unusual are some of Beckett's apparently more conventional portrayals. In his earlier novels, he satirizes many figures to a degree that the characterizations begin to seem more like diatribes.

This, for example, is how the narrator of *More Pricks Than Kicks* describes the Smeraldina:

> The wretched little wet rag of an upper lip, pugnozzling up and back in what you might nearly call a kind of a duck or a cobra sneer to the nostrils, was happily to some extent amended by the wanton pout of its fellow and the forward jaws to match—a brilliant recovery. The skull of this strapping girl was shaped like a wedge. The ears of course were shells, the eyes shafts of reseda . . . into an oreless mind. The hair was as black as the pots and grew so thick and low athwart the temples that the brow was reduced to a fanlight. . . . But what matter about bodies?[1]

What matter indeed. Having vented his pique, the narrator is perhaps attempting to win back readers by ending on a more moderate note. But is there more here than satire gone sour? The narrator's acerbity drains the passage of humor: the temptation to laugh at the Smeraldina is curtailed by the severity of the attack.

Descriptions of other women in *More Pricks Than Kicks* are at times equally unkind, which leads to another question. Does Beckett's writing reflect an underlying hostility to women? To be sure, the same kind of sarcasm is at times extended to masculine characters such as the homespun Poet and the Polar Bear. Even so, such evenhandedness is not a particularly compelling defense, unless misanthropy is considered a cure for misogyny.

This adds urgency to the question of whether there is more to the characterizations in *More Pricks Than Kicks* than mockery for its own sake. The corrosiveness in some of these descriptions, along with methods like using of definite articles before characters' names, seems to dehumanize Beckett's writing. Moreover, it becomes difficult to believe in the people who figure in the novel when they are so broadly portrayed.

An early reviewer—a famous one—raised a similar question about *Murphy,* the novel Beckett published after *More Pricks Than Kicks.* Here is what Dylan Thomas had to say about Neary, one of the characters in the novel: "The Dublin Professor, whose mental adventures and adventurous conversations are loud and lively and boisterous, is a slap stick, a stuffed guy, when he moves; his mind is Mr. Beckett's mind, and is full of surprises, but his figure that of a taped and typed 'eccentric professor' of music-hall and cartoon."[2] If Thomas is right, Beckett is vulnerable to a charge that his characterizations are at times no better than stereotypes. To this can be added a related charge—that his satire at times degenerates into caricature, particularly in his delineations of women. But these questions must be carefully considered: in Beckett's case, hasty conclusions can often lead to misunderstandings.

In the "Cyclops" chapter of *Ulysses,* James Joyce deals with a related question about stereotyped characterizations. Here the first-person narrator, like Homer's Polyphemus, is one-eyed, and his physical disability becomes a metaphor for an intellectual one—his narrow understanding of human reality. The narrator's limited perception of other people reduces them to stereotypes. Joyce, on the other hand, provides a stereoscopic view of human events, reflecting his ability to see more than one side of an issue. In dissociating himself from the bigoted views of the narrator, Joyce does not forget that even repugnant characters should be presented in depth.[3]

Beckett has often spoken of his admiration for Joyce's artistry, and his friendship with Joyce is well known.[4] Such factors make it likely that Beckett was aware of Joyce's ideas about stereoscopic characterization. Beckett too is capable of multi-dimensional portrayals: in plays like *Happy Days, All That Fall,* and *Not I* his central characters—women— are depicted with compassion and sensitivity. It is worth considering, then, why Beckett so often does create characters who seem stereotyped.

Even before Dylan Thomas's observations, Beckett himself suggested that such characters were stereotypes. For example, in *Murphy,* when Cooper becomes maudlin, the narrator says, "All the puppets in this book whinge sooner or later, except Murphy, who is not a puppet" (122).

But this statement needs to be reexamined because, as it happens, Murphy does whinge. Early in the novel the narrator describes how

Murphy "threw his voice into an infant's whinge"[5] (27). The comment raises difficulties: is the narrator saying that all the characters, including Murphy, whinge and that all of them, with the exception of Murphy, are puppets? Or is this one of the places (there are many others) where the narrator's account becomes unreliable?[6]

Another hint about Beckett's stereotyped characterizations comes in *More Pricks Than Kicks*. Here, particulars in the narrator's descriptions of women in the novel are often repeated. In the following examples, specific details about Lucy and the Frica can be matched with excerpts from the passage about the Smeraldina cited earlier:

> Her thick short hair went back like a pennon from her fanlight forehead [from a description of Lucy, 105].

> The horropilating detail of the upper-lip writhing up and away in a kind of duck or a cobra sneer to the quivering snout . . . [from a description of the Frica, 75].

The lack of variants in some of these reiterated phrases makes it unlikely that the repetition is accidental. For example, in each instance the article *a* occurs three times: "*a* kind of *a* duck or *a* cobra sneer." Moreover, there one can find many similar examples of recurring details in descriptions of the heroines in *More Pricks Than Kicks*.[7]

Beckett uses a similar kind of repetitive characterization in his later works. In this example from *Molloy* the words *grey* and *wizened* recur:

> Once I touched with my lips, vaguely, hastily, that wizened grey pear [Molloy is describing his mother's head, 24].

> In that wizened, grey skull what raging and rampaging. . . . [Moran is describing Martha, 132].

Many masculine figures similarly possess recurring attributes. Thus Molloy speaks of his testicles "dangling at mid-thigh," and Moran says his testicles "swing a little low."[8] The narrator of *The Unnamable* provides the beginnings of an explanation for such similarities when he refers to different characters as "two phases of the same carnal envelope" (60). If conventional characterization requires that characters be easily differentiated, Beckett is clearly following a different course.

Another attack on traditional characterization comes in Beckett's technique of revealing little about the physical appearance of central figures like Murphy and Watt. The Nixon-Hackett conversation in *Watt* indicates that a characterization of the hero is deliberately being withheld; but Evans and Severn, figures who play very minor roles in the novel, are described in elaborate detail.

At times, the narrator of *More Pricks Than Kicks* calls attention to his refusals to provide physical descriptions of the characters:

There was nothing at all noteworthy about his appearance (27).

But it would be a waste of time to itemise her (105).

It is impossible to describe the matron (168).

Bodies don't matter, but hers went something like this . . . (176).

But what matter about bodies? (177).

A more detailed disclaimer of this kind appears in Beckett's first novel, the unpublished *Dream of Fair to Middling Women:* "The effect or concert of effects, unimportant as it seems to us, and dull as ditchwater as we happen to know, that elicited the Smeraldina-Rima, shall not, for those and other reasons that need not be gone into, be stated" (10). Such comments hint at an idea that is central in Beckett's fiction: in mocking a particular character, he is often also conveying the sense that the very notion of characterization—of summing up a person in a few paragraphs—is ludicrous.

In Beckett's earlier novels this idea leads to a number of unusual effects. At times the protagonist's mind is depicted while those of the remaining characters are not; this corresponds to the idea that we can apprehend our own thoughts better than those of other people. In *More Pricks Than Kicks* Belacqua's mind is described at length, and an entire chapter is devoted to the hero's mind in *Murphy;* but many of the minor characters in these novels are stereotypes whose thoughts are never revealed. Mr. Endon represents an ideal of mental existence that Murphy aspires to; but if Mr. Endon's appearance is described, no thoughts—or even lines of dialogue—are attributed to him. In lieu of giving a conventional description of Celia, the narrator of *Murphy* provides readers with a long list of measurements, such as "Neck. 13 ¾. Upper arm. 11. Forearm. 9½ " (10). Celia is in many ways morally superior to the other characters in *Murphy,* but we can learn this only from her words and actions: her thoughts usually remain private.

This selective reporting introduces a sense of irony. The ethical point of view in the early works initially seems sympathetic to that of the protagonist: the hero's defects are slighted while those of the other characters are emphasized and mocked. With careful reading, however, the narrator's distortions begin to emerge. Belacqua may loudly bemoan the lack of compassion in the world, but he is treated with great compassion by the women in *More Pricks Than Kicks*. It is in his repeated refusals to return this compassion that a sense of his moral shallowness is delineated.[9] Murphy, similarly, at first seems in most ways superior to Celia; but as eventually emerges, he is her inferior both ethically and in terms of sensitivity.

Beckett conceals Murphy's flaws in such a way that the underlying moral reality in his novel remains concealed, at least initially. For example, Celia's honesty and kindness are demonstrated by the narrator's observation, "She kept nothing from Mr. Kelly except what she thought might give him pain, i.e., next to nothing" (11). It takes careful reading to notice that the very opposite is true of the way Murphy deals with Celia: "Nor did she know anything of his heart attacks, which had not troubled him while she was with him. He now told her all about them, keeping back nothing that might alarm her" (30).

Such patterns of irony are maintained throughout the earlier novels. Many of the characters in these works, including the protagonists, are shallow, egocentric, and hypocritical; but their high-minded principles are celebrated even as the charitable acts of other characters are dismissed. In Beckett's fiction, as in the world, hypocrisy often eclipses virtue.

With the introduction of first-person narrative in his fiction, Beckett's writing becomes increasingly introspective, and his presentation of minor characters undergoes a related transformation. At the outset, Beckett's trilogy of novels—*Molloy, Malone Dies,* and *The Unnamable*—seems to be about people and events in the outer world. But the secondary characters in these novels can also be seen as figures invented by the first-person narrators and therefore reflections of their own personalities.

Thus Moran eventually realizes that Gaber, the messenger who brings him directives, is a figure he has created to flesh out a volitional entity within himself. As Moran says: "The voice I listen to needs no Gaber to make it heard. For it is within me" (180). In the same way, Molloy equates his own thoughts with the dialogue of a minor character he encounters, a police sergeant: "And then sometimes there arose within me, confusedly, a kind of consciousness, which I express by saying, I said, etc., or, Don't do it, Molloy, or Is that your mother's name? said the sergeant, I quote from memory Or which I express without sinking to the level of oratio recta, but by means of figures quite as deceitful" (119).[10]

Like the lack of differentiation among characters, this again is part of Beckett's attack on traditional fictional methods. Not only is conventional characterization a futile enterprise, but it becomes misleading when it presupposes imaginary individuals who can exist independent of a central persona. Characters are fragments of an author's personality;

any contrary suggestion is deceptive. The narrator of *The Unnamable* therefore considers it a mistake to deal with a character "as if he really existed, in a specific place" (118).

In the trilogy, Beckett is less concerned with representing people as they exist in the outer world than with depicting them as reflections of such people in the mind of a persona. Fantasy is at the base of characterization. This helps to clarify another element in Beckett's descriptions of women. In contexts where Beckett's protagonists have an interest in initiating sexual relationships, the women are often remarkably beautiful, as in *More Pricks Than Kicks* and *Murphy*. But when the idea of sexual expression is threatening, the women become repulsive.

Thus Molloy, remembering the women with whom he made love, says, "My memory confuses them and I am tempted to think of them as one and the same old hag, flattened and crazed by life. And God forgive me, to tell you the horrible truth, my mother's image sometimes mingles with theirs, which is literally unendurable, like being crucified" (79). The crucifixion is again associated with an oedipal situation in *Malone Dies*, when Macmann becomes involved with Moll, a maternal figure with a tooth that has been carved to represent the crucifixion (93). Reading the description of Moll's tooth is painful; this pain evokes in readers a sense of the unendurable emotions Molloy referred to earlier.

Another facet of Beckett's method is to create and negate, to establish characters and later admit that they are fabrications. Moran says: "What a rabble in my head, what a gallery of moribunds. Murphy, Watt, Yerk, Mercier and all the others. I would never have believed that—yes, I believe it willingly. Stories, stories" (188). Malone, thinking about his impending death, lists himself together with some of the characters who preceded him in the Beckett canon: "Then it will be all over with the Murphys, Merciers, Molloys, Morans, and Malones, unless it goes on beyond the grave" (63). Similarly, the narrator of *The Unnamable* says: "All these Murphys, Molloys, and Malones do not fool me. They have made me waste my time, suffer for nothing, speak of them when, in order to stop speaking, I should have spoken of me and of me alone" (21).[11]

The narrator of *The Unnamable* often uses derogatory terms in referring to such characters; this underscores the idea that they are unsatisfactory attempts to create surrogates.

> delegates (12)
> mannikins (25)
> troop of lunatics (27)
> moribunds (28)

vice-exister (37)
caricature (37)
avatars (38)
formenters of fiasco (70)
wretches (71)
dirty pack of fake maniacs (113)
the same gang (118)
cogener (127)
renegades (131)
bran-dips (145)
old buffers (145)

The narrator in *Murphy* calls the characters puppets; the narrator of *The Unnamable* does the same—three times (4, 52, 100). Introducing a new character, the narrator of *The Unnamable* says, "Now I'll have to find a name for this latest surrogate" (147).

The way Beckett names his characters is also unusual. An addendum in *Watt* suggests "Change all the names" (253). This anticipates another of Beckett's techniques in the trilogy: he often changes the names of the characters, again to hint that they are not people in the outer world but surrogates of an underlying persona.

A clue to the arbitrariness of the naming process comes in the way the protagonists of the trilogy continually profess uncertainty about names:

> Dan was my father's name perhaps. . . (21).
> Her name must be Molloy too, I said (29).
> Christian name something like Sophie. . . (44).
> Perhaps the name was Edith (76).
> I've lost her name again, Rose, no. . . (113).
> Christian name? I don't know (9).
> Moran's boss. I forget his name (33).
> what is his name, what was his name, in his jar . . . (152).

In some instances Beckett uses similarities in a succession of character's names—Molloy, Moran, Malone, Macmann—to undercut a sense of the fixity. In another series—Mrs. Loy, Lousse, mother Molloy, Mollose—such euphony is used in contexts that stress uncertainty about names:

> Mrs. Loy . . . or Lousse, I forget . . . (44).
> perhaps I knew nothing of mother Molloy, or Mollose . . . (153).

At times Beckett introduces a related idea by using names that are obviously unrealistic, such as Pim, Bom, Krim, Kram (in *How It Is*), or Jolly and Draeger Praeger Draeger (in *All Strange Away*).

Proper names are less important in such works as *The End, The Expelled, The Calmative, First Love, Texts for Nothing,* and *From an Abandoned Work.* Here Beckett's method is to introduce an unnamed first-person narrator; to give most of the secondary characters names related to their roles ("my father," "a policeman," "a cabman"); and to reserve proper names only for a few peripheral characters ("Mother Calvet," "Mr Weir," "Mr Nidder"). In referring to the last of these characters, the narrator of *The Expelled* hints that the process of eliminating character's names is a deliberate one: "Mr Nidder, strange how one fails to forget certain names" (*Stories and Texts* 18).

The practice of stripping away naturalistic details continues in Beckett's later works, where the characters again often represent aspects of a single psyche. Here the number of characters diminishes and the proper names are replaced by pronouns. Thus in *Fizzle 3, Fizzle 4,* and *Enough,* the two principal figures are called "I" and "he." In *Company,* a voice addresses "one in the dark" as "you." In *Ill Seen Ill Said,* the protagonist is "she." In *Fizzle 6,* there is only one character, a first-person narrator.

Beckett introduces a different technique for diminishing the effects of conventional characterization in another group of late works. Here figures called "bodies" are presented in spare and obviously unrealistic settings. Examples include the "lost bodies" roaming in a cylinder in *The Lost Ones,* the "two white bodies" inhabiting a rotunda in *Imagination Dead Imagine,* the "little body" surrounded by ruins in *Lessness,* the "expelled" standing "amidst his ruins" in *Fizzle 8,* and the "body" occupying "a place" in *Worstward Ho.*

Beckett gives few particulars in depicting these figures. They are usually isolated, featureless, deprived of words or thoughts. Such terseness adds to their universality: such characters can represent embryonic existences or fragmented components of the self or much larger entities, such as all of humanity.

Emerging from such examples is a sense of Beckett's consistency of purpose, of his continual movement away from the type of portrayal that strives to represent people as they appear in the world. The same rule does not hold for his drama: in plays like *Happy Days* or *All That Fall,* he does depict people as they appear in the outer world.[12] The givens of a theatrical performance—actors observed by spectators—make it less suitable than fiction for representing introspective processes.

This is perhaps another reason why the focus in Beckett's fiction is so often on the interplay between a persona and the figures this persona creates. This fictional process stands for the way we try to understand ourselves by creating surrogates for an essentially unknowable entity.

Beckett's fictional characterizations often illustrate two postulates that are usually ignored—in practice if not in principle—by most writers. The first of these postulates specifies that because we have direct access only to our own thoughts, our representation of another's thought is always distorted by subjectivity. The second postulate specifies that, because the mind acts both as subject and object simultaneously, essential components of one's own psyche can never fully be perceived. In other words, a comprehensive understanding of the human psyche—of one's own or another's—is impossible.

Many of the apparent oddities in Beckett's fiction are corollaries derived from these two principles. For example, Beckett seldom reveals very much about his characters' motives. Such omissions are based on the idea that we can never identify, except in the most superficial way, the underlying elements of our own volitional processes. If we were truthful about how little we knew even about our simplest choices, we would admit that discussions of motivation are mainly based on conjecture.

Even so, we continually ascribe motives not only to ourselves but also to others. In the latter instance our conclusions are even less trustworthy than when we are being introspective. We perceive others through distorting filters: of language, illusion, error, mendacity, and the subjectivity that continually tempts us to see what we want to see. A character in fiction is therefore an unfathomable blend of images from the world and imaginary figures.

In Beckett's earliest novels—*Dream of Fair to Middling Women, Murphy,* and *More Pricks Than Kicks*—a growing distrust of conventional novelistic devices leads to two distinctive types of characterization, based on subjective and objective perception. Subjective portrayals are reserved for the narrator or the protagonist and correspond to the way we invoke images of ourselves; the remaining characters are portrayed objectively, that is, in a mode corresponding to the way we observe other people.

Each mode reveals the advantages and limitations inherent in that type of perception. The protagonist's thoughts are marked by the depth and immediacy which correspond to our experience of direct thought; at the same time they are distorted by a haze of egocentricity and self-justification. The characterizations of secondary figures in these works are distorted both by superficiality and by emotions (such as hostility or sexual feelings) originating in the observer.

In his later fiction Beckett introduced a variety of devices—first person narratives, the renaming of characters, the vague figures called "bodies"—that move even further away from traditional characterizations. Because even such devices are inadequate for representing human thought and feelings, Beckett's narrators repudiate their own creations. But if the reality of his characters is undercut, Beckett's main target is the idea of characterization itself.

I have so far left unanswered the question of how to judge Beckett's most caustic descriptions of women, such as those in *Dream of Fair to Middling Women* and *More Pricks Than Kicks*. Certainly, understanding his ideas about characterization can explain some of the disturbing factors in these works. And it is true that over time Beckett made less use of stereotyped characters.

But even so, I am made uncomfortable by passages like the description of the Smeraldina cited at the beginning of this essay. I admire Beckett's work and often see, or hope to see, an element of perfection in it. It is probably for this reason that I find myself wishing Beckett had never written these passages. For all the mitigating circumstances, their rancor still jars.

Beckett was reluctant to have *More Pricks Than Kicks* reprinted and has so far withheld permission for the publication of *Dream of Fair to Middling Women*. I would like to think that he now also regrets having written these caustic passages.

NOTES

1. *More Pricks Than Kicks* (1934; rpt. New York: Grove Press, 1970), 176–77. Subsequent references in the text to Samuel Beckett's works include *Company* (New York: Grove Press, 1980); *Dream of Fair to Middling Women,* Dartmouth Library TS; *Molloy* (New York: Grove Press, 1955); *Malone Dies* (New York: Grove Press, 1956); *More Pricks Than Kicks* (1934; rpt. New York: Grove Press, 1970); *Murphy* (1938; rpt. New York: Grove Press, 1957); *The Unnamable* (New York: Grove Press, 1958); *Stories and Texts for Nothing* (New York: Grove Press, 1967); *Watt* (1953; rpt., New York: Grove Press, 1958).

2. Dylan Thomas, "Documents: Recent Novels," *The English Weekly,* March 17, 1938, 454–55, rpt., *James Joyce Quarterly* 8 (Summer 1971), 290–91.

3. Thus William York Tindall, after describing Joyce's attacks on bigotry in the "Cyclops" chapter, says, "But two-eyed Joyce observes man's virtues, too." Tindall, *A Reader's Guide to James Joyce* (New York: Noonday Press, 1959), 190.

4. Beckett, of course, wrote an essay defending *Finnegans Wake* and has often spoken about his debt to Joyce. For example, Beckett said to Richard Seaver, "Joyce taught me what it meant to be a real artist." Seaver, "Introduction to Samuel Beckett, *I Can't Go ON, I'll Go ON* (New York: Grove Press, 1976), xxiii.

5. *To whinge* means to whimper.

6. A discussion of the unreliable narrative in *Murphy* is given in chapter 9 of my book, *The Development of Samuel Beckett's Fiction* (Champaign: University of Illinois Press, 1984).

7. For more examples of these recurring traits and a discussion of their significance, see *The Development of Samuel Beckett's Fiction*, 37ff.

8. *Molloy*, 47, 215. As a number of critics have pointed out, the trilogy contains many other parallels of this kind. A discussion of these parallels is given in a paper I presented at the Stirling University Beckett conference in August 1986. This paper, "Repetition and Underlying Meanings in Samuel Beckett's Trilogy," will appear in *Rethinking Beckett,* a collection of essays from the conference edited by Lance Butler.

9. A more detailed explanation of how Beckett accomplishes this is given in chapter 5 of *The Development of Samuel Beckett's Fiction.*

10. This passage refers to another, in which the sergeant is presented as a conventional character, that is, as a person with an existence independent of Molloy's; the passage, "Is that your mother's name? said the sergeant," appears there for the first time (29).

11. There are many other places where characters in the trilogy refer to those who preceded them. In *Molloy* there are references to Watt (103) and to Murphy, Watt, and Camier (230). In *The Unnamable* there are frequent references to Malone (5, 6, 7, 9, 10, 11, 14, 15, 16, 23, 33, 44, 163) and also to many other characters—for example, Molloy (5); Murphy (6); Mercier and Camier (11); Murphy, Watt, and Mercier (53); Mercier and Moran (163)

12. Beckett sometimes gives clues about whether the setting of a play is external in naming his characters and describing the lighting. When the names are conventional and the lighting strong, the setting is in the outer world. Thus characters in *Happy Days* have conventional names (Winnie, Willie) and the stage directions call for "blazing light." On the other hand, in *What Where* the characters are named Bam, Bem, Bim, and Bom and the stage is "dimly lit, surrounded by shadow."

Cartesian Man and the Woman Reader
A Feminist Approach to Beckett's Molloy

CAROL HELMSTETTER CANTRELL

> In beginning, therefore, to speak from where we are as women, we can be-
> gin to make observable at least some of the assumptions built into the socio-
> logical discourse. Its own organized practices upon the world have treated
> these assumptions as features of the world itself.
> > Dorothy E. Smith, "A Sociology for
> > Women," in *The Prism of Sex: Essays in
> > the Sociology of Knowledge*

To be a woman reader is constantly to test within one's own experience
the double assumption that both readers and discourse are gender-
neutral. These assumptions are powerful and pervasive: virtually all disciplines presume that gender is as irrelevant to thought as the color of
one's hair and as easily dismissed; indeed, in the sciences and social sciences, validity rests on this presumption. When women trained in professional fields learn to transform "the immediate and concrete features
of [their] experience . . . into the conceptual mode" of their disciplines,
gender neutrality seems to be confirmed.[1] But as soon as women readers
begin to move back and forth between their experience as women and
the assumptions of the discourse they study, the act of reading changes.

For women reading literature the difference can be a shift of emphasis rather than of strategy, for much literature thematizes sex and/or
gender.[2] However, most scientific and philosophical discourse is not
"about" gender; indeed, these discourses are governed by rules which
exclude gender, for they seek to transcend the particular, the personal,
the situational, and the historical in favor of the general or the universal.
Women reading as women in these fields have had to confront directly
the gap between the structure of their experience and the structure of
the discourse they study. The result has been a number of studies in
feminist epistemology which open up not the subject matter but the history and structure of discourse to gender analysis.[3] This body of work
has enormous relevance to literary study. It is of particular importance
for genres and texts whose surfaces present "the human condition" more

or less directly and which, like philosophical discourse, have strategies for getting beyond the stories of day-to-day life.

Samuel Beckett's *Molloy* is a classic example of such a text: the events in the novel defy location in history or geography; the character(s) are hard to construe except as operations of the psyche or operations of language. *Molloy* is not about men and women; it is about what is left of humanity when all that can be stripped away has been stripped away.[4] It is thus both resistant to a feminist reading and demanding of one, for it names and defines human reality. In this essay I will gather together materials and methods from feminist epistemology which, like a light held at an oblique angle to a seemingly flat plane, throw into sharp relief the contours of a language of gender informing *Molloy*.

> The trouble is all in the knob at the top of our bodies. I'm not against the body or the head either: only the neck, which creates the illusion that they are separate.
>
> Margaret Atwood, *Surfacing*

The assumption that readers and texts can be gender-neutral is nested within the long history of the privileging of mind over body in Western culture. In this complex tradition the division between mind and body is hierarchical, implying that human nature "makes its distinctive character most strongly felt in a certain kind of knowledge . . . which contemplates universals."[5] Reason, the faculty of mind which handles universals, is, according to this tradition, unaffected by the bodily situation of the knower. At the same time, reason is strongly associated with the male and just as strongly dissociated from the female.[6] This paradox does not seem paradoxical because the masculine is "unmarked"—that is, it is taken to be the normative or inclusive condition, while the feminine, in contrast, is "marked" as deviant or exceptional.[7] Thus a feminist analysis of the concept of reason suggests that, far from being a privileged human activity free of the taint of gender, reason has served simultaneously to enforce and to deny the reality of gender hierarchy.

Even if reason were gender-neutral, it is defined in relation to pairs of terms that are not. The designation of woman as lesser or partial man is reinforced by the analogous valuation of body as inferior to mind.[8] Both pairs are located with a large and interlocking network of polarities[9] articulating a system of values so pervasive they seem to exist within nature itself.[10] These numerous pairs, which organize and assign values to perceptions and conceptions, include, for example,

male	female
mind	body
culture	nature

reason	emotion
objectivity	subjectivity
public	private
invention	reproduction
form	matter

This system of polarities is not a group of archetypes; its terms are not eternal and unchanging but rather fluid and at times inconsistent,[11] and each pair has its own complicated history.[12] In fact, as a group, these pairs act rather like a language in which gender is a central term.[13] In Iris Young's words, "Gender is not merely a phenomenon of individual psychology and experience. In most cultures it is a basic metaphysical category by which the whole universe is ordered.... [G]ender differentiation is primarily a phenomenon of symbolic life, in both the individual consciousness and the general metaphysical framework of a culture."[14]

As a governing principle of the symbolic life of a culture, then, gender differentiation, and the language of dualisms in which it is embedded, leaves its traces within the discourses which participate in that symbolic life.[15] To anticipate my later argument, Beckett's *Molloy* is a particularly clear example of how a language of dualisms functions within a literary text, for *Molloy* embodies Cartesian dualisms with an uncanny clarity and consistency, as I will show. Before turning to Beckett's text, however, I want to sketch out a feminist reading of the Cartesian shift, with special emphasis on its import for the woman reader.

As feminist philosophers and historians of science have shown, the Cartesian shift affected both the context and the content of gender differentiation. While Descartes clearly considered the *cogito*—that is, the "thinking mind, neither person nor body"—to make human beings equals, the effect of his thought was to rigidify and intensify the split between the two sides of the traditional system of polarities by redefining the nature of knowledge and the nature of matter.[16] First, his method, which makes the mind's detachment a precondition for real knowledge, drove a wedge between subject and object, self and other, mind and body, reason and emotion. The historical significance of this wedge can be demonstrated by contrasting Descartes' detachment with Plato's picture of the knower as driven by passion and striving for union with the object of knowledge.[17] Second, Descartes' reduction of matter to the measurable and the inert intensified the hierarchical relationship between the two sides of the system of polarities. Again, if we contrast Descartes' thought with a prior tradition—in this case, of the long-standing conception of the earth as a living being—we can see the effect of his thought. For after Descartes, veins in human bodies and veins of ore, both living elements in the Renaissance microcosm and macrocosm, are composed of "dead, inert particles moved by external, rather than inherent forces." The "death of nature," as Carolyn Merchant has named this mechanical conception of the world, sanctions its manipulation.[18]

The relationship between subject and object produced by the Cartesian shift affected man's relationship to nature and man's relationship to woman. In Genevieve Lloyd's words: "We owe to Descartes an influential and pervasive theory of mind, which provides support for a powerful version of the sexual division of labor. Women have been assigned responsibility for that realm of the sensuous which the Cartesian Man of Reason must transcend, if he is to have true knowledge of things."[19] The "Man of Reason" can live at the necessary remove from the material world in which, after all, his body is embedded, only with substantial support from those who tend to bodily needs and smooth over the difficulties of life outside the circle of reason. This division of responsibilities amounts to a translation of the language of dualisms into private and public social roles. (In Dorothy Smith's analysis, "At almost every point women mediate for men the relation between the conceptual mode of action and the actual concrete forms in which it is and must be realized, and the actual material conditions upon which it depends."[20]) The modern sexual division of labor typified by the complementary labors of doctor and nurse has been bolstered by an analogous sexual division of personality—women seen as naturally more emotional, more passive, more connected to others; men as more analytical, more active, more detached.[21] Man's impartiality has qualified him to be judge, doctor, scientist, administrator; women's partiality has disqualified her. To a great extent her role has been limited to realms where her main labor—care—is all but invisible.[22]

The extent to which the symbolic life of Western culture absorbed Cartesian assumptions and made self-evident the natural rightness of Cartesian divisions is demonstrated rather dramatically in a nineteenth-century painting described by L. J. Jordanova: "A group of men stand around the table on which a female corpse is lying. She has long hair and well-defined breasts. One of the men has begun the dissection and is working on her thorax. He is holding up a sheet of skin, the part which covers her breast, as if it were a thin article of clothing—so delicate and fine its texture. The corpse is being undressed scientifically, the constituent parts of the body are being displayed for scrutiny and analysis."[23] In this image, virtually all the terms of the language of dualisms are presented with a clarity that results from their interchangeability, which in turn confirms the value system they articulate in unison. Woman equals nature equals body equals object of study:

" '[s]he' becomes 'it'—and 'it' can be understood. Not through sympathy, of course, but by virtue of the very object-ivity of the 'it.' "[24] Woman/body/nature is a passive object devoid of mind, while man/mind/scientist stands above her/it in the act of analysis.[25]

> I am endangered by motherhood. In evacuation from motherhood, I claim my life, body, world as an end in itself.
>
> Jeffner Allen, "Motherhood: The Annihilation of Woman," in *Mothering: Essays in Feminist Theory.*

> But she said despite all this activity, the woman lay alone. She lay alone in labor... *We said it was so clear to us where and how to touch her. We said that to hold back this caring would have been a violence to ourselves.*
>
> Susan Griffin, *Woman and Nature: The Roaring Inside Her*

Being in a body is not a neutral fact for a woman reader, for the female body and the terms associated with it are not neutral or normative but "marked" in the life she lives, in the discourses she reads. If she chooses to think of herself as a neutral, bodiless reader, she regards herself differently than a text regards her. If she chooses to be a "marked," or embodied, reader, she is proceeding in violation of the text's expectations. Seeing her relationship to a text as a problem forces her to reconsider the question of the relationship between body and mind, as mind is represented by texts and readers.

Her location is a function of a complex interaction between symbol system and biology; and in this interaction, analogy is destiny. Analogy, that is, interprets and valuates anatomy: woman is to nature as man is to culture, or, more complexly, woman is closer to nature than man; her labor mediates nature for culture.[26] Her biological rhythms and her capacity to give birth are taken to define her, for they confirm that her alignment with nature is natural. Biology, screened through the grid of her culture's symbolic structures, seems to lock her into her body while loosening the relation of man to his.[27] This asymmetrical relationship of gender to body is an instance of the feminist insight that, as Gayle Rubin has put it: "The idea that men and women are more different from one another than either is from anything else must come from somewhere other than nature.... Far from being an expression of natural differences, exclusive gender identity is the suppression of natural similarities. It requires repression: in men, of whatever is the local version of "feminine" traits; in women of the local definition of "masculine" traits."[28] Thus if woman is defined by her biological rhythms, man in contrast is defined by his disjunction from nature, from natural cycles and processes. Analogy is destiny for him, too. If woman is located on a map of cultural analogies as being close to nature, man must strive to distance himself from nature. Cartesian man, in particular, strives for detachment at both the personal and cultural level in his effort to escape the female/body/nature and to become wholly autonomous; his separation from body, from nature, Susan Bordo argues, "can be seen as a 'father of oneself' fantasy on a highly abstract plane. The sundering of the organic ties between person and nature—originally experienced as a chasm between self and world—is reenacted, this time with the human being as the engineer and architect of the separation."[29]

This sundering gestures in the diretion of what has been torn away, as culture defines itself in opposition to the nature it transcends. For a woman reader the presence of a language of dualisms within the texts she reads means that she is represented in these texts at critical moments of suppression and valuation. She is thus in a position to use these dualisms in a double way as a reader. First, she can use them as guides to what is being opposed, to find the hidden, the unspoken, the denigrated in her life and analogous lives. At the same time she can use her developing understanding of her experience as a standpoint from which to read gendered structures wherever they appear. Such a process of reading, which moves between dominant symbolic structures and the undocumented, devalued, and obscure experience on which those structures depend, can allow a woman reader to read as a woman a novel like *Molloy* within a framework she shares in common with it but without being swallowed up by it.

She has a model for this sort of reading in Susan Griffin's *Woman and Nature: The Roaring Inside Her,* a poet's history of Western civilization, which parallels and anticipates the major issues and discoveries of feminist history and philosophy of science; in this book the voices of Western intellectual history are placed in a space where women hear and respond to them and gradually initiate their own speech.[30] Its beginning point is a series of passages tracing Western intellectual history in which Griffin implicitly locates speaker and virtually silent listener on a map of cultural analogies. Statement and response, speaker and listener, are thereby shown to be in relation to one another. Within that relationship both the speech and the silence subtly change: the listening silence becomes a voice in a dialogue. That specific silence is a starting point for a feminist reader.

> And there was another noise, that of my life become the life of the garden as it rode the earth of deeps and wildernesses. Yes, there were times when I forgot not only who I was, but that I was, forgot to be. Then I was no

longer that sealed jar to which I owed my being so well preserved, but a wall gave way and I filled with roots and tame stems. . . . But that did not happen to me often, mostly I stayed in my jar which knew neither seasons nor gardens.

Samuel Beckett, *Molloy*, 65

It is hard at first to know what to make of the strange, implausible, ridiculous, sporadically beautiful book *Molloy*, but having read it in conjunction with Griffin, our woman reader is struck at once with what seems to her its central feature: it is a monologue, or rather two monologues.[31] The very typography of the book—the great bulk of it a few long uninterrupted paragraphs—tells her that this is a voice that talks but does not listen, a voice that has little concern for, or even awareness of, how his words might affect others. It is a voice that circumscribes her world, for there seems to be no place in the monologue for all that it excludes.

At the same time the book is split in two; it is composed of two sections, one Molloy's and the other Moran's. And indeed the book is riddled with Cartesian splits and divisions which seem to proliferate in it like a monomaniacal genealogy.[32] Mind is divided from body, self from world, father from son, head from feet, man from nature, son from mother, action from desire, attribute from object. And the more she looks at this unity and division, the more each seems to be a function of the other. For in the world of *Molloy* the unity of the self depends on the absorption of or division from all other elements. Thus it is that Molloy's "region is so vast [he has] never left it and never shall" (88) and that at the same time "the Molloy country" is a "narrow region whose administrative limits he had never crossed and presumably never would" (183).

The Molloy country derives both its narrowness and its completeness from its transcendence of the natural world: sense impressions are unreliable; desire for the sensual world is suspect. Moran resents "the spray of phenomena . . . which happily [he] know[s] to be illusory" (15); Molloy has "no reason to be gladdened by the sun and . . . take[s] good care not to be" (39). Molloy successfully remains unaware of seasonal change, and in his eyes distinguishing features of rooms in a house, of cities, of countries, all disappear. When he says, "in my region all the plains looked alike, when you knew one you knew them all" (123), he might as well be describing virtually any category of observable phenomena. In his generalizing eyes, gender distinctions collapse, and whether Lousse might be a man, whether Ruth was a man, become problems of logic, not observation. In any case he and his mother are now so old, as he sees it, that they are sexless and unrelated (21). His visit to the seashore is a masterful exercise in transcendence: while ignoring the ocean, he turns his pleasure in sucking stones into a logical puzzle, taking from the stones their sensuous attributes and transferring his pleasure in them to the mental sphere of problem-solving, effectively obviating his desire for them at all (93–100). Moran would seem to speak for Molloy too when he praises the delights of total separation of mind from body in a "local and painless paralysis": "To be literally incapable of motion at last, that must be something! My mind swoons when I think of it. And mute into the bargain! And perhaps deaf as a post! And who knows blind as a bat! And as likely as not your memory a blank! And just enough brain intact to allow you to exult! And to dread death like a regeneration" (192). This immobilized body is a piece of "a world collapsing endlessly, a frozen world" (53), for the "world dies too, foully named" (41), mind separated from matter rendering lifeless everything that is not mind.

Yet even if regeneration of what our woman reader recognizes as "the death of nature" were a goal for Molloy or Moran, insuperable difficulties appear to stand in the way. For this death is a consequence of the division of mind from body, but union between the two is unstable at best. This she sees in the flickering possibility/impossibility of union between Molloy and Moran. Moran increasingly is Molloy by virtue of sensations and feelings he shares with him, like the pain in his leg and an overwhelming feeling he sometimes has when he thinks of Molloy: "Then I was nothing but uproar, bulk, rage, suffocation, effort unceasing, frenzied and vain" (155). But when Moran thinks about thinking about Molloy he actuates the inevitable doubt that splits mind from body: "Perhaps I had invented him, I mean found him ready made in my head" (152–53); thus the unclosable gap between the Molloy "I stalked within me" and the object of the quest outside the self, "the true Molloy" (157) who exists in some real world outside the imagination.

For our woman reader, alert to the history of gender-related dualisms, the divisions of mind from body in *Molloy* are by analogy divisions from the cluster of associations (the sensuous, the affective, and so forth) in which the language of dualisms locates her. She knows that she can't fit herself into the genderless sphere of mind posited by the text and by the tradition behind it, but she is wary of this strategy and pursues instead the path of her own gendered reading of the book. For she knows that what has struck her most forcibly about this narrative is not its calm rationality but its violence. Detachment, it seems to her, is here propelled by animus. Molloy's narrative gets underway with mother battering ("thumps of the fist" on his mother's skull for supposed communication (22–23); Moran's with child abuse (a punitive enema he administers to his son (162)), though "child abuse" and "battering" are her names, not the narratives', for these events.

The trajectory of violence reaches a climax in murder in each of the monologues: Molloy kicks to death an unconscious charcoal burner, and Moran, not remembering how, kills a stranger (207). The clinical detachment of Molloy's systematic attack on the completely objectified body evokes the image of a dissection:

> This is how I went about it. I carefully chose the most favourable position, a few paces from the body, with my back of course turned to it. Then, nicely balanced on my crutches, I began to swing, backwards, forwards, feet pressed together, or rather legs pressed together, for how could I press my feet together with my legs in the state they were? ... I swung, that's all that matters, in an ever-widening arc. ... I rested a moment, then got up, picked up my crutches, took up a position on the other side of the body and applied myself with method to the same exercise. I always had a mania for symmetry. (114)

And the coldness and technical curiosity of this passage in turn remind our woman reader of Molloy's comedic "love-making" with Ruth, characterized as it is by a combination of his indifference, curiosity, and speculation (76–77).

In the context of the narrative's indifference or antipathy to the body, to life itself, our woman reader finds Molloy's description of his own birth especially disturbing: "Unfortunately it is not of them I have to speak, but of her who brought me into the world, through the hole in her arse if my memory is correct. First taste of the shit" (20). She experiences this passage as a hostile rewriting of the actuality of her body and her experience. Life as waste, birth as defecation—these devaluations of the whole matter/body/nature side of her culture's dualisms find their focus in a vengeful distortion of the female body, her body. The experience of birth is reduced to entrapment in excrement, in matter, by virtue of Molloy's inaccurate reconstruction of his mother's body.[33] In a parallel act of renaming, Molloy calls his "Ma" "Mag," "because for me, without my knowing why, the letter g abolished the syllable Ma, and as it were spat on it, better than any other letter would have done" (21).

From the woman reader's point of view, the movement of the novel compels this hostility toward the female, for it seems to her that a drive for freedom from the body, from nature, from generation and mortality, sanctions violence against her body, which represents all these things. And a drive towards such freedom governs *Molloy*. Its many separations and divisions assert mind's freedom from and superiority to body, which is mightily present in the narrative as an enemy, an impediment, an aching and defective weight that must be swung around on crutches: the more complete the divorce between mind and body, the better. What is called for is a rebirth into transcendence rather than materiality, and this the woman reader finds in Moran's sly suggestion at the end of his monologue that his story has been a complete fiction: he has made himself his own author. If Descartes may be seen as writing a "father of himself fantasy on a highly abstract plane,"[34] so may Moran and, even more easily, Molloy. For when Molloy finally emerges from the dark forest through which he has been crawling, the forest ends in a ditch. He opens his eyes and bursts into the light (122); he is virtually reborn. Having had this experience, he too sits down to write and begins by renaming himself and his mother.

> [Woman] became the embodiment of the biological function, the image of nature, the subjugation of which constituted that civilization's title to fame. For millennia men dreamed of acquiring absolute mastery over nature, of converting the cosmos into one immense hunting ground. It was to this that the idea of man was geared in a male-dominated society. This was the significance of reason, his proudest boast.
>
> Max Horkheimer and Theodor W.
> Adorno, *Dialectic of Enlightenment*

Reading these grand words, the woman reader smiles. For do they not show, by contrast, what pathetic and powerless creatures Molloy and Moran are? Molloy controls, dominates nothing; he owns virtually nothing, succeeds at nothing, leaves his imprint nowhere. Similarly, Moran is stripped of property, reputation, even his son. These are heroes shorn of everything—except their detachment. Molloy's achievement is to rise above his desire for his sucking stones; Moran's, to rise above his attachment to his possessions. It is not power but freedom from attachment, from the claims of convention, of family, of the body, of desire, that they seek. Perhaps they are nothing more than the tail-end of a tradition of heroism defined by the domination of nature. Or perhaps this minimalism is the guarantee of power—the power to define essential human reality.

For as she reflects on the very minimalism of these claims to the heroic, the woman reader considers that in *Molloy* a substantial portion of her experience has been jettisoned in the name of trimming life down to bare necessity. Just as the novel excised and renamed her reproductive system, so it castigates and then eliminates the work of care which the sexual division of labor has assigned to her—care of the body, of the shelter, of the children. Somewhat to her surprise she finds that each monologue dwells at length on a rejection or inversion of this kind of care. For Molloy, the middle third of his monologue is taken up with his resistance to being cared for by the woman he calls Lousse; for Moran, the first two-thirds of his monologue bump repeatedly into the son as obstacle, and child-care shades in and out of neglect and abuse. In both narratives, the labor of human care is devalued as an impediment to freedom.

The preparation of food is an easy example of the mediation of the material world which comprises much of the labor of care, and each monologue registers a protest against it. Molloy feels sure that Lousse is poisoning his food, underlining the significance of the poison with an inaccurate reference to Ulysses being drugged by Circe. He responds to the food she makes for him by ignoring it or snapping it up like a dog (71–72). Moran, who is the caretaker himself, reverses the activity of nourishing his child with the enema he gives him before their journey. These monologues caricature and invert a more fundamental activity of caretaking—that of attentiveness to another person's needs, which in both narratives becomes a version of voyeurism. Lousse does all that she can to keep Molloy around "just to feel me near her, with her" (63), and spies on him constantly. Even though "with Lousse my health got no worse, or scarcely" (74), he does not need her in any way; on the contrary, her food, shelter, and, above all, her attention threaten to smother him: "me too she would have buried" (50). Moran, with his desire to maintain unquestioned authority, is as watchful of his son as Lousse is of Molloy; he is wary of his every movement and mood. The result is to reproduce the value system which creates and fosters separation; the son inevitably leaves his father. Connection with others is as threatening to freedom as is connection with the body.

The essential life of Molloy and Moran, then, cannot be located in the world they share with other people. The essential life is the lonely life of the quest. When Molloy leaves Lousse, the change is abrupt and absolute: "Outside in the road the wind was blowing; it was another world" (80). Both monologues articulate a sharp contrast between the petty comforts of domestic life and the lonely rigors of the quest. There is something a little odd about these rigors, though—they are mainly failures of the body rather than difficulties of terrain or weather. Food and shelter seem to take care of themselves. "But did I at least eat, from time to time? Perforce, perforce, roots, berries, sometimes a little mulberry, a mushroom from time to time, trembling, knowing nothing about mushrooms. . . . In a word whatever I could find, forests abound in good things" (115). This is a pretty minimal pastoral scene, but it suffices to eliminate the work of gathering and preparing food, a task associated with the likes of Lousse. Safe in the forest, the hero's autonomy is not challenged by any obvious dependency on the material world or those who might mediate it for him by providing food and shelter. In fact the violence dominating both narratives may be a measure of the recoil, even revulsion, against dependency and helplessness, for it is directed against those who are themselves helpless and who remind the narrator of his own potential for dependency: mother, son, the unconscious body.

This crabbed pastoral is of central importance to the woman reader in another way as well, which she sees most clearly when she thinks about Lousse's house and Molloy's forest as a dualism. For in this pair of opposites, the forest represents nature and Lousse's house represents culture, thus reversing the more usual association of man with culture, woman with nature. Yet the reversal does not bring about a recognition of her achievement as a maker of culture. Far from it. Lousse's "culture" is genteel female culture: it is "chock-full of pouffes and easy chairs, they all thronged about me, in the gloom" (50). Molloy wakes to find himself in a nightdress—"pink and transparent and adorned with ribands and lace" (58). What could be more unnatural? Molloy obviously does not belong here; this world is antithetical to him. He belongs rather out there, in the world of nature away from her artifice and control. He is natural man, and he scratches, farts, and stinks to prove it. And what is the nature of natural man? "It was I who was not natural enough to enter into the order of things" (58). He is separated man, split man, hierarchical man—in a word, Cartesian man.

The woman reader reflects that this implicit claim to the universal and normative has shadowed her reading of *Molloy* from the first. The book's structure is, in Dorothy Smith's words, "determined elsewhere than where she is."[35] The woman reader is present in the book by negation; its structure of discourse sanctions and perpetuates dualisms which exclude her. At the same time, she notes the possibility that the text offers a critique of this structure, for she is aware of a distance between the author and the characters he has created; at times she glimpses a narrator behind the narrator. "Lousse," for example, is a name Molloy gives to a woman whose given name is "something like Sophie" (44). Yet Sophie is not wise, or if she is, Molloy does not or cannot tell us so; there is no way out of the hall of mirrors of the self-reflexive narratives of Molloy and Moran. If Beckett's narrative implicitly offers a critique of the Cartesian split, it also treats that split as an inescapable condition of human life.[36]

The woman reader, on the other hand, feels a release from this claim. She thinks again about her favorite passage from *Molloy,* the passage about the sealed jar, and, reflecting on the history of dualisms, remembers that the thinking jar who knows neither seasons nor gardens is embedded in both nature and culture, just as she is; that the jar is the invention of a certain historical moment; and that it is subject to all sorts of pressures, to "deeps and wildernesses," "roots and tame stems" (65).

She wonders about the force of certain marginal elements in the book. For there are a few moments when the jar is cracked: Molloy, leaving the forest, listens to the birds singing; Moran writes that he could not have survived without his son's help (216). The achieved harmonious life in the book, represented by the tableau of the shepherd and the sheep (217–19), is impossibly remote; the chasm of the shepherd's silence is not to be broached, not by Moran. No, the challenge to the division between self and other, to the ensuing hierarchy of mind over matter, comes, she thinks, from Moran's bees. Without his attentive care, they die, and he feels the connection with and the loss of life: "I put my hand in the hive, moved it among the empty trays, felt along the bottom. It encountered in a corner, a dry light ball. It crumbled under my fingers. They had clustered together for a little warmth, to try and sleep. . . . They had been left out all winter, their honey taken away, without sugar. . . . My bees, my hens, I had deserted them" (239).

NOTES

I am grateful to Linda Ben-Zvi for encouraging me to undertake this project and thank her and Sue Ellen Charlton for generous and perceptive readings of early drafts. Many thanks also to the students of my spring 1987 Women's Studies seminar for their spirited discussions of the main issues discussed in this essay.

1. Dorothy E. Smith, "Women's Perspective as a Radical Critique of Sociology," *Sociological Inquiry* 44, no. 1 (1974), 7–13; quote on 8.

2. The contribution of much feminist literary criticism of male authors has been to foreground sexism as a major theme—e.g., "Styron's novels—and the distinction is important—are not oppressive but about oppression, not racist but about racism, not anti-Semitic but about anti-Semitism, and, I shall argue, not sexist although, in the instance of *Sophie's Choice* especially, are presistently about sexism." See Carolyn A. Durham, "William Styron's *Sophie's Choice:* The Structure of Oppression," *Twentieth Century Literature* 30, no. 4 (1984), 449.

Generally, however, "feminist literary scholars have turned their attention to the study of . . . literature produced by women, chiefly about the nature and lives of women themselves." Ellen Carol DuBois et al, *Feminist Scholarship: Kindling in the Groves of Academe* (Urbana: University of Illinois Press, 1985), 58.

3. These writings do not provide a unified theory of feminist epistemology, nor do they try to do so. They might be described as an "extended family" of writings, with some branches clearly distinguished by their disciplinary or theoretical lineages. For explorations of the difficulty or even the desirability of unifying feminist theory, see Sandra Harding, "The Instability of the Analytical

Categories of Feminist Theory," *Signs* 11, no. 4, (1986), 645–64, and *The Science Question in Feminism* (Ithaca, N. Y.: Cornell University Press, 1986), esp. 136–96.

4. *The Norton Anthology of English Literature: The Major Authors,* ed. M. H. Abrams (New York: Norton, 1986), a standard classroom text, describes Beckett's heroes: "They take no action, they preach no doctrine, they know nothing save their own ignorance. . . . And yet in some dark way they represent mankind. . . . [T]hey bear witness, as more comfortable folk could not, to the essential holiness of existence" (2543).

5. Richard Rorty, *Philosophy and the Mirror of Nature* (Princeton, N.J.: Princeton University Press, 1979), 43.

6. Sandra Harding, "Is Gender a Variable in Conceptions of Rationality? A Survey of Issues, "*Dialectica* 36, no. 2–3 (1982) rpt. in *Beyond Domination: New Perspectives on Women and Philosophy,* ed. Carol Gould, (Totowa, N.J.: Rowman and Allenheld, 1984), 43–63; Lynda Lange, "Woman Is Not a Rational Animal: On Aristotle's Biology of Reproduction," in *Discovering Reality: Feminist Perspectives in Epistemology, Metaphysics, Methodology, and Philosophy of Science,* ed. Sandra Harding and Merrill B. Hintikka, (Dordrecht, Holland: D. Riedel, 1983), 1–15; Janice Moulton, "A Paradigm of Philosophy: The Adversary Method," in *Discovering Reality,* 149–64; Kathryn Pyne Addelson, "The Man of Professional Wisdom," in *Discovering Reality,* 165–86; Evelyn Fox Keller, *Reflections on Gender and Science* (New Haven, Conn: Yale University Press, 1985), esp. 75–79; Genevieve Lloyd, *The Man of Reason: "Male" and "Female" in Western Philosophy* (Minneapolis: University of Minnesota Press, 1984), with a useful bibliographic essay, 123–33; Elizabeth Young-Bruehl, "The Education of Women as Philosophers," *Signs* 12, no. 1 (1987), 207–21, esp. 212–14.

7. See Judith Shapiro, " 'Women's Studies': A Note on the Perils of Markedness," *Signs* 7, no. 3 (1982), 717–21. The unmarked/marked distinction extends to other species, even invented ones: a regular Smurf is a Smurf; a female Smurf is a Smurfette.

8. Caroline Whitbeck, "Theories of Sex Difference," *The Philosophical Forum* 5, no. 1–2 (1973–74), 54–80; rpt. in *Women and Values: Readings in Recent Feminist Philosophy,* ed. Marilyn Pearsall (Sacramento: California State University Press, 1986), 34–50.

9. I would argue that we could not even construe a passage like the following if we did not know that the terms "woman," "nature," "passive," "nurturing," (to note only a few) were in certain rhetorical circumstances interchangeable:

> In [woman's] nature lies the healing power which replaces that which has been used up, the beneficial rest in which everything immoderate confines itself, the eternal Same, by which the excessive and the surplus regulate themselves. In her the future generation dreams. Woman is more closely related to Nature than man and in all her essentials she remains ever herself. Culture is with her always something external, a something which does not touch the kernel that is eternally faithful to Nature." Nietzsche, "The Greek Woman," quoted in Lloyd, *The Man of Reason,* 1–2.

Similarly, the history of one of these pairs entails the others: "Public and private are imbedded within a dense web of associational meanings and intimations and linked to other basic notions: nature and culture, male and female. . . . Another scholar might explore the same issues—those having to do with women and politics—by tracing the meaning of nature and culture through the centuries." Jean Bethke Elshtain, *Public Man, Private Woman: Woman in Social and Political Thought* (Princeton, N.J.: Princeton University Press, 1981), 5.

10. See especially the germinal essay by Sherry B. Ortner, "Is Female to Male as Nature Is to Culture?" in *Woman, Culture, and Society,* ed. Michelle Z. Rosaldo and Louise Lamphere (Stanford, Calif.: Stanford University Press, 1974), 67–87, rpt. in *Women and Values,* 62–75.

11. Carol P. MacCormack, "Nature, Culture and Gender: A Critique" in *Nature, Culture and Gender,* ed. Carol MacCormack and Marilyn Strathern (Cambridge, England: Cambridge University Press, 1980), 1–24, esp. 6–11.

12. See two works by L. J. Jordanova, "Natural Facts: A Historical Perspective on Science and Sexuality," in *Nature, Culture and Gender,* 42–69; and "Naturalizing the Family: Literature and the Bio-Medical Sciences in the late Eighteenth Century," in *Languages of Nature: Critical Essays on Science and Literature,* ed. L. J. Jordanova (New Brunswick, N.J.: Rutgers University Press, 1986), 90–116. See also A. E. Pilkington, " 'Nature' as Ethical Norm in the Enlightenment" in *Languages of Nature,* 55–85; the pioneering studies by Raymond Williams, *The Country and the City* (New York: Oxford University Press, 1973); and Mary Ellmann, *Thinking about Women* (New York: Harcourt, 1968).

13. "Language" here refers to a system of signs regulated by laws of combination and selection, "discourse" to a social/historical formation of language. See Jean-Michel Rabaté, *Language, Sexuality and Ideology in Ezra Pound's Cantos* (Albany, N.Y.: SUNY Press, 1986), 14–16, for a concise discussion of these terms.

14. Iris Marion Young, "Is Male Gender Identity the Cause of Male Domination?" in *Mothering: Essays in Feminist Theory,* ed. Joyce Trebilcot (Totowa, N.J.: Rowman and Allenheld, 1983), 129–46, esp. 135.

15. For an analysis of the effect of traditional rational thought on feminist discourse about abortion, see Kathryn Pyne Parsons, "Moral Revolution" in *The Prism of Sex: Essays in the Sociology of Knowledge,* ed. J. Sherman and E. T. Beck (Madison: University of Wisconsin Press, 1979), 189–227.

16. Elshtain, *Public Man, Private Woman,* 173, n. 48: Lloyd, *The Man of Reason,* 44–50.

17. See Lloyd, *The Man of Reason,* 6 and 4–41; Keller, *Reflections on Gender and Science,* 23–32.

18. Carolyn Merchant, *The Death of Nature: Women, Ecology and the Scientific Revolution* (San Francisco: Harper and Row, 1980), 193.

19. Lloyd, *The Man of Reason,* 50.

20. Smith, "Women's Perspective," 10.

21 See Keller, *Reflections on Gender and Science,* 75–94, and Susan Bordo, "The Cartesian Masculinization of Thought," *Signs* 11, no. 3 (1986), 439–56, esp. 441, 455–56.

22. See Smith, "A Sociology for Women," 163–69; Sara Ruddick, "Maternal Thinking," *Feminist Studies* 6, no. 2 (Summer 1980), 342–67; shorter version rpt. in *Mothering*, 213–30. Joan C. Tronto, in "Beyond Gender Difference to a Theory of Care," *Signs* 12, no. 4 (1987), 644–61, provides a useful guide to feminist writings about this issue, though her emphasis is on claims within feminism to the ethical value of care rather than its invisibility.

23. Jordanova, "Natural Facts," 57.

24. See Bordo, "The Cartesian Masculinization of Thought," 452: "Now, in the same brilliant stroke that insured the objectivity of science—the mutual opposition of the spiritual and the corporeal—the formerly female earth becomes *res extensa:* dead, mechanically interacting matter."

25. The assumptions behind the treatment of other beings as objects suggest to some feminists an essential link between the domination of woman and of nature. See Leonie Caldecott and Stephanie Leland, eds., *Reclaim the Earth: Women Speak Out for Life on Earth* (London: The Women's Press, 1983); Ynestra King, "The Ecology of Feminism and the Feminism of Ecology," *Harbinger: The Journal of Social Ecology* 1 (Fall 1983), 16–22; Jane Coleman, "Reflections on Feminism and Ecology," *Harbinger* 3 (Fall, 1985), 41–44. Many thanks to Karen Wedge for sharing the *Harbinger* articles with me.

26. Ortner, "Is Female to Male as Nature Is to Culture?" 67–87.

27. See *Women Look at Biology Looking at Women: A Collection of Feminist Critiques*, ed. Ruth Hubbard, Mary Sue Henifren, and Barbara Fried (Boston, G. K. Hall, 1979).

28. Gayle Rubin, "The Traffic in Women: Notes on the 'Political Economy' of Sex," in *Toward an Anthropology of Women*, ed. Rayna Rapp Reiter (New York: Monthly Review Press, 1975), rpt. in *Feminist Frameworks*, ed. Alison M. Jagger and Paula S. Rothenberg, 2nd ed., (New York: McGraw-Hill, 1984), 155–71, esp. 165.

29. Bordo, "The Cartesian Masculinization of Thought," 452; see also Keller, *Reflections on Gender and Science*, esp. 79–94.

30. Susan Griffin, *Woman and Nature: The Roaring inside Her* (New York: Harper and Row, 1980).

31. Samuel Beckett, *Molloy*, tr. Patrick Bowles and Samuel Beckett (New York: Grove Press, 1955). References to *Molloy* will be indicated parenthetically in the text.

32. Though this essay is not an influence study, it is useful to note that Beckett read Descartes' works in his academic studies, and based his poem *Whoroscope* on a biography of Descartes. See Linda Ben-Zvi, *Samuel Beckett* (Boston: G. K. Hall, 1986), 12.

33. What Molloy calls "love" momentarily restores at least the vagina, if not the rest of the female reproductive system: "She had a hole between her legs, oh not the bunghole I had always imagined, but a slit," but this recognition of difference is short lived, for Molloy soon speculates about whether his partner didn't really have testicles after all (76).

34. Bordo, "The Cartesian Masculinization of Thought," 452.

35. Smith, "Women's Perspective," 13.

36. Martin Esslin argues that "the whole mighty *oeuvre* of Samuel Beckett . . . never ceases to dismantle and deconstruct the Cartesian '*cogito ergo sum.*'" See "Modernity and Drama" in *Modernism: Challenges and Perspectives,* ed. Monique Chefdor, Ricardo Quinones, and Albert Wachtel (Urbana: University of Illinois Press, 1986), 54–65, esp. 59. Esslin is making the case that Beckett, like Nietzsche, questions assumptions implicit in saying "I think"—e.g., it is I thinking, there is such a thing as I to whom thinking is causally related, and so forth. In that sense of the word *deconstruct,* this essay is also an attempt to show how Beckett works out the implications of the *cogito,* but its emphasis is on examining the values ensconced in the *cogito* as a given, however problematic.

The Magna Mater Myth in Beckett's Fiction: Subtext and Subversion

ANGELA B. MOORJANI

That every text repeats other texts, which repeat still other texts and so forth ad infinitum, is nowhere more dramatically evident than in Beckett's writing. Indeed, the dizzying abysmal structure of his novels, which heaps fragment upon fragment upon fragment, provides no foundation or end that might anchor or limit the text. Of the novels' reverberating myths, this essay examines the subtexts related to the Magna Mater and explores how they function within the fiction.[1]

Of the many attitudes writers can take to the subtexts they manipulate, Beckett's is almost without exception ironic or antagonistic. The many texts his fiction quotes directly or indirectly are rewritten, mocked, superimposed one on the other, only to be erased. Beckett's de-mythologization thus joins his other debunking activities which, in contesting language from within language, genre conventions from within genre, and mythic categories from within myth, are—as Roland Barthes would have it—what writing is all about (16–17). In the process, readers are challenged to question one after the other the categories that make up their conceptual universe, the archeology of the mind, to reflect on the consequences of the old ideologies, and to hear the whispered call of something as yet untried. Within a diologic dimension, then, in Beckett's fiction the infinite store of stories that readers bring to the reading process is subverted along with the rest as a web of illusions.

The following discussion of the Magna Mater fragments concentrates on *Molloy* (1951), whose mythical reverberations have been long noted, and on *Ill Seen Ill Said* (1981).[2] The narrator of the first part of *Molloy* carefully stages what he calls his "unreal journey" (16) toward his mother as a descent into the psyche, the poetic descent into the underworld. The narrator/writer, then, after fraying a path into the embedded archives of the mind, transcribes the tracings of multiple inner texts made up of layer after layer of inscriptions. Such textual travel/travail brings to mind similar inner autobiographies, not least of which Dante's

Commedia, that other journey through the mind's book toward the celestial rose and divine light, those partial translations of the ineffable.

The first inner landscape of *Molloy* features a bare white road at evening undulating through pastures in which cows are chewing. The town and the sea are not far off. After a brief stay in the town and a night passed in a ditch, on approximately the third day, Molloy runs over a dog and, having entered its owner's domain, remains there a year or so before continuing his wanderings. The description of this one-year cycle in Sophie Loy-Lousse's garden bristles with mythic allusions and functions as a micronarrative reduplicating the narrative that surrounds it. Embedded within Molloy's inner journey to his mother, then, is the mythic realm of a maternal divinity.

The triple-named Lousse calls to mind a whole cluster of deities, among whom the Greek lunar trinity of Artemis, Selene, and Hecate, particularly the latter associated with the waning moon. The triple-bodied Hecate is the mother of witchcraft and the goddess of death and rebirth who with her hounds guards the gates of Hades. Dog-sacrifices were offered to her at crossroads. The key, the dagger, the dog, and the cross were among her symbols (Spretnak 65–77, Jung 369–71). One need only recall the long description of the moon, Lousse's sorcery evoking Circe along with Hecate, the mysterious garden gate, the death and burial of the dog, the knife and cruciform knife-rest Molloy takes from the house, to recognize Hecate within Lousse.

In his *Symbols of Transformation* (179), the first version of which appeared in 1912, Jung links Hecate to the bad mother and the sphinx, a role the hag-like Lousse plays by keeping Molloy captive in her underworld prison and by preventing his journey to his mother. That she also saves him from being torn to bits by the surly crowd that gathers after the dog's death, that she loves and nourishes him in her paradisaical garden, point to Lousse as the good mother, blending the negative with the positive.

The repeated allusions to the dead dog as Lousse's child, whom Molloy replaces, suggest, however, the Graeco-Asian Magna Mater, predating classical myth by thousands of years, whose divine child suffers death or a descent into the underworld and a return to life, in imitation of the seasonal cycle of growth, decay, death, and rebirth. The Sumero-Babylonian Ishtar and Tammuz, the Phoenician Astarte or the Cypriote Aphrodite and Adonis, the Phrygian Cybele and Attis, the Egyptian Isis and Osiris, and the Greek Demeter and Persephone and later Dionysus are all versions of the Great Mother and her dying and resurrected child. Outranking her child in importance, this Magna Mater, the embodiment of creative power, controlled birth, vegetation, and fertility and taught humanity law and divine worship. Among her emblems were the dove, the lion, the fish, and she was associated with life-giving waters (James 186, 237f.). Although Beckett could have thought of any or all of the above myths, or of others still, certain elements found in the Lousse episode would make it appear that the Cybele-Attis rites as portrayed by Frazer in *The Golden Bough* are the text to which he alludes, a connection first pointed out by Aldo Tagliaferri (53). According to Frazer, one of several versions of the legend has Attis, the son and lover of Cybele, bleed to death after castrating himself under a pine tree (264). Frazer glosses this as an attempt to explain the presence of eunuch priests, whom he describes as "unsexed beings in . . . Oriental costume," in the service of the divinity (265–66). Other writers have pointed out that such self-mutilation was motivated by the desire "to secure complete identity with the Goddess" (James 167). The main festival of Cybele and Attis, which took place at the vernal equinox, consisted of bringing a pine tree wreathed with violets into the Magna Mater's sanctuary, for these flowers "were said to have sprung from the blood of Attis, as roses and anemones from the blood of Adonis" (Frazer 267). Frazer speculates that it was during the ecstatic death and resurrection rites around the tree that the self-emasculations took place, adding that the mutilated worshippers would thereafter put on female attire (268–70).

In returning to Beckett's novel, we find Lousse burying the dog Teddy, whose divine nature is hinted by his name signifying "gift of god," under a larch, whose green needles appear speckled with red, while Molloy contemplates ridding himself of his testicles: "So the best thing for me would have been for them to go, and I would have seen to it myself, with a knife or secateurs, but for my terror of physical pain and festered wounds, so that I shook" (36). This passage, of course, is an example of Beckett's self-destructive texts, for no sooner identified with Attis, Molloy becomes an anti-Attis. Further hints, however, link him to the Cybele myth: he awakens in Lousse's house shaven of his beard, dressed in a frilly pink nightgown, served by an Oriental, and feeling like a sacrificial victim. When he leaves Lousse's garden at the end of a year, the weather is warm, and multi-colored flowers are growing on Teddy's grave. These details and Molloy's continued identification with the buried dog point to the motif of the year-god, particularly Attis and Dionysus, and to Lousse as a Great Mother of birth, death, and rebirth. Of Lousse's garden Molloy tells that it appeared to change very little "apart from the tiny changes due to the customary cycle of birth, life and death" (52). That he merges with this garden's life in a mythic return to the womb of the Earth Mother emphasizes his oneness with the Magna Mater, a oneness evident in his symbolic emasculation and in the blended names Molloy/Loy and Mollose/Lousse. He is, as it were, reabsorbed in the mother awaiting rebirth.

At the same time, though, as we have seen, Molloy is the son-lover of the mother goddess. That, as a consequence, he identifies Lousse both with his mother, Mag (a blend of "Ma" and "hag"), and with another triple-named crone, Ruth-Edith-Rose (an anagram of "Eros"), does not prevent him from thinking that she is perhaps male or at least androgynous—an observation echoing the dual gender of Cybele and of the earliest known divinities (James 166). An androgynous Magna Mater and her hermaphroditic child, moreover, question and confound the rigid male/female polarities of patriarchal religions, which devalue the female principle. From an archetypal perspective, this androgynous image shifts Lousse beyond the Magna Mater into the primordial archetype in which opposites are undifferentiated (Neumann 7–8).

In linking Lousse to the lunar triad and the Magna Mater, we have far from exhausted this fragment's intertextual reverberations, for in Sophie Lousse, there are also echoes of the gnostic Sophia or divine Wisdom in female form. That Beckett playfully manipulates gnostic concepts has been pointed out by a number of commentators, although not in relation to the Sophia myth (Morot-Sir 81–104, Busi 76f.). For the gnostics, Sophia combined the attributes of the Graeco-Oriental moon-, mother-, and love-goddesses into one figure, encompassing the whole spectrum from the most spiritual to the most sensual. She was known accordingly as "Sophia-Prunikos" or "Wisdom the Whore" (Jonas 176–77). That the ancient Sumero-Babylonian Ishtar was similarly called both "Queen of Heaven" and "Harlot" shows that the blending of spirituality and sensuality was a constant of goddess worship (Langdon 81f.). (In relation to Beckett, one cannot help but think of *Murphy* and the novel's punning reference to Celia as a celestial whore.) The dove, which became the symbol of the gnostic Sophia in her role of Holy Spirit, provides a further link to the ancient Mother- and Great Goddess (Walker 951).

In returning to Beckett's Sophie Lousse, we find that the elements linking her to Sophia are treated with particular ridicule. Lousse, whose soliloquies Molloy finds harder to understand than her parrot's obscenities in which the word *putain* ("whore") stands out (37), is a travesty of Sophia-Prunikos. The French word for "parrot," *perroquet,* moreover, is close enough in sound to "Paraclete" (Holy Spirit) to make me suspect a multilingual pun.

Certainly, *Molloy's* ironic treatment of Sophia, and of the Magna Mater she represents, parallels the gnostic attitude toward her, for gnosticism—or, more precisely, the older Syrian-Egyptian or emanationist

gnostic tradition—makes the distinction between an unknowable, unnamable, and hidden divinity, on the one hand, and the divinity's degraded emanations, the creators of an evil world, on the other. Among
these creators comes first the androgynous Sophia followed by a demi-
urge born of her and commonly identified with the biblical Yahweh.[3]

In order to clarify the parallels between the gnostic bisexual creation
myth and *Molloy*, it is necessary to situate the Lousse text in the two-part
novel. As we have seen, in chronicling a mother quest within a mother
quest, the Lousse fragment is embedded, indeed more or less centered,
in the main narrative of the novel's first part, which, in turn, is contained in the novel's second part, featuring a patriarchal order. The second part repeats the first by rewriting its maternal discourse in terms of
the paternal.[4] Since the female order is thus everywhere traceable within
the male, just as the mother-identified Molloy is within the father-
identified Moran, the novel's second part is an example of an androgynous text or palimpsest.

Once the formidable Magna Mater/Sophia figure of part 1 has been
rewritten as a tyrannical pater, a parody of Yahweh, in part 2, however,
these two discourses, echoing the multiple mythic representations of the
female and the male, are equally subverted by the narrators. The androgynous nature of the text, giving equal status to the maternal and paternal
law, which we might prefer over the uniquely patriarchal, does not end
the quest. All totalizing solutions, archetypal or otherwise, are rejected,
for the quest, one of an infinite series, spirals on to the unnamable.
Thus, at the end of his self-narration, Moran no longer identifies the
voice he hears with the paternal Logos, and Molloy, rejecting the maternal law (Loy/law), listens to the small voice telling him to leave Lousse's
garden. It is this anonymous call that might free them perhaps from the
violent maternal and paternal inscriptions of the past and undo writing's
ties to a degraded creation mystique.

And finally, as is well known, the narrators proceed with a more dras-
tic negation, that of their own discourses and by extension of the texts
they contain, all of which they dismiss as lies, as fictions of fictions,
which like all language are the faulty translations of what cannot be
named.

The fictions, visions, or transcriptions that the narrators of *Molloy*
produce during their journey through the psyche are, however, not so
easily blotted out. Thirty years or so after *Molloy*, the landscape and figure of *Ill Seen Ill Said* evoke the Lousse fragment and its multiple subtexts. As in the first part of *Molloy*, the landscape is pastoral, containing
unshepherded white cows, in whose form the divine mother is frequently pictured. The sea is nearby. The garden, however, is replaced by

a circular area of stones within whose nonexistent center stands a cabin. The deathly whiteness of stone and snow in the light of the moon increasingly invades the terrain. The unnamed old woman, a silhouette of white and black like so many recent Beckettian figures, alludes particularly to Ishtar, the ancient Great Mother. Like the Magna Mater, Beckett's silent apparition is linked to the planet Venus as the morning star; associated with the moon; attended by male guardians (here a cyclical or zodiacal twelve), linked with a stone pillar or menhir (replacing the sacred tree), has the fish as an emblem, and flowers a mysterious tomb (Langdon 53f.). She is foremost a mater dolorosa, the mother sorrowing for her lost lover and child (here recalling the divine shepherd Tammuz) during the desolate seasons of the year. As a mater dolorosa, she evokes Mary, the mother of Christ, to whose sacrifice this, as most Beckettian texts, makes direct reference and with which Beckett associates his own birth.

Unlike the narrator of *Molloy*, whose tone is mocking in relation to Lousse and whose comments playfully undermine the discourse he is producing, this later narrator's tone varies from panic to weary sadness at the tenacity of the illusory maternal trace, which like all the other figments of the mind, all lying traces of lying traces, is the "ill seen ill said" transcription of the still unnamable.

These Beckettian texts, then, in displacing the usual male/female oppositions, in subverting the mythic network imprisoning female and male, and in contesting language from inside language, join with contemporary theoretical critiques of self-presentation, as so well exemplified by Hélène Cixous in *La Jeune Née:* "Men and women are caught up in a network of millennial cultural determinations of a complexity that is practically unanalyzable: we can no more talk about 'woman' than about 'man' without getting caught up in an ideological theater where the multiplication of representations, images, reflections, myths, identifications constantly transforms, deforms, alters each person's imaginary order and in advance, renders all conceptualization null and void" (Marks 96).

NOTES

1. "Subtext" is here defined as "an already existing text (or texts) reflected in a new one" (Taranovsky 18). For a discussion of the concept, see Rusinko.

2. For references to other mythic subtexts in *Molloy*, see Moorjani 96–120.

3. This cosmogony is described in the *Apocryphon of John*, written in approximately 95 A.D., and since the second century one of the most widely known gnostic tractates. Renewed interest in the work has come with the discovery of

the Nag Hammadi codices. For the text of the *Apocryphon,* see Robinson 98–116; for further discussions of Sophia, see Rudolph 72–84, and Pagels 57f.

4. To illustrate how the second part of *Molloy* rewrites its maternal subtext, one might mention that Molloy's wrangling over the distribution of his sixteen sucking stones (maternal substitute objects) reappears in the second part as Moran's preoccupation with sixteen irreverent theological questions of a patriarchal nature (Moorjani 114). For an analysis of the intricate relation between the two parts, see Moorjani 39–48, 99–118.

WORKS CITED

Barthes, Roland. *Leçon.* Paris: Seuil, 1978.

Beckett, Samuel. *Mal vu mal dit.* Paris: Minuit, 1981/*Ill Seen Ill Said.* New York: Grove Press, 1981.

————*Molloy.* Paris: Minuit, 1951/*Three Novels: Molloy, Malone Dies, The Unnamable.* New York: Grove Press, Black Cat, 1965.

Busi, Frederick. *The Transformations of Godot.* Lexington: University Press of Kentucky, 1980.

Cixous, Hélène, and Catherine Clément. *La Jeune Née.* Paris: Union Générale d'Editions, 10/18, 1975.

Frazer, Sir James G. *The Golden Bough.* 3rd ed. 1914; rpt. London: Macmillan, 1966. Part 4. Vol. 1.

James, E. O. *The Cult of the Mother-Goddess.* New York: Barnes and Noble, 1959.

Jonas, Hans. *The Gnostic Religion.* Boston: Beacon, 1958.

Jung, Carl G. *Symbols of Transformation.* 2nd ed. Princeton: Princeton University Press, 1967.

Langdon, Stephen. *Tammuz and Ishtar.* Oxford: Clarendon Press, 1914.

Marks, Elaine, and Isabelle de Courtivron, eds. *New French Feminisms: An Anthology.* Amherst: University of Massachusetts Press, 1980.

Moorjani, Angela B. *Abysmal Games in the Novels of Samuel Beckett.* Studies in the Romance Languages and Literatures. Chapel Hill: University of North Carolina Press, 1982.

Morot-Sir, Edouard. "Samuel Beckett and Cartesian Emblems." In *Samuel Beckett: The Art of Rhetoric.* Ed. E. Morot-Sir et al. Studies in the Romance Languages and Literatures. Chapel Hill: University of North Carolina Press, 1976. 25–104.

Neumann, Erich. *The Great Mother.* 2nd ed. Princeton: Princeton University Press, 1963.

Pagels, Elaine. *The Gnostic Gospels.* New York: Random House, Vintage, 1981.

Robinson, James M., ed. *The Nag Hammadi Library in English.* San Francisco: Harper and Row, 1981.

Rudolph, Kurt. *Gnosis.* Trans., ed. Robert McLachlan Wilson. San Francisco: Harper and Row, 1983.

Rusinko, Elaine. "Intertextuality: The Soviet Approach to Subtext." *Dispositio* 4 (1979), 212–35.

Spretnak, Charlene. *Lost Goddesses of Early Greece*. Boston: Beacon, 1981.

Tagliaferri, Aldo. *Beckett et la surdétermination littéraire*. Paris: Payot, 1977.

Taranovsky, Kiril. *Essays on Mandel'štam*. Cambridge: Harvard University Press, 1976.

Walker, Barbara G. *The Woman's Encyclopedia of Myths and Secrets*. San Francisco: Harper and Row, 1983.

Homage to the Dark Lady
Ill Seen Ill Said

LAWRENCE GRAVER

Most readers looking for the main source of the drama and the interest of *Ill Seen Ill Said* are likely to locate it where it is customarily found in Beckett's fiction since *The Trilogy:* in the scene of the writing; in the narrator's fevered, indeflectable effort to flesh out a figment, to embody in language the ghostly figure of a dead old woman who haunts him. The action as usual takes place in the speaker's skull (that "ivory dungeon") where his different perceptual faculties are engaged in a psychic civil war—eye and mind unable to distinguish between what is remembered and what imagined, and language as always the most suspect, persistently indicted of expressive instruments. In what the speaking voice calls this "farrago of eye and mind," each faculty and instrument is continually accused of betraying itself and others: "The mind betrays the treacherous eyes and the treacherous word their treacheries." The result is a narrative of almost unendurable (and yet miraculously endured) pressure. The miracle, as we've come to expect from late Beckett, is in the astral beauty of the language—a prose as compacted, luminous, and densely resonant as any he has ever written.

But what makes *Ill Seen Ill Said* unique in the Beckett canon is less the drama at the scene of the writing, or the narrator's travail, but rather the subject embodied in that astonishing poetic prose—the old woman who is a most singular figure among Beckett's creations. As many of the other essays in this volume demonstrate, nearly all the women in Beckett's fiction are satiric targets or long-suffering victims (and often both). Those seen from a distance (in the early fiction, for example) are usually mocked through irony as frisky, libidinous, threatening figures who create and/or sustain life and won't let the beleaguered male protagonist cultivate his solipcism or get on with his dying. In *The Trilogy* the mockery (though still comic) becomes more corrosive and grim, approaching at times a kind of Swiftian ferocity. For Molloy all women become "one and the same old hag, flattened and crazed by life. And God forgive me, to tell you the horrible truth, my mother's image sometimes mingles with theirs." And by the time we hear the Unnamable, there are only "two cunts into the bargain, the one for ever accursed that ejected me into this world and the other, infundibuliform [funnel-shaped], in which, pumping my likes, I tried to take my revenge." Even Malone's Moll, despite her amiable lubricity and blasphemous dental work, is also seen through the lens of a grotesque, if comic, disgust.

No matter how they are perceived, though, the women of the novels are nearly all ancillary figures; the women of the plays (especially after the opening of *Happy Days* in 1961) are more important. Those seen or heard close-up (Maddy Rooney, Winnie, the wife and mistress in *Play*, Mouth, May, and the Woman in *Rockaby*) are—for all their splendid differences—long-suffering, sometimes self-deluded, always self-divided, often extravagantly resilient but ultimately unfulfilled and incomplete; indeed, in the famous, repeated image, not properly born; or, as in the case of the spectral May of *Footfalls*, not even there. Obvious exceptions exist: the affectionately drawn, prominent Celia in *Murphy* is the most notable; and if you read the narrator of *Enough* as a woman, so is she; but on the whole these broad generalizations hold up.

What makes the old woman in *Ill Seen Ill Said* unique is that she is entirely exempt from irony—neither mocked nor exposed—and she is given a dignity matched by very few, if any, figures (male or female) in Beckett's work. The main source of her dignity is that she both embodies in her physical being and enacts in her behavior values that for Beckett—despite his unremitting skepticism—have always been positive. And, in several mysterious ways, she seems also to be one of the most significant of the elusive others that his narrators have for more than half-a-century been trying to track down.

The woman's ancient frame, frail yet rigid and erect, everywhere reflects what Beckett once described in a tribute to his friend, Avigdor Arikha, as indelible "marks of what it is to be and be in the face of." She appears to have endured the immemorial afflictions of her species and registers them in a way that generates a shivery respect and even wonder. "The long white hair stares in a fan. Above and about the impassive face. Stares as if shocked still by some ancient horror. Or by its continuance. Or by another. That leaves the face stonecold. Silence at the eye of the scream"(28–29). Long white hair is perhaps the most familiar feature of the late Beckett protagonist, and the old woman of *Ill Seen Ill Said* shares it with May of *Footfalls*, the male figures in *That Time, A Piece of Monologue,* and *Ohio Impromptu,* and the shadowy inhabitants enclosed in Beckett's hermetic *Residua.* But her most unforgettable and expressive signature is the faintly bluish white face that impassively yet all at once registers the shocks of past, present, and future adversity.

The old woman is never heard to speak; she no longer even talks to herself. Yet if in her silence we are prompted to imagine the chilling "eye of the scream," we perceive other very different things as well. Despite her great age and the marks of suffering, she is described as moving with a stately purposefulness that makes her seem monumental. When the hovering eye closes in on her eating her slops in the dark, he sees how, "at last in a twin movement full of grace she slowly raises the bowl toward her lips while at the same time with equal slowness bowing her head to join it."

The beauty of this depends in large measure on the sense that the grace has been hard won through countless, unimaginable vicissitudes, the suffering a kind of refining fire. At another point the woman's face is compared to "a calm slab worn and polished by agelong comings and goings. . . . How serene it seems this ancient mask. Worthy those worn by certain newly dead." Indeed, throughout the narrative, the woman is perceived as substantial *and* spectral, as being in time and yet in ways beyond it—beyond surprise and human need—which has always been something of a hallowed state in the Beckett universe, a state that partakes at once of the mysteries of presence and absence.

The powerful, eerie sense of the woman being at the same time here and elsewhere is reinforced throughout the text by the repeated emphasis on her paradoxical monumentality and wraith-like delicacy. Indeed, just after the image of her face as a serene and ancient mask, the narrating eye startling reminds us of those jet black lashes that are the remains of the brunette she once was, "perhaps once was. When yet a lass." Or even more startling is this scene of the woman at her husband's tomb:

> Seated on the stones she is seen from behind. From the waist up. Trunk black rectangle. Nape under frill of black lace. White half halo of hair. Face to the north. . . . Voidlike calm as always. Evening and night. Suffice to watch the grass. How motionless it droops. Till under the relentless eye it shivers. With faintest shiver from its innermost. Equally the hair. Rigidly horrent it shivers at last for the eye about to abandon. And the old body itself. When it seems of stone. Is it not in fact ashiver from head to foot? Let her but go and stand still by the other stone. It white from afar in the pastures. And the eye go from one to the other. Back and forth. What calm then. And what storm. Beneath the weeds' mock calm.
> (29–30)

In addition to catching so memorably the strength and vulnerability of the "old so dying woman," this passage illustrates the provocative kinship between the perceiver and his subject. As David Read has helpfully observed, the description incorporates a characteristic Beckettian ambiguity into the eye's relationship to external (even if imagined) reality. "Is it the eye's apparent flux that causes the object to shiver—the observed infected with the mobility of the observer—or is it only the eye's perseverance that enables it finally to perceive a shiver that was always present in the object—the observer infected with the mobility of the observed?"[1] But the ambiguity is less an invitation to resolution than a reminder that whether the shiver is caused by the eye or inherent in the object, one effect of so intensely sustained an act of perception is to enlarge and in this instance to ennoble the thing perceived.

Equally important in the process of expansion is the fact that the shadowy old woman is both votary and protestant. Morning and evening she worships Venus, standing rapt before the sky, marveling; and many of her days are spent on bone-wearying journeys from her cabin back and forth across the zone of stones, carrying a cross or wreath to the tomb of someone she venerates—a tomb formed of a stone very much like her in shape and size. It seems natural enough to think of the tomb as her husband's—as many readers have done—but its identity is never confirmed. Similarly, she herself seems to be the object of ritual attendance by a ring of obscure figures called the Twelve—a typically Beckettian piece of provocation—for that highly charged number suggests not only the Apostles and the festival of the Epiphany but also (as Marjorie Perloff has remarked) the signs of the Zodiac; but it too is never made explicit and is finally as elusive as the stone tomb itself.[2]

Like any Beckett character in good standing, the old woman will sometimes protest against her existence, railing against the sun and savoring Venus's revenge when it rises as the sun sets. But for most of the narrative her fury remains bottled, and she is increasingly seen as a paradoxically frail yet commanding, almost mythological, figure in touch with lambs and birds, and someone for whom natural processes bend and stop. Once, when she visits the stone tomb, the sun stands still, and when she heads for home, "Time slows all this while. Suits its speed to hers." Indeed, it is not far-fetched to be reminded of Wordsworth's Lucy rolling "round in earth's diurnal course,/With rocks, and stones, and trees"; even if Beckett's old woman can hardly be described as "a thing that could not feel/The touch of earthly years."

Many of the objects associated with her seem in provocative ways sanctified or preternatural. Her tarnished silver pisciform buttonhook hangs from a nail and trembles faintly without cease, as do her house key (trembling and shimmering in the light of the moon) and the greatcoat hanging as a curtain in the cabin. "Same infinitesimal quaver as the buttonhook and passim." At the end, when she is approaching death, another one of her nails is described as "set to serve again. Like unto its glorious ancestors. At the place of the skull. One April afternoon. Deposition done."

This allusion to the crucifixion is part of the old woman's own deathbed scene and is one of only half-a-dozen overt allusions in *Ill Seen Ill Said*. But the most notable of these allusions also work to magnify the frail old woman by linking her to real or legendary figures who are associated with passion, suffering, and acts of great magnitude. King Lear and Gloucester are evoked when the old woman's eye is called "vile jelly"; and Job's question, "Hast thou eyes of flesh,/Or seest thou as man seeth?" is echoed in her "eyes of flesh." The stone tomb has a rough-hewn air, as if it were the product of some human hand forced to desist, "as Michelangelo's from the regicide's bust," a reference to the great unfinished bust of Brutus in the Bargello—that incarnation of fortitude, resolution, and inner torment. And finally, at the close of the passage quoted earlier describing the old woman lifting the bowl of slops, she strikes "the rigid Memnon pose," a reference to the great statue at Thebes, which was famed for making a musical sound at day break when Memnon greeted his mother, Eos, the goddess of the dawn.

That all these are masculine figures associated with passion and power (and that there are no women at all alluded to in the narrative) tells us something vital about Beckett's views of magnitude and indomitability. Although figures like Maddy Rooney in *All That Fall* and Winnie in *Happy Days* are gritty and flamboyant survivors, they are continually seen as comic in their rhetorical extravagance. Women like Mouth in *Not I* or May in *Footfalls* are not viewed comically, but they are perceived as integrally defective, incomplete. In *Ill Seen Ill Said* it is the men associated with uttermost striving, ultimacy (and rarely with laughter)—Lear, Job, Michelangelo—who provide the touchstone for measuring Beckett's conception of the protagonist's hardihood.

Nowhere is this seen more vividly than in the description of the old woman's last moments, a chillingly graphic and yet lyrically fulfilling sequence in which microscopic delineations of bodily collapse exist along with gleams of hope and sweet foretastes "of the joy at journey's end." As the narrator's steely yet still-ill-seeing eye closes in on death, a constant yet merciful process of denudation begins. All that is left to his distilling gaze is the woman's inscrutable, unyielding face ("Of the rest beneath its covering no trace.") Painstakingly, he moves past the "slumberous collapsion" of the cabin to record the sensory details of her dying moments: unexplained sounds and "sigh upon sigh till all sighed quite away. . . . Last sighs of relief." Conflating past, present, and future, he examines the sclerosis-inflicted eyes of the old woman. And then suddenly "farewell say say farewell. If only to the face. Of her tenacious trace." The phrase "tenacious trace" is in this context an honorific term for Beckett, because it captures just about the most of what (in his world) one can hope to remain—a vestige, a barely discernible indication of some quality, characteristic, or expression—and yet (if lucky) tenacious, stubbornly, persistently held.

And then, unexpectedly, in the astonishing close, comes not a victory of the residual, of the barely remaining, but a triumph of voracious desire and perhaps the closest thing to fulfillment any Beckett character has ever achieved.

> Farewell to farewell. Then in that perfect dark foreknell darling sound pip for end begun. First last moment. Grant only enough remain to devour all. Moment by glutton moment. Sky earth the whole kit and boodle. Not another crumb of carrion left. Lick chops and basta. No. One moment more. One last. Grace to breathe that void. Know happiness. (59)

Much of the power here comes from the surprising exuberance—what might even be called the gusto—of Beckett's threnody. Death is described not in terms of deprivation but of heartily satisfied appetite: to devour the world, breathe the void, and die—this surely is the consummation devoutly to be wished by so many of Beckett's desiring questors.

In *Ill Seen Ill Said,* then, the achievement of ultimacy is given to a woman, as it is nowhere else in Beckett's work. But if the "old so dying woman" and the ritual conduct of her last solitary days are exempt from irony, some aspects of the narrator's responses to her are not. Although the woman achieves fulfillment in dying, she is a product of the narrator's insatiable need; indeed, she exists only through his fiercely focused efforts to imagine her accurately. Thus she remains in more ways than one the inquiring narrator's subject. His struggle to embody her mirrors her gallant journey across the zone of stones, her vigil at the tomb, at the window, and elsewhere. Her enterprise and his are correlative; and even his insistence on her being unseeable and unmakeable is a tribute not only to her mystery but to his own minimalist mastery. As Christopher Ricks has observed: "How much dignity of mystery remains unviolated even after the most imaginative exploration. When all is said and done."[3] So for all her grace, vigilance, and nobility, it is the narrator's achievements at the scene of the writing—his ability to respect her unfathomability and to give her the death she desires and deserves—that the majority of readers are most likely to celebrate. "Imagination at wits end" *has* spread "its sad wings."

And there are, too, some important questions that someone looking at *Ill Seen Ill Said* from feminist and/or psychoanalytical perspectives might ask: what, for instance, is the significance of the fact that the narrator's struggle to express depends on bringing a dead woman back to life, on obsessively charting the last days of her suffering, and reproducing her death? Given the ardor with which the old woman is described and the dignity she is granted, she is clearly an idealized form whose reincarnation in language is a necessary stage in the narrator's search for the other. And the other is powerfully associated with idealized forms of both the mother and of death.

As Susan Rubin Suleiman observes in a recent essay, "Writing and Motherhood," psychoanalytic theory often views artistic creation (like motherhood) as the child's drama.[4] "In both cases," she says, "the mother is the essential but silent Other, the mirror in whom the child searches for his own reflection, the body he seeks to appropriate, the thing he loses or destroys again and again, and seeks to recreate." And one recalls, too, Melanie Klein's theory of artistic creation, in which the writer is impelled by the "desire to rediscover the mother of the early days, whom [he] has lost actually or in [his] feelings."[5] The work of art itself suggests the mother's body, restored or "repaired" in the act of creation. Klein's image, incidentally, appears often in recent criticism, most vividly perhaps in *The Pleasure of the Text,* where Roland Barthes (speaking of language and "the mother tongue") describes the writer as "someone who plays with his mother's body . . . in order to glorify it, to embellish it, or in order to dismember it, to take it to the limit of what can be known about the body."[6]

It is well known that Beckett—in his seventies—wrote a sequence of works *(Footfalls, Rockaby, Company,* and *Ill Seen Ill Said)* that drew on memories of the elusive figure of his mother and that these texts remind nearly all who read them of May Beckett, or of their mothers or of some archetypal image of *the* mother. Speculation about the biographical significance of this cannot go very far until scholarly studies tell us a good deal more than we now know about the fiery relationship of May Beckett and her son. But at this point it is worth observing how extraordinary it is that the mother-haunted *Ill Seen Ill Said* should be—for all its provisionality and anguish—arguably the most conclusive and serene of the old master's works.

NOTES

1. David Read, "Beckett's Search for Unseeable and Unmakeable: *Company* and *Ill Seen Ill Said,*" *Modern Fiction Studies* 29, no. 1 (Spring 1983), 111.

2. Marjorie Perloff, "Between Verse and Prose: Beckett and the New Poetry," *Critical Inquiry* 9 (1982/83), 419n.

3. Christopher Ricks, "The Hermit of Art," *Sunday Times* (London), no. 8254 (September 12, 1982), 36.

4. Susan Rubin Suleiman, "Writing and Motherhood," in *The (M)other Tongue,* ed. Shirley Nelson Garner, Claire Kahane, and Madelon Sprengnether (Ithaca: Cornell University Press, 1985), 352–77.

5. Melanie Klein, "Love, Guilt, and Reparation," reprinted in *Love, Guilt, and Reparation and Other Works, 1921–1945* (New York: Doubleday, 1977), 334.

6. Roland Barthes, *The Pleasure of the Text* (New York: Hill and Wang, 1975), 37.

Male or Female Voice: The Significance of the Gender of the Speaker in Beckett's Late Fiction and Drama

CHARLES R. LYONS

This volume directs its attention to the image of the female in the works of Samuel Beckett, and the specific focus of this essay is the question of the gender of the speaker in the late prose and drama, specifically *Ill Seen Ill Said, Company, Worstward Ho, Rockaby,* and *A Piece of Monologue.*[1] Each of these texts consists of a narrative that describes an action observed or imagined in the present. Each also suggests that the action described or dramatized is a repetition of a sequence of regularized patterns of behavior that re-enact or respond to episodes from a past that remains largely undisclosed. For example, the first paragraph of *Ill Seen Ill Said* ends with the statement, "All this in the present as had she the misfortune to be still of this world" (8). The obvious difference between the late drama and fiction is that the plays house their narratives in specific images of character. The fiction reads like the drama with the introductory descriptions of character and scene removed, that is, these prose pieces do not position their narratives in any situation other than an event of speaking/writing by an undefined subject. In the dramas the physical presence of the actor provides a mimetic context for the words spoken while the performer occupies a tangible if almost completely non-referential space and speaks through a moment that is defined only as the duration of performance.

What I would like to do in this brief essay is to pose certain questions: Is the voice that speaks the narratives in the late prose works a male voice, as I assume? And if so, is the female voice we hear in *Rockaby* identical, similar, or antithetical to the male voices that speak the texts of the other late plays and pieces of fiction? What is the relationship of these prose and dramatic narratives to their implied speakers—whether the speakers be dramatic characters who voice the text in the plays or the more purely functional subjects who speak the prose narratives? For example, what is the connection between the voice that speaks the story of a woman's progressive retreat from the search for another and the character, Woman, who rocks in the chair, invoking and listening to the rhythmic story of the movement from street, to upstairs room, to lower room and the station of the chair? What is the relationship of that voice to the speakers of the late fiction, whose immediate situations are not grounded in the physical presence of character and space as in the drama?

Since the trilogy, Beckett's prose fiction has worked to undermine the image of a narrative consciousness. For example, in the third novel the speaker suggests that the writer/protagonists of the earlier two novels are personae that once inhabited his imagination. Beckett implements conventional strategies to establish the identities of the writer/protagonists Molloy, Moran, and Malone and then lines them out with the announcement that they are merely rhetorical images that play within the consciousness of the narrator of *The Unnamable*. Of course, after being deceived into believing, on an aesthetic level, in the existence of Molloy, with his delightfully idiosyncratic voice, we resist believing unequivocally either in the existence of Mahood or in the validity of his claim that Molloy, Moran, and Malone do not exist within the fictions they write. In any case, Beckett's prose—especially the late prose—consistently provokes us to be cautious about making fixed judgments on the relationship of speaker and text. That is why I like to think of this critical exercise as an interrogation rather than an analysis. Beckett's writing establishes a relationship with reader or spectator that invites the kind of questioning I undertake here.

In *Company* and *Ill Seen Ill Said,* the text assumes, in part, the form of a description of space that contains the behavior of a predominant figure. *Company* details the behavior of an old man, lying on his back in the dark, who hears the voice of another who appears to describe events from the past of this old man who lies on his back in the dark. In *Worstward Ho* the spatial field described holds four objective figures: an old man and a young boy, consistently together hand in hand, an old woman who kneels before a tombstone, and a skull whose mouth-like orifice spews forth a consistent emission that may be the text itself. In each of these prose pieces, the text documents the difficulties involved in sustaining the observation or invention of the action and, simultaneously, the difficulties involved in articulating that observation or invention. To use Professor Graver's felicitous phrase: our interest remains focused on "the scene of the writing."[2] Each text reminds us periodically that the objects observed have no existence outside of the language of identifying or describing statements. As arresting as the image of the old woman of *Ill Seen* may be, she remains nothing more—nor less—than a rhetorical figure, a "figment," that provides a continuity of focus that sustains the movement of the discourse and allows the speaker to continue speaking. That is, this old woman is not the subject of the narrative but, rather, an object used by the narrating voice to constitute *his* subjectivity within this immediate act of speaking. Later in this essay I will attempt to defend my choice of the pronoun *his*. While my assignment of gender is tentative, the choice both derives from and informs the kind of questioning I undertake.

Because the process of speaking the text of *Ill Seen Ill Said* is the only action represented unequivocally and because that action makes no reference to the speaker's existence outside of that process, the *character* of the speaker has no implied presence external to the immediate act of speaking. While we recognize, of course, that the narrator of any work of prose fiction has no presence external to the words assigned to him or her as subject, we are accustomed to find referential clues within the text that stimulate us to extrapolate fictional relationships between the speaker's history and the narrative which that subject voices. However, Beckett's fiction consistently dissolves the image of a narrative consciousness beyond that needed to comprehend the text as a series of connected statements. These texts establish the consistency of the subject only by the continuity of the objects described and the recurrent attention of the speaker to the difficulty of assertion. For example, in both *Ill Seen Ill Said* and *Worstward Ho,* the repetition of "On," referring to the forward movement of the discourse, suggests a desire to proceed through and beyond the text into silence. The frequency of this repetition, as well, implies the presence of a resistance that provokes it. The speaking subject here, however, cannot be trusted to identify himself or herself beyond articulating that desire and the equally strong need to deny the validity of any statement made.

Beckett's prose uses language to oppose itself in the fictional subject's attempt to create a temporary, confining, and yet equivocally satisfying field of consciousness by delimiting objects that fill this arena. At the same time, by asserting the problematic status of these very objects, the speaker brings both this arena and his perception into question. The late fiction maintains an irredeemable distance between the male perceiving/speaking subject and the human objects of his sight or invention which are both male and female. The equivocal relationship between subject/narrator and object/character implements a paradoxical strategy: it cuts the object/character free from the idea of a subject/speaker at the same time that it clarifies that the characters of the narrative have no identity—as referent, image, or idea—outside of the immediate process of speaking or writing. Because the *character* of the speaker is more a function than a specific representational presence, the text itself is free to be appropriated by the reader who identifies not with the consciousness of the speaker, as either narrator/character or "implied author," but rather with the perceptual and epistemological difficulties involved in being able to sustain sight and speech with the knowledge that neither may connect to an external structure. That is, the reader identifies less with an implied persona who speaks the narrative than with the problems this voice encounters in sustaining the narrative project itself, more with the speaker as the origin of a particular and unsettling statement than with the speaker as a character whose persona encloses the whole discourse. As well, the character/objects that the speaker uses to sustain speech are invariably enigmatic. They cannot be known because the speaker has no means to ascertain their presence other than as rhetorical figures within the narrative. The differences between perception and invention or between memory and invention are too "subtle-potent" (to use Shakespeare's oxymoron) to situate the equivocal figures of the narrative in any of these categories. The indeterminate relationship between speaker and story, which cannot be resolved, insures that the speaker's and reader's tentative and difficult passage through the narrative becomes an act of both virtuosity and hubris.

Those of us schooled in the interpretative strategies of the Geneva School phenomenologists during the late fifties and sixties have been tempted to identify stylistic conventions and recurrent images that taken together form the Beckettian voice, a prototypical narrative consciousness that writes or speaks the prose texts. However, the strategies that house these works within an image of authorship work against the shifting functions of the narrative and dramatic texts we examine in this essay. We should not create an image of the writer that functions as a *character* whose identity is developed by the words he writes—words that represent him. When we succumb to this temptation, of course, we protect ourselves from the claim that we work in a naive biographical strategy by discussing the "consciousness of the text" or the "implied author." We may identify the strategy as an attempt to deal with Poulet's notion of transubjectivity in which the *I* of the text merges with the sub-vocalized *I* of the reader.[3] However difficult it is to make the leap that Foucault demands—to isolate the text from an image of the subject—it is useful in looking at Beckett to identify the ways in which the text itself questions the notion of a unique subject and frees the narrative to exist as a speaking, an event tied neither to the personal history of the subject as the representation of the speaker nor to his or her story.[4]

While Foucault's project cannot, ultimately, succeed with those of us who are grounded in the idea of the text as the manifestation of a movement in consciousness, be it the writer's or the reader's, his insistence can temper the tendency to use the image of the consciousness of the speaker to sentimentalize the notion of the perceiving subject or the objects upon which the speaker fastens. Frequently, Beckett's fiction and drama have been discussed as representations of the search for the self. In a sense that search for the self has been conducted by the critics who seek a conventional image of the subject in order to locate the narrative consciousness of the prose or the characters of the drama within a more comfortably orthodox process of representation. However, Beckett's fiction and drama display the concept of subjectivity as a problematic (to use Lukács's term) in its refusal to see the self as anything more than an instrument of rhetoric. As well, the writing frequently voices a desire for freedom from the conventional fiction of the *I*.

From *Not I* onward, Beckett's plays of narrative recitation feature characters who tell "their" story in the third person. The woman's voice in *Rockaby* and the male speakers of *That Time* and *A Piece of Monologue* recite narratives that speak of themselves as she and he. We make the assumption, primarily through visual clues, that the characters to whom they refer are identical with themselves. That is, the physical appearance of the actor aligns with the description of the principal voiced in the narrative. To see *Ill Seen* and *Company* as analogous to *Rockaby* and *A Piece of Monologue,* we would have to assume that the texts are spoken by the old woman who traverses the stony terrain and by the old man who lies on his back in the dark. That method of reading would be easier in *Company* because the speaker details the old man's thoughts, and the woman in *Ill Seen* remains an object whose behavior is described. I suspect that *Ill Seen* will be performed, if it hasn't been already, and I know that *Company* has been.[5] Performing these pieces of prose fiction as dramatic events, however, creates serious aesthetic problems because the interplay between the non-existence, the intangibility, of these *characters* and the self-denying speaker constitutes their action. That is, these texts attempt to undermine the hypothetical presence of the narrative itself as an object in the speaker's imagination; as well, they insistently question the status of the speaker's existence.

Performance situates the speaker in a physical presence that automatically establishes inextricable connections among consciousness, body, and language. While systems of overt theatricality may aggressively remind spectators that the event they witness is a fiction, the reality of the event qua event makes the project of equivocation and the epistemological critique that is always present in the fiction very difficult to represent in the theater. In very simple terms the continuity of the actor's presence and the very palpable concreteness of his or her body grounds the experience of the play as an object in the spectator's imagination, whereas the fiction can turn itself on itself with a kind of self-denial that is impossible to replicate in the theater. The individual character can, of course, go through a process of self-cancellation. The metonymic mouth of *Not I,* for example, appears to represent a process of speaking which the implied consciousness perceives as nothing but sound. But that illuminated mouth has undeniable presence as a witnessed, present phenomenon throughout the performance. The voice in *The Unnamable* can undercut its subjectivity by identifying the narrative *I* as a mere rhetorical space inhabited by a series of transient personae. Reading this novel becomes a process of gaining and losing a sense of subjective presence as the reader speaks/reads a decidedly unfixed first-person pronoun. The character in the theatrical space, however, remains a fixed objective presence even though spectators may witness the dissolution of his or her self-consciousness. Confronting the fundamental difference between the representation of presence in narrative and drama has shaped my work with the following basic question: to what degree are the extended prose statements of the late non-dramatic narratives different in kind from the late narrative dramas, and how does that difference relate to the issue of gender? The following statement offers highly speculative and self-consciously hypothetical answers to that question.

1. The object/characters of the late fiction hold a paradoxical relation to the subject that speaks the words that establish them: they are free of that elusive subject primarily because of the equivocal relationship between speaker and character, and yet they have no existence apart from the speaking. The woman of *Ill Seen,* for example, has no formally disclosed relationship with the speaker who tells her story and is, in that sense, free from that voice. However, she has no existence external to the act of narration itself. In the dramas, of course, there is no all-inclusive speaker: no narrator whose functional presence contains the characters as objects of perception, invention, or memory. The components of these theatrical events are the figure on the stage and the recitation the character either speaks or hears. The audience, grappling with the visual image and the words voiced, relates to the objectified image on the stage in a process that is analogous to the speaker of the prose narratives. The words of the speaker identify the object/characters as "figments," nonpresences; and the action of the fiction is the attempt both to fix and to release these images. The dramas, which present only the tangible presence of the object/character, have no speaking subject that either establishes or invalidates their image. The spectator, like the speaker in the fiction, must fix these enigmatic objects in relationship to the text that the character either speaks or hears. The performance provides an event in which the spectator perceives an object—the figure in the theatrical

arena—whose identity is largely unclear but whose presence holds a limited referentiality sufficient to provoke a partial, extrapolated history. The physical presence of the actor is tangible; the presence of the actor as *character* is suggestive but elusive. Correspondingly, the presence of the *character*—for example, the woman of *Ill Seen*—is, for the speaker of that narrative, tangible as a rhetorical figure, as an instrument of the process of story-telling. However, the relationship between speaker and *character* remains elusive, not concretely determinable as memory, invention, or dream. The absence of an established relationship between narrator and *character(s)* severely limits the function of the narrator as a participating *character.*

By diminishing the sense of the speaking subject, the fiction releases the object/characters to the process of reading. That is, the figures gain presence only as read because the speaker does not refer them to a fictive situation (or reality) outside of the speaking or the reading. These pieces of fiction confine their characters to the text. Dramatic performance first gives the object/characters over to the actors and then to the perceiving consciousness of the spectator. However, the refusal to place these figures within a scene more referential than the space in which they confront a narrative recitation holds these images of character within the boundaries of that narrative text and the minimalist scene. In Beckett's late prose fiction, the relationship between narrator and the human objects he describes remains slippery. In the corresponding dramatic form, the slippery relationship between perceiving subject and equivocal object becomes the relationship between the witnessing spectator and actor/character who plays within a functionally unreferential theatrical space.

2. The narrative spoken by the old man of *A Piece of Monologue* shares with the late fiction the male speaker's use of a female figure to inscribe readable but subtle patterns of relationship, loss, and renunciation. The old man details a ritual, apparently no longer performed, of a nightly vigil that includes staring at a wall that once held family photographs, ostensibly destroyed years before. The vigil described encompasses the invocation and renunciation of images of the funerals of relatives—always referred to as "he all but said of loved ones." The repetitious discourse works toward the articulation of the following: "Till whose grave? Which . . . he all but said which loved one's? He? Black ditch in pelting rain . . . Bubbling black mud. Coffin on its way. Loved one . . . he all but said loved one on his way. Her way"(269). The sense of this statement—and the transition from *his way* to *her way*—suggests that the death of the female loved one is the critical event of this partial and oblique story. Or, more accurately, the attempt to speak of this specific event and renounce it from memory is the most significant behavior represented in the narrative spoken by the actor.

3. *Company* and *Monologue* exercise rhetorical structures that enigmatically refer to an undocumented history that includes a male child and parents, and the presence of this triad seems to figure largely in the undisclosed history of both narratives. *Worstward Ho* may implement the same triad. Whereas *Company* uses the figure of the child and mother, hand in hand, coming from "Connolly's Stores" and uses the image of the father separately, *Worstward Ho*—the more fragmented text—puts the man and child together, isolates the woman, and seems to identify the grown child/speaker with the skull.

Ill Seen Ill Said focuses upon the old woman as a sexual creature in a description of her self-stimulation: "The hands. Seen from above. They rest on the pubis intertwined. Strident white. . . . They tighten then loosen their clasp. Slow systole diastole. And the body that scandal. While its sole hands in view. On its sole pubis" (31–32). A few lines later: "It is now the left hand lacks its third finger. A swelling no doubt . . . of the knuckle between first and second phalanges preventing one panic day withdrawal of the ring. The kind called keeper"(32). Here the reference to the lost finger and wedding ring follows the description of the hands at the pubis. The relentless journeys to and from the tombstone, with these references, suggest that the old woman as object in the observation/ invention of the speaker operates as a sexual image or the residue of a sexual image. The triad of speaker, old woman, and the occupant of the grave may, or may not, suggest the triad of son, mother, and father. However, the pervasiveness of the triad suggests the possibility that the speaker of *Ill Seen* is male. The speaker of *Company* maintains a kind of identification with the old man lying on his back in the dark, and the tone of that identification suggests that the relationship between speaker and object reflects an ironic, if uncertain, self-reflexivity. The irony of the rhetoric of *Ill Seen* directs itself to the processes of perceiving and speaking, not to the behavior of the woman; and the language maintains a distance between the subject speaking and the object described that does not seem to reflect self-consciousness but, rather, the difference between perceiver and perceived. It seems highly unlikely to me that the woman of *Ill Seen* is an objectified image of the speaker (herself).

4. The clearly male voices of the speakers of *Company* and *Worstward Ho* focus on female objects. While these women appear in some sense to be sexual creatures, they function more as maternal figures than as lovers. The voice of *Ill Seen* speaks of the *trace,* to use Beckett's word, of a familial structure, attenuated as it may be. The Woman of *Rockaby,* the single female voice of this sequence, if the voice of *Ill Seen* is, indeed, male, sustains no memory of a family history other than the death of her mother, which she re-enacts. Unlike the voice of *Not I,* she does not

detail her orphan status, but her search for another like herself may be based, in part, on the absence of her mother. Her search is not hetero-sexually erotic, but, rather, for the reflection of herself—"another crea-ture like herself / a little like." As an object we observe, this character exists within an increasingly limited world. As the representation of a subject, she listens to the narrative of her attempt to find another and, then, her attempt to function as another for herself, and, finally, her effort to give up the fiction of her objectified image of herself.

In *A Piece of Monologue* we witness a male speaker who rehearses, at some attenuated level of consciousness, an earlier confrontation with the painfulness of the death of a female. Whereas the establishment of that moment is, indeed, indistinctly formed, the shift from male to female loved one is telling in the simplicity of the performance. The paradigm of male speaker / female object is clear in this text and its performance, even though that relationship is substantially more undisclosed than revealed. If the narrative represents a desire, it represents a desire for silence, particularly about that relationship. The text of *Ill Seen*, em-phatically in the last paragraph, seems to represent a desire for silence and, in that sense, a release from the obligation to speak of the woman who is the principal of the story. The final paragraph, in my opinion, suggests not just a simple desire to be released from the phenomenon of self-consciousness but also a wish to be freed from the image of the self possessed by the image of this female object. In *A Piece of Monologue* the female loved one is both painfully attached to the speaker's discourse and painfully absent, slipping away into the grave and into the attenuation of failing memory. The image of the woman in *Ill Seen* also maintains that curious attachment in absence.

The female object we spectators witness in *Rockaby* is dressed in clothes and ornaments that suggest erotic provocation, but the figure is isolated from sexuality unless the search for another like herself and her re-enactment of her mother's death in the rhythm of rocking have an erotic charge. The painfulness of her narrative, however, is not specifi-cally sexual; her rehearsal of isolation and loneliness provokes a response in both male and female spectators. However, the woman in the rock-ing chair is both isolated and inaccessible—that is, the character is self-enclosed within the routine of her movement. That self-enclosure, within the highly constricted space of the area illuminated by the stage lights, is analogous to the movement of the woman in *Ill Seen* within the larger but still restrictive topography of the story. Both figures are inac-cessible in their confinement. Both are female, and the inaccessibility becomes more problematic if the sexual role of the narrator in *Ill Seen* is male. I would not assign an exclusively male role to the spectators of

Rockaby, however, even though I make that connection between the speaker of the prose narrative and the spectators of the drama. If we consider that the woman has searched for a sexual duplicate in her attempt to find another creature like herself, the failed effort to find a mirror image that confirms her womanhood would be particularly painful for the women in the audience, whose presence ironically belies her perceived isolation. Her attempt to find that reflective confirmation in the re-enactment of her mother's death isolates her from the potential community of other women. And, for the men in the audience, the woman remains the elusive sexual other in her confinement within a search for a sexual reflection rather than a sexual opposite. For both sexes, of course, the woman provides a figure of their own isolation.

5. Beckett's later prose fiction and drama continue to exercise processes of ending. Our skepticism about the idea of the speaker as *character* should encourage us to guard against too strong an emphasis upon the achievement of the ending silence in the narrative texts. They may rehearse endings rather than represent them—"for to end yet again." The end of *Ill Seen Ill Said,* like the end of *Rockaby,* seems to reach a point of termination; but as a work of prose fiction and a work of drama, each narrative can be taken up again. Some people read the ending of *Ill Seen* as the representation of the death of the woman upon whom the speaker has focused. The emphasis here, in my opinion, is not upon the death of the woman as an event in her story but, rather, as the opportunity for the speaker to complete the process of telling the story and release himself from this female figure as object. The penultimate paragraph ends: "No more tear itself away from the remains of trace. Of what was never. Quick say it suddenly can and farewell say say farewell. If only to the face. Of her tenacious trace"(58–59). The final paragraph begins: "Decision no sooner reached or rather long after than what is the wrong word? For the last time at last for to end yet again what the wrong word? Than revoked"(59). The final sentences of this paragraph do not focus upon an end but, rather, upon the moment immediately preceding an end. Thereby, the speaking extends that moment of ending indefinitely: "First last moment. Grant only enough remain to devour all. Moment by glutton moment. Sky earth the whole kit and boodle. Not another crumb of carrion left. Lick chops and basta. No. One moment more. One last. Grace to breathe that void. Know happiness.

In my opinion the sense of calm implicit in this paragraph refers not to the state of mind of the dying woman but, on the contrary, to the pleasure of the speaker, who has succeeded in moving through the narrative to the point at which he has finished with the woman as the object of his perception / invention / memory and is "done with that." The use of the phrase "for to end yet again" from an earlier prose piece confounds the sense of termination, of course, and suggests the possibility of another movement through the recitation.[6] If the "decision" refers to the possibility of renouncing the object and the narrative and is subject to revocation, the peace achieved may be a temporary stasis between recitations. The recorded narrative of *Rockaby* voices the woman's statement, "saying to herself / no / done with that . . . ," as a prelude to a death-like silence. However, because that statement is contained within her recitation, the text suggests that it, as well, may be a repetition of a previous action and not the representation of her abandonment of the recitation and death. As in *Endgame,* the ending of *Rockaby* and *Ill Seen* may (or may not) point toward the potentiality of the action beginning again.

In the later narrative dramas, as in *Not I,* we discover the present figures reciting or listening to a narrative that does not engage their minds with the vitality of a story freshly composed but, rather, moves in the rhythm of repeated re-telling. While the event represented has the vitality of the presence of actors, the performances enact an attenuated solipsism, displaying the residue of a failed narcissistic project. *Rockaby* seems particularly confined because the Woman's search aims at a mirror object and eventually transforms her into the image of her mother. The fact that this dramatic event restricts itself to one sex increases the intensity of the image of containment and isolation. *Ill Seen Ill Said* traverses a more detailed geography, the variety of the farm rather than the serial regularity of the city, and possibly details the fascination and elusiveness of a sexual opposite—the attracting and repelling of difference, and the need for the opposite to constitute the identity of the voice and, correspondingly, the desire to be free of that other. *Rockaby* uses the image of the mother as the instrument of self-objectification and conflates the Woman and her perception of the mother. If the female object of *Ill Seen Ill Said* is a maternal image and the speaker functions as a male—and if the female object works, as I propose, as the agency of the self-constituting activity of speaking—then the narrative implements the fixing and deleting of the sexual other as the significant strategy of the text. If the critical behavioral phenomenon of the narrative of *A Piece of Monologue* is the climactic speaking of the phrase *her way* in the section I quoted, this dramatic work also shows the tenacious hold of a female image in the language of a male and, as well, the voiced desire to be free of that image. As I said above, these comments are speculative. I offer them with the self-conscious recognition that they approach the texts they address with the particular biases of a male reader—and a reader who is fascinated with the differences between the operation of narrative and dramatic texts.

NOTES

1. See Samuel Beckett, *The Collected Shorter Plays* (New York: Grove Press, 1984); *Company* (New York: Grove Press, 1980); *Ill Seen Ill Said* (New York: Grove Press, 1981); *Worstward Ho* (New York: Grove Press, 1983); "All Strange Away," *Rockaby and Other Short Pieces* (New York: Grove Press, 1981). Each of these plays I have discussed elsewhere. See Charles R. Lyons, *Samuel Beckett* (New York: Grove Press, 1983), and "Perceiving *Rockaby*—As a Text, as a Text by Samuel Beckett, as a Text for Performance," *Comparative Drama* 16 (Winter 1982–83), 297–311; Barbara S. Becker and Charles R. Lyons, "Directing/Acting Beckett," *Comparative Drama* 19 (Winter 1985–86), 289–304; Charles R. Lyons, "Beckett's Fundamental Theater," *Texts for Company* (London: Macmillan, 1986).

2. Lawrence Garver, "Homage to the Dark Lady," in this volume, 142.

3. Georges Poulet, "Criticism and the Experience of Interiority," *The Languages of Criticism and the Sciences of Man,* ed. Richard Macksey and Eugenio Donato (Baltimore: The Johns Hopkins Press, 1970), 62–63.

4. Michel Foucault, *The Archaeology of Knowledge and the Discourse on Language,* trans. A. M. Sheridan Smith (New York: Pantheon, 1972), 21–30.

5. The French text, *Compagnie,* was performed in Paris in 1984, opening November 15, in a production directed by Pierre Chabert, with Beckett's cooperation, at the Théâtre du Rond-Point. S. E. Gontarski directed a version of the English text, *Company,* at the Actors' Theatre (Half Stage) in February 1985. Katharine Worth produced her adaptation of *Company,* directed by Tim Pigott-Smith, at the Edinburgh Festival in 1987; it was awarded one of the "Fringe Firsts" by the *Scotsman* and was later presented at the Warehouse Theatre in London.

6. "Fizzle 8 / For to end yet again," *Fizzles* (New York: Grove Press, 1976), 55–61.

The Femme Fatale on Beckett's Stage

RUBY COHN

In Western tradition the femme fatale is a woman of lethally erotic power, but Beckett implies a more literal reading of the phrase; the women of his drama (as opposed to his fiction) are fatal because they live intimately with death—more intimately than his male characters. In contrast to those feminists who valorize women's sexuality and mother-hood, Beckett reminds us that birth begins a long day's dying. His stage women, often mothers, do not take sexuality as their springboard. For the most part their bodies are hidden under long garments. Even con-cealed, however, those bodies exude frailty, vulnerability. Aware that they propagate the human race, Beckett's stage women are excruciat-ingly sensitive to the mortality of that race.

In an early scene, the 1936 *Human Wishes,* death seems to have caught Beckett off-guard. His first attempt at a play was intended to dramatize love rather than death, and toward this end he took many notes on the relationship between Dr. Samuel Johnson and Mrs. Henry Thrale. As a matter of historic fact, these two individuals met in 1765, when Dr. Johnson was fifty-five, and Mrs. Thrale twenty-four years old. For fifteen years after that meeting, Dr. Johnson was a welcome guest of the Thrale family, spending weekdays at their estates and return-ing to his home in London only on weekends. In 1781 that home was Bolt Court, which was occupied not only by Johnson, but by five poor, lonely, and irascible people who would otherwise be homeless: Dr. Rob-ert Levett, who was not a doctor; Francis Barber, who became Johnson's heir; and three women—blind Anna Williams, Mrs. Desmoulins from Johnson's native Litchfield, and Polly Carmichael, who may have been a prostitute.

Despite his many notes Beckett composed only a single scene of the four acts he outlined. Beckett's scene (published in *Disjecta*) stages four inhabitants of Bolt Court (five if we include the cat of unmentioned sex), who were pithily etched by their host in his March 1778 letter to

Mrs. Thrale: "Williams hates everybody. Levett hates Desmoulins and does not love Williams. Desmoulins hates them both. Poll loves none of them." Into that loveless household death intrudes.

Still unwritten, the play already carried the title *Human Wishes,* after Dr. Johnson's poem "Vanity of Human Wishes." Although Beckett's scene is chary of information about the set and costumes, the implication is that they are true to the period. When the curtain rises, three women are seated, presumably encircled by the long gowns of the time. Mrs. Williams is meditating, Mrs. Desmoulins is knitting, and Miss Carmichael is reading. During the course of the scene the latter two rise and temporarily leave their seats, but Mrs. Williams's actions are confined to striking the floor with her stick. Although Beckett does not describe her, Mrs. Williams draws her own vivid self-portrait: "I may be old, I may be blind, halt and maim, I may be dying of a pituitous defluxion, but my hearing is unimpaired." It is above all Mrs. Williams who fulfills Beckett's penchant for a frail female body on stage.

Midway through the scene the lone male appears; Dr. Levett is drunk and tries to weave his way inconspicuously upstairs, after emitting "a single hiccup of such force that he is almost thrown off his feet." The three women "survey him with indignation," but they ostentatiously refuse to discuss him. Instead, their words turn toward death—Dr. Goldsmith, Queen Anne, a clergyman of uncertain surname, and perhaps Hugh Kelly. Increasingly, Mrs. Williams dominates the scene, with a reverse weekly calendar of the dead and a delayed reaction to the death of her father. Toward the end of the scene she ponders what Polly Carmichael reads aloud uncomprehendingly—from Jeremy Taylor's *Rule and Exercises of Holy Dying.*

The *Human Wishes* scene is a harbinger of playwright Samuel Beckett's later works in several ways, not least in assimilating three actual women into an analogue of the three mythic fates. Whereas Beckett's Levett is a figure of farce, his three women look as though they might have emerged from tragedy. Their dialogue—especially Mrs. Williams's lines—occasionally recalls Restoration comedy, but its substratum is human mortality, without hope of restoration. Beckett's celebrated ambiguity is heard in Mrs. Williams's seriocomic references to death:

I am dead enough myself, I hope, not to feel any great respect for those that are so entirely.

I know they are dead, their deaths are come to the notice of my mind.

I know if death would be content to enter into me by a horsehair, or by any other manner of hair for that matter, I should be very much obliged to him.

As in later Beckett drama, tension builds between the still stage picture and the funny, moving lines of dialogue.

Nearly three decades after *Human Wishes* Beckett again staged three women—in his 1965 *Come and Go* (whose final version is printed, thanks to Breon Mitchell, only in *Modern Drama*, September, 1976). These three women have vaguely floral names that do not individualize them—Flo, Ru, and Vi. Although they are garbed in different colors, their garments also do not individualize them. Like the eighteenth-century gowns of the *Human Wishes* scene, their coats reach from throat to foot; moreover, their faces are obscured by broad-brimmed hats. Only their hands reveal pale frail flesh. Like the three women of *Human Wishes*, those of *Come and Go* spend much of their brief stage time seated, but their bench is invisible (to the frustration of many a lighting designer). In Beckett's production the three women glided silently and separately out of the light and back into it—like dreams or ghosts. Only on the invisible bench were their gestures clearly articulated—move toward center, head turned to whisper, finger raised to lips, and final interweaving of three pairs of hands.

Unlike the three historical women, the floral women share memories—of sitting "together as we used to" and dreaming of love. The silences, repetitions, and minimal motions of *Come and Go* are more strictly patterned than those of *Human Wishes*. Rather than the latter's explicit references to death, *Come and Go* spirals delicately around absence and threat; we never hear the whispered secrets that evoke the tonally distinct "Oh"s, trailing pious hopes for divine mercy. And we never see the faces of the doomed trio. What Beckett achieved in the three decades between his two brief scenes is a stage presentation in which the unstated compels at once attention to his medium and mythic extension.

In *Come and Go* Beckett brings mathematical precision to speeches, pauses, postures, gestures—"Holding hands . . . that way." No sooner do we absorb the basic stage picture of three faceless women seated on an invisible bench than the dialogue explicitly recalls the witches of *Macbeth*: "When did we three last meet?" but Beckett displaces the Shakespearean future to the fictional past. By the end of what Beckett has called a "dramaticule," his witches take a position that recalls the Three Graces. Pivoting on secrets and absence, Beckett's trio are at once Fates, Graces, and creatures gracefully subject to fate.

I have broken chronology to juxtapose Beckett's female death-brushed trios that are separated by three decades, but Beckett dramatized other women before *Come and Go*. His first full-length play was written in French in 1947, but the title, *Eleuthéria*, is Greek for freedom. That play is, by the wish of its author, unproduced and unpublished. In its cast of seventeen characters are a number of grotesque women, but the three-act play centers on a man, young Victor Krap, who has left his bourgeois home to live in indigence but freedom. The play's women try to lure him back to the family home, which he views as a tomb. Into his wretched hotel room three dowagers arrive seriatim—his mother, Mme. Krap; his aunt, Mme. Piouk; and his mother's friend, Mme. Meck (French slang for pimp). Beckett's satire of these diversely ailing women (as well as Victor's fiancée, Mlle. Skunk) is the nadir of his stage femininity.

Written only a year later, *Waiting for Godot* is bare of women, but the passivity of waiting characterizes female behavior, rather than male. In *Godot* erections arise from hanging, not women; honeymoons stem from the color blue, not women. But as we travel chronologically past *Godot* in the Beckett canon, women reappear on his stage, playing increasingly vital—and deadly—roles. Still, little vitality is displayed by Nell of *Endgame*, whose name puns on *knell* as well as *nil*. Entombed like her husband Nagg in an ashbin, she alone is "perished" with cold, and she alone used to laugh as though she "would die." In her single appearance from the ashbin, she speaks "wearily," and after she utters her last word—"Desert"—Clov reports that she has no pulse. Is Nell dead? "Looks like it," declares Clov.

Nell contrasts markedly with another woman Beckett created in that same year (1956)—Maddy Dunne Rooney of the radio play *All That Fall*. A small child, sex unspecified, is the only one to fall to death in *All That Fall*, but metaphorically many females fall toward death. Maddy's daughter Minnie is long dead, and Maddy recalls a mind doctor's lecture about a little girl who died although "she had never really been born." Christy's wife and daughter are ill, and Mr. Tyler's daughter has just had a hysterectomy. Mr. Slocum manages to keep his mother out of pain, but we hear the squawk of pain when he runs over a hen. A nameless old woman in an empty house plays Schubert's "Death and the Maiden." Of herself Maddy affirms: "I am not half alive nor anything approaching it." For all that, however, she endures volubly as she trudges, stumbles, climbs in and out, up and down, in sun and in rain. Neither coming to nor going from the train station does she fall. Invisible on the air waves, she makes an epic journey that is conveyed through sound effects, but the dialogue surrounds her with death. Even her name, Maddy Dunne Rooney, puns on a mad old woman who is done for and ruined.

Five years after Maddy—in 1961—Beckett created a younger version for the stage in Winnie of *Happy Days*. Both women offer tenderness to minimally responsive husbands; both are sensitive to the nuances of their respective environments; despite the twenty-year difference in their ages—Winnie is in her fifties, Maddy in her seventies—both are elegiac about the past, and yet they peer through gloom to redeem the present. Maddy claims to be "not half alive," but Winnie is half-buried in Act I of *Happy Days,* and by Act II only her head is unburied. In perhaps his most relentless stage image, Beckett burns her burial into our vision, and burial suggests death.

As Act II of *Godot* is bleaker than Act I, as Maddy's homeward journey is bleaker than her setting out, Act II of *Happy Days* is bleaker than Act I, and Winnie knows it: "To have been always what I am—and so changed from what I was." By Act II Winnie can no longer imagine any relief, and she can no longer pray, as she did at the play's start. Although she still intones the phrase "happy day," it no longer triggers her smile. And yet she pursues her discourse; she addresses her unresponsive husband, Willie; she again summons to memory the Shower/Cooker couple; but she no longer recalls Mr. Shower's exclamation that he would dig her out with his bare hands. Until the climactic crawl of her husband Willie, Winnie's main resource in Act II is the story of a little girl, Milly, who screams with the terror that Winnie forbids herself to show. Beckett's portrait of a lady in *Happy Days* is as brave as that of Henry James.

Nell, Maddy, and Winnie are a succession of long-wed wives, precise in their perceptions, nostalgic about love, and eloquent in their individual rhythms. All three breathe the atmosphere of death, but Maddy and Winnie endure. Physically, Winnie resembles Nell, each head prattling away. Yet we see more of Winnie: she lingers longer on stage, and her busy hands make greater claims on stage space. Winnie may live a kind of death in the life she calls "old style," but even in quotation she does not utter that dread word.

Rival women take second place to the man of *Play* (1963)—the man who declares that he "could not live without" the one woman and "could not go on living without" the other but nevertheless exclaims: "God what vermin women." Beckett divides the printed text into Narration (of an earthly triangle) and Meditation (on the theater present). In both parts the three characters are confined to urns, with "faces so lost to age and aspect as to seem almost part of urns." Each of the three thinks that he or she alone is summoned by the light to speak, while the other two live on elsewhere; each thinks he or she alone is a restless ghost.

The Narration apprises us of the banal plot of a thousand plays, even while the language parodies that plot, but the Meditation immerses us in what I call theatereality and what Paul Lawley calls "the medium made manifest" (*Journal of Beckett Studies* 9:29). In the theater darkness the characters are triggered by the spotlight into speech, and each of the characters personifies the light, each actor responding to it. *Play* is the first of Beckett's plays in which the actual and the fictional, the physical and the metaphysical virtually converge.

Although we see all three characters in funeral urns, and although the man protests that he cannot live without each woman in turn, it is the women who brush more closely by death. Not only does W1 threaten both her own life and that of W2, but W1 describes herself as "Dying for dark," and W2 affirms, "I felt like death." As so often in Beckett, the loose clichés assume an eerie literality.

Nell, Winnie, and the characters of *Play* trace Beckett's fascination with that old folk motif, the talking head, and from that motif he derived the boldest image he ever staged: a faceless mouth spouts words in *Not I* (1971). The spotlit mouth shapes a story that is difficult to follow in the theater. In the study, however, one can impose a rough chronology on events in the life of a nameless woman: premature birth and abandonment, religious education in an orphanage, silent shopping in a supermarket, silent appearance as a defendant in a law court, occasional shameful winter bursts of speech, ambiguous tears in a meadow, and (five times evoked) sudden speech at age seventy on an April morning. Beckett's *Not I* describes that speech and contains that speech— theatereality.

Instead of style being the man, the style of *Not I* is the woman—an asyntactical rush of rhythmic phrases irregularly interrupted by questions. Never uttering the titular "not I," the voice explodes four times in four symmetrical syllables—two interrogations and two exclamations: "what? . . . who? . . . no! . . . she! . . . " As Keir Elam has noted, these syllables mark the progression within her wordstream: curriculum vitae, discovery of speech, doom to speech, running out of material (*Beckett at 80*, 137). Like Winnie, Mouth utters pious platitudes about great and tender mercies, and like the two women of *Play*, Mouth entertains the possibility that her situation is a punishment for some mysterious sin. However, Winnie and the two women of *Play* occasionally escape from the bright theater lights; Winnie can close her eyes and the *Play* rivals are only erratically spotlit, whereas Mouth absorbs and is absorbed in the unrelenting beam of light we see and hear about—theatereality. At the extreme limit of Beckett's fragmented human residua, Mouth is as gracefully feminine as the "she" of her narration. (The enlarged mouth of television is hypnotically vaginal, but unlike some male critics, I never saw this likeness in the theater.) The stage image of the nervous fluttering mouth of *Not I* seems to reside in another order of reality, perhaps beyond the grave.

Having stripped a woman's body to its ultimate vulnerability in *Not I*, Beckett returned the female form to full height in *Footfalls* (1975), but a "worn grey wrap" hides her contours. Behind that wrapping Beckett's femme fatale soars to a metaphoric pinnacle, even while he confines an actress to a board nailed down on the stage board. Played in half an hour, *Footfalls* nevertheless contains four distinct movements, marked off by blackouts, successively fainter chimes, and successively dimmer lights. In the first three movements a woman paces back and forth on a narrow strip of board—nine steps and turn, nine steps and turn. From scene to scene, we perceive fewer steps, dimmer light, fainter chimes; the first three movements of *Footfalls* describe a theater asymptote, a metaphor for entropy. The fourth and last movement comes very close to zero, since we see the board and a vertical line of light (not in the published text), unbroken by human trace.

The words of *Footfalls* dramatize mothers and daughters. In the first movement we hear a dialogue between an invisible invalid mother and a grey, stooped daughter, who ceases her pacing when she speaks. The second movement, a monologue by the invisible mother, seems to be a flashback that explains her daughter May's compulsion to pace on the board, while other girls are out playing lacrosse. The third movement, a monologue by the daughter, is itself divided into three parts: the Sequel, the Semblance, and a scene involving old Mrs. Winter and her daughter Amy, anagram of May. In these three verbal scenes both women speak of pain—the ubiquitous pain of "it all."

In *Footfalls* Beckett has written a modern mystery play. The suffering mother of Movement 1 refuses the comforts of biblical resonance— dressings, sponge, lip-moistening, and prayer. The suffering daughter of the Movement 2 narration paces on the bare floor—boards nailed as in a cross—while other girls are "out at . . . lacrosse." The suffering daughter of the Movement 3 Sequel, a ghost who can enter a locked church, pities Christ's pain as she paces; the fictional daughter, Amy Winter, is absent from the evening church service, and yet her mother hears her say "Amen." To our eyes in the theater it is the mother who is absent, but in Movement 2 the daughter is said to be absent from lacrosse as in Movement 3 she is said to be absent from Vespers. A literal mystery, the play hammers at what is hidden. Beckett was brought up as a Christian; he could not sustain his faith, but he nevertheless dramatizes an "Amen" to a "loving God and the fellowship of the Holy Ghost." And he does this by exalting woman. Rather than the Father, Son, and Holy Ghost of Christianity, *Footfalls* conveys a ghostly mother and daughter who brim with compassion before the final fourth movement, which is bare of the "tangle of pale grey tatters," or humanity.

Irena Jun in *Footfalls*

Footfalls weaves a tapestry from tatters of Beckett's earlier portraits of haunted ladies. Like the trios of *Human Wishes* and *Come and Go,* the single figure of *Footfalls* is clothed from foot to throat. Like Nell, Maddy, and Winnie, this mother and daughter observe their worlds sparely but precisely. Like Mouth, this mother and daughter utter confessions in the third person—not I. The trios of *Human Wishes* and *Come and Go* concentrate down to the maimed trinity of *Footfalls*—visible daughter, invisible mother, and the ghostly mother-daughters of the enfolded narrative. *Footfalls* presents a feminine caritas before the obliteration of all human residue. These footfalls, like those in Eliot's "Burnt Norton," echo in the memory, but rather than lead to a rose garden, they hammer at human pain.

Rockaby (1981) might be Act II of *Footfalls,* but mother and daughter coalesce into a shifting "she." As in *Footfalls* we see a single actress, and we hear a woman's voice from an invisible source. The text stipulates that the voice (heard on voiceover) belongs to the woman in the rocking-chair—a black-clad woman seated in a light wooden rocker. Again the woman is covered from foot to throat, but she also wears an "incongruous flimsy headdress." As the grey-clad woman of *Footfalls* paced to and fro on a wooden board, the black-clad woman of *Rockaby* rocks to and fro in the arms of her light wooden rocker. As we simultaneously see and hear about a pacing woman in *Footfalls,* we simultaneously see and hear about a rocking woman in *Rockaby.* But the woman in black conducts only a sporadic dialogue with the recorded words she triggers by the monosyllabic "More." The repeated, accreted phrases constitute her memory, but seven times the rocking woman lifts her voice to a three-syllabled duet with the voiceover—"time she stopped."

The rocking woman's four "More"s introduce the brief play's four movements, through which the pitying, pitiable mother/daughter fugues are damped to stillness. In *Rockaby* the pronoun "she" reaches out to mother, daughter, and rocking actress, all in black.

Purer than *Footfalls* with its interrupted pacing and abysmal fictions, *Rockaby* chants a simple complex tale that gradually narrows to the rhythm of the rocking woman. "All eyes" dwarfing her pale face, the living actress wears a black evening gown and a rakish black hat. No Whistler's sober "Mother," she cajoles light to glitter on her sequins, as she is rocked to and fro. Bright black ornaments glisten, and light polished chair gleams; her steady rocking yields a wayward scintillation in the steady light. Yet we cannot forget that in our culture black is the color of mourning.

The first movement of *Rockaby* describes a farflung search for "another like herself," even while the living woman agrees that it is "time she stopped." In the second movement she searches from her window, with continued admonition that it is "time she stopped." The third movement limits and ends the window search. The fourth and longest movement traces a descent from the upstairs window down to the rocker where a mother "all in black/best black" died and where a living actress sits and rocks. The moving chair, "mother rocker," lulls its occupant to death.

The chanted woman goes gentle into that good night, as her mother did, "head fallen/ . . . rocking away." The last "More" softens to a sigh as the chair continues to oscillate in the rhythm of a heartbeat. When "live eyes" have closed, the voiceover objects "no" to still another repetition of "time she stopped." "Done with that," we hear, and the voiceover emits three abrupt imperatives: "rock her off/stop her eyes/fuck life," to summon death.

"Time has stopped," thought Vladimir in *Waiting for Godot,* but legless Nell can still ask, "Time for love?" Winnie ruefully realizes that time is "old style," and the invisible mother of *Footfalls* marvels that her daughter is "as though she had never been." The nameless rocking woman of *Rockaby* is more ruthless: "time she stopped." Like a tipsy angel of death, the figure in black is finally enfolded in the rocker/cradle/coffin. In Billie Whitelaw's performance her head falls softly to the side, face miraculously childlike as if born into death. "They give birth astride of a grave," rages Pozzo in *Waiting for Godot,* and with exquisite nuance Beckett has staged those fatal births.

The Transformational Grammar of Gender in Beckett's Dramas

SHARI BENSTOCK

As an ontological concept that deals with the nature of Being, along with a whole nebula of other primitive concepts belonging to the same line of thought, gender seems to belong primarily to philosophy. Its raison d'être is never questioned in grammar, whose role is to describe forms and functions, not to find a justification for them. It is no longer questioned in philosophy, though, because it belongs to that body of self-evident concepts without which philosophers believe they cannot develop a line of reasoning and which for them go without saying, for they exist prior to any thought, any social order, in nature. So they call gender the lexical delegation of "natural beings."

> Monique Wittig. "The Mark of
> Gender," in *The Poetics of Gender*

One might begin a discussion of the role of gender in Beckett's plays by arguing that gender itself is not clearly designated in the dramas, that it seems not to be a major factor in any of Beckett's works: there are few female characters in the plays, and with the exception of Winnie in *Happy Days* and Mrs. Rooney in *All That Fall,* none of these women exhibits characteristics that make gender an issue.[1] Indeed, most of Beckett's figures appear to be androgynous, their sexual identities either absent or disguised. Beckett's interests are in *human* nature, and—according to the dictates of Western culture—woman is subsumed under the category "man." That is, a feminist reading of Beckett's plays might merely confirm the playwright's participation in a culture that repeats rather than rewrites the myth of Genesis: female is a derivative of male; man takes priority over woman; woman serves man as his mirror, his temptress, a seductress of the evil powers of his own unconscious.

But in Beckett's world woman is denied even the mystery of sexual curiosity that has sustained our interest in Eve and her responsibility for the human condition that Beckett's works so meticulously analyze: the minimal sexual force at work in these plays belongs to the male, apparent in the double entendres of the language, the male gaze, and in standard sexual symbolism—guns, boots, bananas, parasols, and so on. The sexual is suggested but somehow never embodied, hinted at but never enacted. Indeed, one is left to wonder how these creatures—not clearly either male or female—came to inhabit the universe Beckett's work describes. Were they produced by some extra-sexual force?

At least two questions arise from the assumptions I have just delineated: (1) the relation of gender to sexuality and its consequences for character development in Beckett's plays; (2) the assumption that feminist readings can find in literary texts only a rewriting of that which is already present in culture: an inscription of woman as derivative of and dependent on man, her place consigned to the domestic, to a language of the familial and nonintellectual, her body a mechanism for producing the offspring that feeds the patriarchal cultural machine. If one were to undertake a feminist reading of Beckett's plays, where would one begin? Not just with which texts, but with what assumptions? Here we find something that feels familiar in Beckett, the philosophical concerns of the post-Modernist universe that provides a starting place, a meeting ground of the two different sets of questions our undertaking must trace. We are less interested in readings that examine the ways in which woman is inscribed in male texts than in discovering the laws that underwrite those texts. How do grammar and gender come together under the law of genre?

To illustrate the differences between a genderized reading that searches for cultural definitions of the feminine in literary texts and a reading that examines the ground rules of literary genres, we can begin with Winnie, who is situated not so much *on the ground* of generic premises as embedded in it. She is, according to Beckett's explicit stage directions for *Happy Days*, found to be "embedded up to above her waist in exact centre of mound," which is composed of "scorched grass"(2272).[2] Her emplacement here—stuck in the mud, so to speak—seems an all-too-predictable, clichéd version of woman's place in Western civilization; indeed, it is precisely this demi-immersion in the earth's crust that is the "given" of the drama. From this, all else derives. The play constructs its drama between the gender positions of male and female and between the "elemental contrast of earth and air" (Knowlson and Pilling 94). Winnie is described by Beckett as being "like a bird" (Cohn 94). Imbedded in the earth, she dreams of flying or floating; she hopes "that perhaps some day the earth will yield and let me go, the pull is so great, yes, crack all round me and let me out"(2281). Is it purely chance, or the playwright's whim, that it is the woman who has lost mobility, while it is the male who has lost—almost—the ability to speak? That while he retains the ability to move (he crawls) but risks the loss of speech, she has nothing but speech, her movements restricted to those of the upper body—a body over which she is progressively losing control? What is the allegorical meaning of Winnie's earth-bound imbeddedness, her paralysis, her loquaciousness?

Surely we would respond to the play differently if the roles were reversed, if Winnie were transformed into a male and Willie into a female. Is there something about Winnie herself, Winnie as woman, that explains her condition in this drama? Would it be possible to work a transformational switch, a recoding of the grammatical law, such that Winnie and Willie would be interchangeable? Out of Winnie's capacious black shopping bag she pulls the essential items that ensure her survival for the two hours on stage. Many of these items—her handkerchief, the mirror, the parasol, the lipstick, the ornate brimless hat—are typically feminine accoutrements. Playing out the cultural script, she tries to maintain a cheerfulness in face of the incomprehensible logic of the universe. She appears at first to avoid the overwhelming questions ("Why am I stuck in this mound of mud?" "Why is my husband living in a hole?"), instead filling her happy days with housewifely patter. That is, she survives as most wives, and housewives, survive—by not questioning the givens of their existence but focusing on daily necessities, coping hour-by-hour, minute-by-minute. As James Knowlson has commented, "Winnie substitutes pattern for purpose"(107). In so doing she duplicates what is for many women—outside of Beckett's script but inside the cultural text—the only known method of survival: the pretense that meaning exists, even though the reality of daily living constantly puts into question the very premises on which this question might be posed; the hope that ritual might actually bring about revelation—a moment in which the carefully construed pattern of details might add up to something, a figure emerging from the jigsaw of life's puzzle; the effort to fill up time, kill time, not waste time, as though time itself were the elixir of life.

Time has been construed as woman's particular enemy—that which robs her of youth, beauty, and sexual attractiveness. The passage of time can only tell her that, from the perspective of patriarchy, she loses value on the exchange market from puberty on. This is not a "biological fact," but the effect of gendered cultural values that make Winnie, like all women, items of economic and sexual exchange in order to shore up patriarchy's institutions, first among which is marriage. Eventually she will be replaced by other—younger—women, ones not "shopworn" by time, women whose youth allows them the temporary fiction that they are unique, their charms enthralling, their seductive powers enchanting, their position secure. Patriarchal time will unwrite that fiction as it inscripts on woman's face and body the story of her disenchantment, the effects of a cruel reality that forces her to realize that she is not unique. Rather, she is part of a chain in which commodities are passed from hand to hand, a chain in which woman's fate is sealed by fathers and husbands.

Holding up her mirror to put on her lipstick, Winnie asks, "What is that wonderful line? Oh fleeting joys—oh something lasting woe"(2274). The image of the woman holding the mirror to her face is all too familiarly female. Does she hold the mirror to confirm that she is still the "fairest of them all," as the wicked queen asked her mirror? Is it to determine whether telltale signs of aging have disappeared after a good night's sleep? Is it to see whether the process of deterioration has worsened since yesterday? Is it to confirm that she is still alive? Winnie's comment is multiply self-reflexive of woman's condition. But in reading the line—which (typically feminine) she can only half remember—she is rewriting Milton's script in a gender reversal. In *Paradise Lost,* the line "O fleeting joys / Of Paradise, dear bought with lasting woe" belongs to Adam, not to Eve. We will return to Paradise and the implications of this reversal.

Mirror, Mirror on the Wall,
Who's the Fairest of Them All?
"Snow White"

First, we must look again in Winnie's mirror. Sandra Gilbert and Susan Gubar have suggested, in a provocative feminist reading of "Snow White," that the mirror into which every woman peers for confirmation of her beauty, her worth, her identity, is not a mirror that reflects woman's own image but rather a mirror that reflects the patriarchal simulacrum of that image. In answer to the queen's question, "Who's the fairest of them all?" the answer is provided by the (absent) king, the very representative of patriarchy, the paternal figure from which all power— of identity, of naming, of creativity—flows. In *The Madwoman in the Attic,* Gilbert and Gubar write that the king

> surely, is the voice of the looking glass, the patriarchal voice of judgment that rules the Queen's—and every woman's—self-evaluation. He it is who decides, first, that his consort is the "fairest of all," and then, as she becomes maddened, rebellious, witchlike, that she must be replaced by his angelically, innocent and dutiful daughter, a girl who is therefore defined as "more beautiful still" than the Queen. To the extent, then, that the King, and only the King, constituted the first Queen's prospects, he need no longer appear in the story because, having assimilated the meaning of her own sexuality (and having, thus, become the second Queen) the woman has internalized the King's rules: his voice resides now in her own mirror, her own mind. (38)

The Gilbert/Gubar argument, which provides the groundwork for a significant part of American feminist criticism, argues not only that art and literature have traditionally belonged to man but that man has inscripted woman into an art that frames her in his image of her and silences her voice, so that, even when she presumably interrogates her own image in the mirror, the answer comes not from herself but from the internalized masculine and patriarchal values. Even the questions the queen poses of the mirror are questions of concern to the patriarchy, to which the patriarchy provides the answers.

Such a reading would suggest perhaps that Winnie, like all women, must turn to the mirror in a gesture of reconfirmation—of identity, of desirability, of the very reality of existence. The answer that must echo back from the mirror is not only the reassurance of sexual attraction—of being "fairest of them all"—but the necessary fiction that *this woman* is uniquely attractive, the most attractive, holding a position of grace in a kingdom in which the king pronounces that which is valuable and that which is not. The answer is designed—for the moment at least—to restate the patriarchal claim and to stop the movement along the chain of substitutability. Thus woman must ask the question again and again, as each tick of the temporal clock can initiate another movement of the chain, as occurs (inevitably, Gilbert and Gubar would argue) in the tale: the queen is replaced by the daughter, who is "more beautiful still." Like Cordelia, this daughter is a threat to the powers of older women; like Cordelia, this daughter's power is underwritten by the father.

But this reading of culture, by now a "standard" feminist reading of the patriarchal text, does not work with Beckett's text, despite the superficial play of details—mirrors, questions, the non-presence of the patriarchal figure—in *Happy Days*. In other words, this Beckett play (perhaps *any* Beckett play) is not a traditional patriarchal script: it does not belong to that genre. Winnie does not consult her mirror for reassurance of her place in the signifying chain or for patriarchal approval. Initially, she uses the mirror to inspect the state of her teeth and gums, in a gesture that suggests the clinical rather than the narcissistic. The series of questions she poses of the mirror suggests a need for understanding the mystery of her condition. The queen, by contrast, asks no questions of the system itself; she does not indulge in a philosophic question but rather seeks to know her place within the system. In a reversal of traditional roles, it is woman here who asks the overwhelming philosophic questions, but she poses them in traditionally "female" terms, in the language of the domestic. That is, these questions are not underwritten with any kind of authority. It is authority they try to comprehend. For example, Winnie asks Willie, "Was I lovable once, Willie? Was I ever

Hanna Marron as Winnie, with Ori Levy as Willie, in *Happy Days*

lovable? Do not misunderstand my question, I am not asking you if you loved me, we know all about that, I am asking you if you found me lovable—at one stage"(2280). This set of questions mimes the patriarchal interrogation (asking for approval, for affirmation of self-worth) as it undermines the philosophical of its reasoned premises.

From a gendered position, Winnie interrogates the "ontological concept that deals with the nature of Being"(Wittig 63), suggesting that the concept of the "lovable" masks the founding terms of love. In appearing to ask for confirmation of her worth (translated as the "lovable"), Winnie also asks for a definition of the lovable—a definition that would use her as the terms of that condition. She specifically sets aside the very issue that grounds the queen's question of the mirror ("Who's the fairest of them all?"—a question that demands comparison among others) in saying "I am not asking you if you loved me." She is not asking for an indication that she must be lovable because he once loved her (a situation that would invest her with worth precisely *because* he loved her) but rather she asks the questions of *intrinsic* worth: was I lovable once? Moreover, her question takes issue with the notion that worth must be constantly reaffirmed over time (if I was lovable yesterday, am I still lovable today?). Winnie explains, "I am asking you if you found me lovable—at one stage." Her remark underwrites the privileging of the temporal in Western civilization by the addition of "at one stage," a remark that suggests the masculine belief in progress and change. We take note of the ways in which the patriarchal script inevitably writes woman *out* of history, precisely because history is man's construct, the story of his conquests; woman occupies separate space, outside of man's time. However, Winnie's question also suggests that she is not interested in whether Willie finds her lovable *now*; in other words, Winnie has escaped the eternal present into which man writes woman. And Willie's presumed answer (never heard on stage, but rather echoed by Winnie) is doubly negative. "No? You can't?" The initial term—"no"—suggests that Willie never found her lovable. Winnie's second question—"You can't?"—implies that Willie cannot answer the question. And the commentary that follows continues that chain of the play's concerns: "Well I admit it is a teaser. And you have done more than your bit already, for the time being, just lie back now and relax, I shall not trouble you again unless I am compelled to, just to know you are there within hearing and conceivably on the semi-alert is . . . er . . . paradise enow" (2280-81).

Again Winnie's comments write a double script. At first glance they appear to underwrite patriarchal concerns—that she needs Willie to confirm her own presence, to assert her own identity and worth. But there is at least one other reading, one that would reverse the generic law. Willie exists because Winnie claims he exists; he exists because she directs her words to him. At the beginning of the second act, Winnie is embedded up to the neck in the mound, and upon awaking, she thinks of Willie ("Say it is a long time now, Willie, since I saw you"): "I used to think . . . [*pause*] . . . I say I used to think that I would learn to talk alone. [*Pause.*] By that I mean to myself, the wilderness. [*Smile.*] But no. [*Smile broader.*] No no. [*Smile off.*] Ergo you are there" (2287). In his Afterword to *Happy Days,* James Knowlson comments that Winnie has rewritten the Cartesian formula: "I need to continue to assert my own existence, therefore you, Willie, still exist"(113).[3] If Knowlson is correct, such a rewriting of the Cartesian formula represents an important revision of the patriarchal script. Woman does not serve to mirror man's identity. She is not his other (in the existentialist notion of self and other) nor is she his Other (his unconscious) as certain feminists have suggested in rewriting Lacan, nor has there been a simple turning of the tables that a popularized notion of deconstruction might posit.

Happy Days does, however, dramatize the human condition in terms complicit with contemporary philosophical and psychoanalytic speculation. As Knowlson and Pilling have commented, the play emphasizes two important Beckett themes: "First is the need for a witness to validate one's own existence. Second is the compulsion to go on saying words 'as long as there are any'" (99). That is, the visual and aural senses, the senses most important to philosophy, are dominant. These senses diminish in their powers as the play progresses: in the second act Winnie can no longer turn her head to verify Willie's gaze at her, nor is she certain he can hear her words. It is also not without significance that the three "lesser" senses, ones so important to contemporary psychoanalysis (taste, touch, and smell), are virtually absent from this landscape, their absence a marker of the forms sterility assumes in Beckett's universe. We are in the wilderness.[4] The scene is one of specularity and speculation, to use the Derridean terms that denote laws of reflection and specular paradoxes. Winnie's "survival kit" includes the mirror, in which she verifies her existence, and her spectacles, through which she reads the world and the word.[5] She is "reflected" in the mirror, but she also reflects on the mirror and its properties, speculates on the eye and its ability to "be-hold" another. Winnie both beholds and is beheld; she is both the object of Willie's gaze, the gaze of validation and verification, and also the gaze that makes woman man's object, the internalized "spy eye" of prison's peephole, the eye of paranoia that traverses the unity of the "I." It is the eye that gives woman the "willies." It is the eye of the king pronouncing judgment on the queen. The "eye" both confirms and splits the "I."

Woman's voice, which calls to man's ear in a most potent form of seduction, is here reduced to banalities, wifely complaints and commentary, no longer that which calls up desire and calls out to the desired. Instead, Winnie's voice drives Willie into his hole or makes him disappear behind his newspaper. Winnie passes the Cartesian formula, "I think therefore I am," through her mirror, the properties of the formula bent in the fold of reflection. It is as though she were saying, "I need to continue to assert my own existence, therefore you, Willie still exist." This proposition hints at the possibility that Winnie's existence is constructed outside Willie's notions of her, and as we never learn what Willie's notions of Winnie might be, the entire play hangs on just the silence of those notions. Winnie wants to know that Willie is "there within hearing distance and conceivably on the semi-alert": a position that most often belongs not to men in this cultural script but to women, a situation of waiting, attending, hanging (however ambivalently) on *someone else's* words. As earlier Adam's line was given to Eve—"O fleeting joys/Of Paradise, dear bought with lasting woe"—Winnie's position of waiting, attending, crawling at the margins of a central, imbedded truth is transferred to Willie. Such reversals of cultural expectations are typical of Beckett and part of the "transformational grammar" of his art. But the reversals are not simple ones, not a mere trading of places and positions. Rather they operate like the mirror by means of an internal bend or fold, a space of specularity or the time of silence: this world is viewed as if through a speculum, heard in the internal recesses of the ear or the womb.

Which is not to say that Willie is feminized, because there is no suggestion that he is. Indeed, Winnie is stereotypically feminine, becoming more so as the play continues. Nor are Willie and Winnie part of the cast of unsexed beings that populate the Beckett stage, characters recognizable neither as male nor female, diminished by a lack of sexuality rather than any kind of androgynous participation in both sexualities. Rather, Willie takes up the position the female has traditionally played in Western society—hidden, silent, called upon to attend. In the first two utterances Willie gives in the play, he pronounces the word "It" in response to Winnie's question: "The hair on your head, Willie, what would you say speaking of the hair on your head, them or it?"(2277). Willie responds to a question of grammar, marking the singular against the plural. Winnie's response is delight, taking his one-word answer as a sign that he will communicate with her today: "Oh you are going to talk to me today, this is going to be a happy day!" That is, she takes Willie's response as a verification of the plural (you and me, us) rather than the singular that addresses the void or absent other. Willie's minimal response evokes an exaggerated pleasure in Winnie, and in this she may be seen as the pathetic·wife awaiting a sign of response from her husband. But a question about grammatical principles might just as well be one that issues from the husband, whose typical expertise is not in language but in mathematics. He comes to his wife, as a child to a teacher, to ask her expertise. The answer—"It"—draws attention to the absent "third gender" in English grammatical laws, that which is neither male nor female but neuter. Again, the text insists on writing both sides of the script, leaving us ultimately unable to decide which of these writings takes precedence. What does it mean that Willie "decided to speak to" Winnie today? We never know, although her reaction suggests that she would take any sign from Willie as a sign of affirmation for her.

> and when I call you my love, my love, is it you I am calling or my love? You, my love, is it you I thereby name, is it to you that I address myself?
> Jacques Derrida, *The Postcard*

> Though I say not
> What I may not
> Let you hear,
> Yet the swaying
> Dance is saying,
> Love me dear!
> Every touch of fingers
> Tells me what I know,
> Says for you,
> It's true, it's true,
> You love me so!
> "I Love You So," Winnie's song, *Happy Days*

What do I mean, then, when I suggest that there is a "transformational grammar of gender" at work in Beckett's texts? The title is something more than playful: it both puts into play the letter of the grammatical law and puts that law into question. I call up this law specifically to raise the issue of woman, to raise the issue of her play in such fictions, to raise the importance of gender to the development of literary genre. The more generalized relation posed by these terms (woman/literature, gender/genre) is grounded in a kind of "common knowledge"—that in French, for instance (and this play was written first in English, then translated by Beckett into French, and he is always walking the lines between two languages, negotiating the distances between them), the word *genre* encompasses and designates "gender." English borrows the generic sense of the word *genre* as it applies to literary forms but relies on a different word—*gender* (whose common genesis with *genre* remains hidden in the Latin root *genus*)—to distinguish biological differences.

Jacques Derrida's essay "The Law of Genre" begins with the pro-
nouncement "genres are not to be mixed," the essay itself demonstrating
the impossibility of *not* mixing genres, of not investigating this proxim-
ity of genre to gender. The essay traces the common thread and uncovers
the hidden assumption that etymologically links gender and genre: the
integrity of biological genders, which cannot be "mixed," whose distinctive, generic forms must remain intact. It is not accidental that I have
chosen a Beckett play that keeps biological identities intact, although
Happy Days, while perhaps a fortunate choice, is not the only Beckett
play that demonstrates my contention. The contention is that the notion
of gender—how it operates in culture and society—is an essential
subject of the play. And, further, that the drama speculates on its own
governing laws, the rules by which the game is played, in terms that
make gender (and genre) an issue. There are two important operations
to be noted, according to Derrida, with respect to genre. The first is
that this figure is feminine: "Now the feminine, or generally affirmative
gender/genre, is also the genre of this figure of law, not of its repre-
sentatives, but of the law herself who, throughout an account, forms a
couple with me, with the 'I' of the narrative account" ("Law of Genre"
225). The second is a "principle of contamination, a law of impurity,
a parasitical economy . . . the trait that marks membership inevitably
divides, the boundary of the set comes to form, by invagination, an internal pocket larger than the whole"(206). One image for this "invagination," a kind of doubled chiasmas, is the hymen, a term that is
sexually marked and refers to the fold of tissue that covers the vaginal
orifice and is the Greek word for marriage. The law of genre is thus
gendered, and it rules in such a way as to uncouple oppositions (he/she;
inside/outside; genre/gender). But such uncoupling, by the very law that
enforces it, is also impossible: the coupled terms can not be divided
from each other cleanly, precisely because they are enfolded into one
another.

Derrida is not speaking of Winnie and Willie, of course, but he
might have been. Their "coupling" through an envisioned dialogue and
their emerging identities within the boundaries of gender are implicit to
the genre, the dramatic form, of this text—to its account and its effects,
to both its beginning and ending. Winnie's speculation and reflection
unfold according to the terms of this coupling. Winnie speaks from her
position as female and wife, but her questions and comments dislodge
the assumptions that inform that positioning. Derrida's theories "shake"
the foundations of culture in order to observe a kind of resettling of
cultural notions. In *Happy Days,* this cultural foundation is the mound
into which Winnie is settling.

What is of crucial importance to the grammar of *Happy Days* is precisely the position from which it questions the system. Winnie speaks from a position of subjectivity (the "I") that is also under the law of genre/gender: she speaks in her female voice but is also spoken by her feminine cultural position. She speaks from *within* the cultural system she interrogates—from the mound that represents not the "earth mother" in the traditional terms of fecundity but rather the sludge, the detritus, of a civilization that both idolizes and inters the female. There is no position *outside* the system, beyond the patriarchal gaze, from which to question the system, and it is this "truth" that *Happy Days* uncovers. In the normal run of things, however, such discoveries are masked by the rhetoric of love, which has as its principle law to keep woman in her "place" as the adored object of male desire. The cultural system can continue to function only when woman keeps to her place, sings to herself, greets each "happy day" as another in a series of happy days. Woman's place is the mound, an extruded womb, a breast made of clay, a burial ground. Woman cannot be allowed movement, she cannot become airborne (as Winnie dreams of flying away). She must be anchored because it is her very fixity that allows the smooth running of the system. She is trapped by her grammatical place in the system (this place is gendered), and it is her entrapment that assures the system's functioning.

(I insert parenthetically Derrida's comments on woman's place in history and her desire to dance. "But I am speculating. . . . Having passed through several detours or stages you wonder how I would describe what is called 'woman's place'; the expression recalls, if I am not mistaken, 'in the home' or 'in the kitchen.' Frankly, I do not know. I believe that I would not describe the place, in fact, I would be wary of such a description. Do you not fear that having once become committed to the path of this topography, we would inevitably find ourselves back 'at home' or 'in the kitchen'? Or under house arrest, *assignation a residence* as they say in French penitentiary language, which would amount to the same thing? Why must there be a place for woman? And why only one, a single, completely essential place?" ("Choreographies" 68). His commentary recalls the terms of our own: a *speculation* on the *place* of woman in the cultural script.)

Gender distinctions situate themselves according to a power structure within the system, a power structure the system denies precisely because it accords privilege to the male. Woman herself is not only the sign of that which the system tries to master; she is also the reminder of that which threatens to undermine mastery. Hers is the sign that both unites and divides, according to the law of genre. Winnie's innocent domestic and feminine questions poke holes in the framework of the system. Caught in its structures she nonetheless insists on rereading those structures, declaring happiness where there is none, claiming love and recognition where love and recognition are in question. From her place, Winnie calls the system to account (for itself), she calls the system to her, and she is rewarded (from her perspective) at the close of the drama, when Willie whispers the first syllable of her name ("Win"), a syllable with ironic echoes. "Win" has its own place in the grammar of the system: it is a verb of action, of triumphing over something. It is a term that suggests sports and war, the playground and the battlefield, a place where men run to exert mastery over opponents and enemies. In this context, however, in the context of the mud mound, the word suggests the metonymy of the feminine by which the woman is recaptured in the cultural script. Willie's cry—"Win"—is a cry in the wilderness, a cry from the place of woman. It is remarked "in the feminine," in the space of the law of genre. Under its terms, the grammar of gender is transformational only from this boundary-line position, from a line that both unites and divides, that both separates gender from genre and renders the two unrecognizable—or recognizable only as each other. Without the system "in place," the overwhelming questions cannot be articulated. Winnie "wins" in bringing the system to its knees, by taking away its voice of authority (which can now only echo her name), but she also "loses" as its central gravity pulls her slowly and inexorably downward.

The "swaying Dance is saying Love me dear," but Winnie's legs are numb. Cultural inscriptions of "love" have entombed her, and it remains unclear whether her song addresses itself to "love" or to "a" love.

NOTES

1. Monique Wittig, like Julia Kristeva and other French theorists, examines the particular complications of the female speaking subject, the one who says "I." She writes: "This act—the becoming of *the* subject through the exercise of language and through locution—in order to be real, implies that the locutor be an absolute subject. For a relative subject is inconceivable, a relative subject could not speak at all. I mean that in spite of the harsh law of gender and its enforcement upon women, no woman can say "I" without being for herself a total subject—that is, ungendered, universal, whole.... But gender, an element of language, works upon this ontological fact to annul it as far as women are concerned and corresponds to a constant attempt to strip them of the most precious thing for a human being—subjectivity. Gender is an ontological impossibility because it tries to accomplish the division of Being" (66).

I do not agree with Wittig's premise that subjectivity is "absolute" or that "Being as being is not divided"(66). The work of Jacques Lacan suggests that *all* subjectivity is divided, this split the very condition of subjectivity (Kristeva's work follows in this line of thinking). However, the "law of gender" that Wittig invokes is also the " law of genre" as discussed by Derrida. This law announces itself through grammar, especially in the use of pronouns. As we will see, Winnie as "split subject" speaks two languages in *Happy Days,* her "monologue"— which is not monologic at all—divided by the requirements of two grammars: she interrogates philosophy (written under the law of a "masculine" grammar) in the language of domesticity. That is, she writes both sides of the Platonic script, disguising the language of the forum—and interrogation of cultural laws— through the feminized, and outlawed, language of the household. What is evident in *Happy Days* is that the two languages are not entirely separate, although some critical reaction to the play suggests that the language of the household so thoroughly masks the language of the law as to produce hostility on the part of certain audiences. See Knowlson and Pilling 98 ff.

2. All quotations are from the Norton Anthology, fifth edition.

3. In another context, Knowlson and Pilling write: "For Winnie touches, however lightly, on many of the central problems that have concerned Western philosophy at least since Descartes: the relationship of the mind and the body; the autonomous existence of 'things' or their dependence on the human consciousness; the power and the limits of the will; the absence or failure to care of any divine Creator; and the status of past experience and its relationship with the present. . . . She experiences these issues as puzzling enigmas, rather than as problems susceptible of solution. So philosophical speculations seem to arise naturally enough out of her specific situation and are expressed in and through carefully structured, yet living, credible human speech and action"(99). While the summary of the Cartesian problems Winnie addresses is quite accurate, Knowlson and Pilling pay little attention to the law of gender/genre that constructs Winnie's philosophical grammar. Her "light touch" and the experience of these problems as "puzzling enigmas" are *effects* of the law of gender under which she operates. It is this rigorously feminine and domestic articulation of these questions that requires—under the law of gender—that her speech be discredited.

4. At one symbolic level, this wilderness is the post-Edenic exile from the garden—an exile brought on by Eve's temptation to the tree of knowledge. This wilderness has its place in Julia Kristeva's examination of masculine and feminine orders: woman (before rational language) inhabits the wilderness; man (in full powers of rational language) stands under the sun. The sun/wilderness division calls forth two orders of Western culture—the Platonic, where sun is the light of reason—and Christian, where the wilderness is the place of exile and suffering, a place of punishment under God's law of unquestioning obedience. What Kristeva and others have shown is the ways in which such a cultural law is gendered. Discussing Kristeva's work, Andrea Nye writes: "It is clear that femininity resists and rebels against the authority of the sun. Women are constrained by logic and subject to it as an alien master. As the passage from Revelation makes clear, their natural habitat is the wilderness to which they will inevitably revert"(670). This linguistic "wilderness" is woman's speech, for which Winnie's speech is exemplary.

5. In a quite different context, an essay in admiration of Nelson Mandela, Derrida describes specular reflection: "But by force of reflection, something else can be understood, beckoning toward the literality of the mirror and the scene of specularity/speculation. Not so much toward the physical law of reflection as toward specular paradoxes in the experience of the law. There is no law without a mirror. And in this properly reversible structure, we shall never avoid the moment of admiration"(14). For discussion of another scene of speculation and the law, see Benstock, "From Letters to Literature."

WORKS CITED

Beckett, Samuel. *Happy Days. Norton Anthology of English Literature*. 2 vols. Ed. M. H. Abrams. New York: Norton, 1962. 2:2271–92.

Benstock, Shari. "From Letters to Literature: *La Carte Postale* in the Epistolary Genre." *Genre* 18 (1985), 257–95.

Derrida, Jacques. *The Postcard*. Trans. Alan Bass. Chicago: University of Chicago Press, 1987.

———."*La Loi du Genre* / The Law of Genre." Trans. Avital Ronnell. *Glyph* 7 (1980), 202–32.

———."The Laws of Reflection: Nelson Mandela, in Admiration." *For Nelson Mandela*. Ed. Jacques Derrida and Moustapha Tlili. New York: Henry Holt, 1987. 11–42.

———, and Christie V. McDonald. "Choreographies." *Diacritics* 12 (1982), 66–76.

Gilbert, Sandra M., and Susan Gubar. *The Madwoman in the Attic*. New Haven: Yale University Press, 1979.

Knowlson, John. Afterword. Samuel Beckett, *Happy Days / Oh les beaux jours*. Ed. James Knowlson. London: Faber & Faber, 1978.

———, and John Pilling. *Frescoes of the Skull: The Later Prose and Drama of Samuel Beckett*. New York: Grove Press, 1980.

Kristeva, Julia. *Revolution in Poetic Language*. Trans. Margaret Waller. New York: Columbia University Press, 1984.

Nye, Andrea. "Woman Clothed with the Sun: Julia Kristeva and the Escape From/To Language." *Signs* 12 (1987), 664–86.

Wittig, Monique. "The Mark of Gender." *The Poetics of Gender*. Ed. Nancy K. Miller. New York: Columbia University Press, 1986. 63–73.

Beckett and Sexuality
(Terribly Short Version)

PETER GIDAL

Sexuality in Beckett is oblivious, or rather, *not* oblivious to the conventions of gender. I mean with respect to the later work. The early writings are hilarious but still partake of sexed figuration—male, female, and the (Warholian) confusions. But in the later writings, like *Not I, Ghost Trio, What Where, Ohio Impromptu, Rockaby,* etc., there's a de-sexing, an un-sexing, to dehumanize the figure. The profound anti-humanist Beckettian project, to put it mildly, is the obliteration of sex in the figure, she/he unheld, *and* the obliteration of possibilities of identification-via-identity, and identiti*es. When* in *Rockaby* there is no possibility of recognition, finally, of Billie Whitelaw as female, in such contingencies as facial gesture, movement of hand, arm, foot, mouth, through the conventions of so-called female speech—"the feminine," tone, timbre, and so on—and when all speech and gesture is also the speaking of presumed author through actress, *then* for the viewer the position is vis-à-vis, and the view*ing* process through, the unsexed. More correctly, all speech and gesture here is not only *not*, but whatever it is, is *also* as to a presumed momentary authorial voice. This then frantic abnegation is simultaneously imbricated by and dialectically engaged with, in resistance to, the viewer/listener's impossible (and constant) attempts at transcendental self-identification/identity. When that goes, *he* goes. The viewer as *she* positions through that (patriarchal identity and its "loss," fright at the loss of the figured hold in representation) differently. Another kind of Realism. The constitution of sexual body, the female, without the endless hysterical male demands for sexed identity-*reassurance*. (Neither male nor female as referred to here eternal.[1]) The confusions for me as a male of stating what (and as) I'm stating are another problem, if not a problematic: a man cannot be a feminist.

It would be voluntarist to assume that through changes of subject position and identificatory mechanism a patriarchal social position could be obliterated. It would be equally idealist to assume that the changing of, for example, economic power positions alone would somehow transform and obliterate the concrete power of patriarchy's ideological positions: both changes being absolutely necessary. So the spectator, and his/her power and powerlessness, is always more than just voice and gesture in vacuo.

As to *Not I:* The denials are of language, i.e., language's denials. And the male romance of non-admission (of the ["Oedipal"?] crisis) is put into the mouth of a woman. The romance of non-admission, the hysteria of that crisis for the male, is enunciated by a woman's speech (by "romance" is here meant that which is allowed but only through non-admission, repression; and as it is motored through repression it is motored hysterically in constant repetitive denial: *"no, she!!!"*). "Without the male romance of non-admission" means not structured through (culturally produced) repressed male Oedipal needs to be Father in the World. Oedipality is not just the Freudian boy wanting to fuck his mother, but the paternal power, and language as power.[2] Hysterical movement is enacted usually as male, in "acts" precisely as consequences of the abnegation of the body and its fears, or in the catatonic silence of male repression or refusal. Such refusal—for example, to talk—denotes speech, and speaking itself, as somehow neurotic, "feminine," in the face of "earnest masculinity." And such male hysteria is of course not usually defined as hysterical. It operates in opposition both to a movement of processes without finalities and to the silences of autonomy, both culturally defined as "female."

The figuring out of this problematic in *Not I's* form engages the viewer in the apparatus of speech-making and positions him/her in a manner that disallows the male voyeur/listener/*doctor.* The non-movement of any figure (no auditor onstage after initial productions[3]) and the constant voice, simultaneous with its constant non-admission ("what? . . . who? . . . no! . . . she!") form for the listener/viewer an untenable position from which to *stop* to "hear" an other's denials (though physiologically we hear the onslaught of voice). Denials are played out on the body of the mouth's voice with speech as the body. Yet one ("I") is given no stable position, no *place from which;* position is untenable, unapprehendable, making that transference impossible. Thus the denial remains unfigured, neither here nor there, and this break of identification is the collapse, impossibility of difference here and there, here to there, there to here. Importantly, a desired collusion of time and space is hereby produced as collapsed, and any illusion thereof reflexivized. (The collapse, not the reflexivity, is what matters.) Positions of sex, sexual power, knowledge are made impossible, *no given "other" onstage,* making identity, indentification, and the repressions of time and space necessary for those ideological (real) mechanisms to take place equally impossible.

This blockage of identification and transference in the theatrically voiced act catatonizes and paralyses the listener/viewer in its (his/her) body, while forcing the mind into production, against consumption. Marx's "productive consumption" necessary for *re*production is here out of the question. There is no other, no different other. The "other" is a myth which to exist has to be containable by the self's norms, complimentary to one.

In reiteration, attempted materialist speech as in *Not I* is not in any way to be somehow held to female biology. It is precisely not an attempt to essentialize or sensationalize as somehow female some kind of fetish of the female which would keep the male position of voyeur firmly intact. Such fetishization/reification would also be yet again to instill a notion of speech-*re*production—reproduction as by the female *for* the male. Somehow, women's speaking, "voice," could be re-acquired neither for "fragmentation and chaos" (whether thereby defined as threat or non-threat) nor for transparency, process-annihilating "communication" (the system we already have). The speaking in *Not I* is a radical tendency—a left-curve in anti-patriarchal/anti-capitalist language and speech production. It is radical positioning, and a labor process, against meaning-as-is. Therein lies its difficult beauty.

NOTES

[For a more detailed version, to which the next essay refers, see Peter Gidal, *Understanding Beckett* (New York: St. Martins Press; London: Macmillan, 1986).—Ed.]

1. Christine Delphy, *Close to Home* (London: Hutchinson; Amherst: University of Massachusetts Press, 1984).

2. All this in the face of Freud's collossal "mental lapses" as characterized by Emmanuele de Lesseps in *Questions Feministes/Feminist Issues (1979)* 1, no. 2 (Winter 1981), 77–102.

3. The auditor written into the published text of *Not I* was as quickly written out by Beckett in his Paris production, which followed the London one. In the latter the auditor was concretely absented through theatrical processes: it was impossible to focus the location of Mouth as to height or depth (the stage a black box vacuum lacking perceptual reference points).

"Her Lips Moving"
The Castrated Voice of Not I

ANN WILSON

> Unfortunately it is not of them I have to speak, but of her who brought me into the world, through the hole in her arse if my memory is correct. First taste of the shit.
>
> Samuel Beckett, *Molloy*

Not I begins as the house lights fade and the sound of Mouth's voice is heard *"unintelligible behind curtain."* For ten seconds the audience sits in the darkened house hearing, straining to make sense of, this voice. When the curtain finally rises, the focus of our attention is directed to the Mouth's lips, the only part of her body lit directly; the rest of her face is in shadow, her body in darkness. The opening moments direct our attention so fully to Mouth that we fail to notice that she is not alone but, as Hersh Zeifman reminds us, shares the stage with another figure: the Auditor (Zeifman 44). Although it is easy to be drawn into Beckett's construction of the action on stage and effectively to erase the Auditor, *Not I,* in the theater, is not a monodrama (Zeifman 40). I would suggest that the theatricality directs the audience's response to such a degree that the piece is not even for two players but for three: the role of the audience is as fully written as that of the Auditor. In fact, the roles of the Auditor and audience are similar, for although our response is not physical, like the Auditor's, it is *"a gesture of helpless compassion."* In the video of the play produced by the BBC, the Auditor is not seen; nevertheless, he remains in the drama, never appearing before the camera's eye precisely because he, like the audience, is the eye of *Not I.*[1]

Given the parallels between the role of the audience and that of the Auditor—we hear the story of Mouth, who is the figure of (a) woman—I am interested in Beckett's stage direction that the sex of the Auditor is *"undeterminable."* Despite the fact that critics tend to use the masculine pronoun "he" to refer to the Auditor, the implications of this ascription of gender are unquestioned. Although the sex of the Auditor

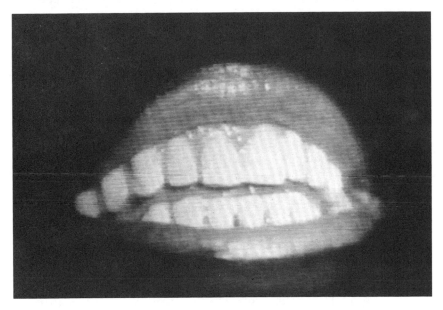

Billie Whitelaw in *Not I*

may be undeterminable (and indeed is not at issue, since the Auditor is a *figure*), his gender, as the use of "he" clearly suggests, is determinable. Within the discursive structure of *Not I* the Auditor is masculine, sexual difference is unproblematically inscribed, and the feminine is constructed only in its oppositional relation to the masculine.

As Enoch Brater notes in his article "Dada, Surrealism and the Genesis of *Not I*," Mouth is "limited to a rudimentary function: words"(49), or perhaps *language* is more appropriate, for in the theater and on film language is not restricted to words but is a complex of aural and visual signifying operations. Mouth is not just a torrent of words uttered so quickly that they are almost reduced to incomprehensible sound; Mouth is also the striking visual image of a pair of lips, divorced from the body, rapidly moving as they articulate the story. The image of lips and the sound of the fractured story issuing from them mutually reinforce the impossibility of Mouth fully constituting identity in language. Mouth is a figure who marks the limits of language, the unfulfilled promise of language to reveal that which ostensibly it represents. She tenaciously maintains her "vehement refusal to relinquish third person" and insists that the story she tells is not her own but that of some other. Her speech is punctuated by ellipses suggesting what is apparent visually: her relation to language is one of such radical alienation that she cannot be embodied in language. Visually and aurally, Mouth is marked by absence.

It is tempting to read Mouth's relation to language as paradigmatic of the relation of woman to language. (Here I use *woman* to name a constructed category rather than to refer to the experience of an individual.) To understand this relation it is necessary to outline briefly, and at the risk of gross oversimplification, the position of psychoanalytic critics that language, the symbolic order, is the Order of the Father.[2] Language acquisition—the entry into the symbolic order—is contemporaneous with the resolution of the Oedipal crisis. The Oedipal phase is precipitated by the child's recognition that (s)he is not the sole object of the mother's desire. This recognition ruptures the exclusivity of the mother/child dyad which hitherto had been the only structure of relations recognized by the child. The recognition of the axis of desire between the mother and the father—an axis from which the child is excluded—results in the child's recognition of the third person: the dyad I/you (child/mother) now opens so that the child's structure of relations includes "he," the father. Because the child, like the father, desires the mother, the child experiences rivalry, and therefore identification, with the father. The child believes the mother desires the phallus which both she and the child lack but the father possesses. The child experiences castration, which is the absence of the phallus. The Oedipal crisis is resolved when the child censures his/her desire for the mother and, in so doing, equates the father with prohibition—the law—and the phallus.[3] This equation of the father, the law, and the phallus introduces an economy in which elements can be exchanged and substituted one for another. This establishes the structure necessary for the acquisition of language, which is an economy of substitution because the signifier stands for the signified. Language is said to be phallocentric because it is bound to the child's recognition of the Father or, more specifically, to the recognition of the Father's desire.

Mouth's speech would seem to "refuse the romanticism of identity," to borrow Elin Diamond's phrase. That is, her speech seems to insist that the identity is always a construct of language and so is marked by the limitations of language itself. Riddled with puns (for example, "godforsaken hole called . . . no matter") which, by definition, subvert the one-to-one correspondence between the signifier and the signified by playing on the ambiguity of meaning, her speech demonstrates the instability of language and suggests the impossibility of constituting a stable, cohesive identity. The gaps in her speech, the holes forsaken by logos, allow her to utter only bits of sentences. These fragments can only constitute a fragmented subject. Mouth steadfastly refuses to inscribe herself as the fully present speaking subject but instead insists that the story is that of "she." Because she insists that the story is not autobiography but the history of someone else, she maintains a tension between the narrative and the speaker. The identity which her story constitutes is the representation, rather than revelation, of the self. In so doing, Mouth refuses to efface the fiction of identity. This refusal, coded in the syntax, is reinforced by the relatively rapid pace of the speech's delivery, which makes it difficult to catch the sense of what she is saying. Throughout *Not I*, the instability of the "I" as subject—an instability which amounts to the impossibility of "I" creating a coherent identity— is pronounced. Peter Gidal suggests that the theatricality of *Not I* forces viewers to confront their desire for art to be meaningful by subverting the construction of a comprehensive interpretation. He argues that *Not I* disrupts the process of signification: "The linkage between every signifier (the mark, or the word, or the image), every signifier being a signified for another signifier, is broken down here, or not upheld. It is kept in process, so as to disallow a process of linkage from taking place"(91). Later he comments: "Thus what we at most may have is *a* subject, and not any imaginary solidity as characteristic fundament. This is a position demanding an anti-patriarchal hold in the word"(93). For Gidal, Mouth's refusal to constitute herself fully within the language of the Father is feminist because her fragmented identity (both aural and visual) protects her from appropriation by the viewers and subjugation under the tyranny of their desire for meaning.

By his own admission, Gidal's interpretation is predicated on the suppression of Auditor's role(91). Later the Auditor figures in the discussion but, the terms having been established by the initial suppression, is then adjacent to the focus of his argument, the role of Mouth. Clearly, the theatricality of *Not I* establishes Mouth as the focus not only of our attention but also of the Auditor's. The Auditor is the ideal audience— he who listens with compassionate attentiveness to Mouth's babble. Given his position on stage, standing between the audience and Mouth, he mediates (actually and figuratively) the audience's response to Mouth. Despite Gidal's suppression of the role, the Auditor is an important figure in *Not I*. Enoch Brater recounts that while

> sitting in a cafe in North Africa . . . [Beckett] observed a solitary figure, completely covered in a djellaba, leaning against a wall. It seemed to him that the figure was in a position of intense listening—what could that lonely figure be listening to? Only later did Beckett learn that this figure leaning against the wall was an Arab woman waiting there for her child

who attended a nearby school. The concept for *Not I* was, therefore, initially sparked by Beckett's preoccupation with that isolated listener, the unidentified Auditor we encounter on stage.[4]

The genesis of the Auditor may have been Beckett's memory of the mother awaiting her child, but the memory of the maternal figure, when translated to the stage, is transformed. Whatever the stage directions indicate, in the absence of her being clearly represented as woman, the discursive structure of *Not I* constructs the Auditor as masculine.

Julia Kristeva suggests that "the *elision* of the object is the syntactic recognition of an impossible object, the disappearance not only of the addressee *(you)*, but of all topic of discourse" (153). Mouth's refusal to recognize the addressee of the story, as Kristeva points out, is the refusal of the structure of discourse: without "you" there can be no "I." Yet, because she does speak, Mouth's refusal is paradoxical, for the very act of speaking necessarily constructs the Other as the object of discourse. Further, she explicitly acknowledges an addressee, a listener, when she responds to the questions which we cannot hear: "what? . . . who? . . . no! . . . she!" Thus the status of her refusal needs to be called into question. Does it mark, as Gidal argues, a refusal to locate herself within a patriarchal discourse? Or is it a mark of humility, the erasure of the self by someone who is before God? Kristeva argues that Mouth's tenacious clinging to the third person "postulates the existence of the other. Here, since it is 'not I', not *you* either, then it must be a *He beyond communication*"(152).

Indeed much in *Not I* indicates that Mouth faces final judgment. Wandering in a field on an April morning, she experienced something which left her insentient and in darkness. Now she is without physical being, save her lips, suggesting that she is in a state which anticipates absolute absence, Death. There is the suggestion that she faces judgment: "what had she to say for herself . . . guilty or not guilty . . . stand up woman . . . speak up woman. . . . " If she is facing judgment, the fragments of her narrative support a reading that she is before a figure of God, the Auditor. Twice she calls into question the collocation of God and mercy, saying, at one point, "brought up as she had been to believe . . . with the other waifs . . . in a merciful . . . *[brief laugh]* . . . God . . . *[good laugh]* . . . first thought was . . . oh long after . . . sudden flash . . . she was being punished . . . for her sins . . . " Surely her laughter—whether out of anxiety over, or at the absurdity of, God's mercy—allows the possibility of reading Mouth's speech as spoken before God, the Father, who is Absolute Presence, the Signified, who cannot be fully represented except through the mediation of the Word. If we follow Gidal's argument, the fragmentation of her speech marks Mouth's refusal to constitute herself unequivocally within patriarchal discourse. But Kristeva's reading of the same syntactical patterns of elision produces an equally compelling, although antithetical, interpretation. She argues that Mouth does not refuse the discourse of the Father but in fact submits so fully that, standing before God, the Father who is Presence beyond representation, Mouth denies herself. It is precisely the ambiguous intention of her refusal to recognize the story as her own history that heightens the importance of considering how other signifying operations construct gender in *Not I*.

Mouth is marked by absence both aurally and visually: the elision of her story, the absence of her body save the lips. Absence is understood as lack, as something missing, and so is recognized only in its relation to what is there. Absence, therefore, is constructed within a structure of differentiation which earlier we named the Order of the Father. In our discussion of the Oedipal complex as a paradigm for the constitution of patriarchal authority, we identified the child's recognition of the father's desire as the intervention which ruptures the dyad of mother and child. This intervention is figured as the phallus (Rose 40). Sexual difference, because it is *difference,* can be explored only within phallocentric discourse. Sexual identification—having or not having the phallus—is not "natural" in the sense that such recognition is possible only within the structure of differentiation which is overdetermined by the phallus. The phallocentrism of the Order of the Father is important for *Not I* because, whether or not Mouth's speech insistently exposes identity as a fiction (and so the problem of constituting feminine identity within the patriarchal order), it is clear that feminine sexuality is unproblematically inscribed. Reportedly, Beckett believes that *Not I,* originally written for the theater, is more fully realized on video, presumably because the technology of the medium allows everything but the lips to be erased (Cohn 200). On video, the visual pun on lips becomes clear, for these lips, from which pour almost ceaseless chatter, are not only the lips of a mouth but suggest the labia of a vagina. The lips are associated with the only other elements of Mouth's identity—words—and so this image, which conflates the lips of a mouth with the labia of a vagina, is an emblem of the erotics of language.

Early in the story, Mouth says, "little girl... into this... out into this... before her time... godforsaken hole called... no matter...." What is the "godforsaken hole" which Mouth will not name (or names "no matter")? As Gidal points out, the syntax of her story prohibits any confident claim of a definitive interpretation; nevertheless, the story seems to support several possibilities. The "godforsaken hole" may be the world into which she was born—a world where there was "no love such as normally vented on the . . . speechless infant," a world which denies the Christian figuration of God as loving and merciful. If God is the Father, then Mouth's world is one which the Father has doubly forsaken, for she experiences neither the love of God the Father nor that of her biological father: "parents unknown . . . unheard of . . . he having vanished . . . thin air . . . no sooner buttoned up his breeches. . . . " Indeed, if the lips are also labia, then the "godforsaken hole" may be an image of the mother's vagina, which was forsaken literally by the father after the act of intercourse which resulted in Mouth's conception.

Perhaps most obviously, the image of lips/labia eroticizes speech; yet critics who recognize the lips as labia seem reluctant to discuss the inscription of feminine sexuality which necessarily must attend such a recognition. The most striking example is the discussion by James Knowlson and John Pilling, in *Frescoes of the Skull*, who suggest that "[i]n the text, the wild stream of words is expressly linked by Mouth with excremental discharge, 'nearest lavatory . . . start pouring it out . . . steady mad stuff . . . half the vowels wrong'(19), just as in *How It Is* the word and the fart have come to be equated"(200). In the next sentence the words pouring from Mouth are characterized as a "form of verbal diarrhea." Knowlson and Pilling slide easily from the possibility of lips as labia to their suggestion that it is excrement which pours from this metaphoric vagina. The slip, which fuses the vagina and anus, is facilitated at that particular moment by the textual ambiguity constructed by rhetorical figures and syntactical elision. The script never allows the illusion that it has a specific referent but instead constantly draws attention to itself as producing a fiction. Words are likened to excrement (but are not excrement); excrement can pour from between labia which are like lips (and lips themselves are only a theatrical figure) because language establishes an economy within which such exchanges are possible. I do not want to argue that Knowlson and Pilling are wrong, because logic dictates that if the lips are labia, then Mouth must bolt to the nearest lavatory to deal with menstrual flow; after all, whatever happens to her apparently occurs only "once or twice a year." Rather, I want to point out that the rhetorical strategies of *Not I,* which Gidal claims prohibit the appropriation of woman, effect the denial of woman by establishing a textual economy within which feminine sexuality is erased. This erasure, so glaringly apparent in Knowlson's and Pilling's equation of words with excrement, is raised throughout *Not I*.

Early in her narrative Mouth says that she was "not exactly . . . insentient" but "feeling . . . feeling so dulled . . . she did not know . . . what position she was in! . . . imagine!" Later, there is the recollection of the recuperation of feeling associated explicitly with the movement of her lips: "when suddenly she felt . . . her lips moving . . . imagine! . . . her lips moving!" This is the moment when the text opens itself to the inscription of the feminine, for the lips moving allows the possibility of pleasure, the sensuality of speech and of masturbation. At that moment feminine sexuality is inscribed as multiplicity which cannot be accounted for within patriarchal discourse. This is not the structure of the masculine auto-affective gesture which effects a clear distinction between the hand which touches and the genitals which are touched.[5] Here, the lips mutually and simultaneously touch and are touched; there is division and unity, for the touching lips are always the indivisible pair. Thus lips and labia are distinct and, at the same time, indistinguishable, within an economy of exchange where there is no exchange. As Luce Irigaray writes in "When Our Lips Speak Together," a piece celebrating lesbian sexuality: "We never separate simply: *a single word* cannot be produced, uttered by our mouths. Between our lips, yours and mine, several voices, several ways of speaking resound endlessly, back and forth. One is never separable from the other"(209).

This moment of the feminine in *Not I* is fleeting, for quickly the pleasure is identified solely with the production of words and so is situated within the Order of the Father: "all these contortions without which . . . no speech possible . . . and yet in the ordinary way . . . not felt at all . . . so intent one is . . . on what one is saying . . . the whole being . . . hanging on its words . . . " Implied is the importance of hearing what is said, of effecting the division of the self into speaking subject and object of discourse so that being—or identity—is constituted. This division paradigmatically enacts the full division of the self as toucher and touched (speaker and auditor) which characterizes the masculine auto-affective gesture and, as discussed earlier, the rupture of the mother/child dyad which occurs with the introduction of the phallus. The informing patriarchal ideology of *Not I*, arguably latent until this point, now is manifest on the level of the script. Mouth is constituted within patriarchal discourse. Theatrically, she is contructed from the outset within a scene of representation which is within the Order of the Father.

Knowlson and Pilling note that the theatrical design of *Not I* is delicate: "If the theatre is too large (like the main auditorium in the Théâtre d'Orsay in Paris, for example) Mouth becomes little more than a distant speck of light in the darkness, and the human dimension which is needed to confer life and emotion on the text is lost. If, on the other hand, the theatre is too small, Auditor appears obtrusive and the image of Mouth becomes too precisely anatomical"(198). Too close to Mouth, the illusion of disembodiment breaks because we would be able to see the theatrical apparatus which produces the image. The script demands that the means of theatrical production are invisible.[6] This aspect of the script seems to counter Gidal's contention that *Not I* displaces the spectators by extricating them "from male sexual superiority into the non-male voice"(96). Contrary to Gidal's claim, the theatricality privileges the spectator's gaze by its implicit demand that the spectator is positioned so that the fragile image can be seen without destroying the illusion. The fragility, as Knowlson and Pilling suggest, is the ambiguity of the lips. If these are only Mouth's lips, and not also labia, then the erotic impulse of the text is suppressed. In effect, the text privileges a few spectators, those sitting close but not too close. The video of *Not I* is powerful because the camera controls the gaze by perfectly positioning the spectator, in effect becoming the eye of *Not I*.

The image of Mouth on video is disturbing: lips and tongue moving rapidly, generating so much saliva that it sprays from Mouth and clings to her lower lip. The sexual overtones of the image are obvious: Mouth is aroused. The viewer's position as spectator is that of the voyeur watching the lips/labia, a position which replicates that constructed by pornography, in which the object of desire (usually female) is the site onto which the spectator (usually male) can project his fantasy. The very ambiguity of the image in *Not I*, and the fact that on video (and, to a lesser degree, in the theater) our position relative to the image is not disrupted, facilitate the element of fantasy. We are constructed as subjects within a structure of desire, which is masculine. What we desire is knowledge, in all its complexity, of Mouth. Key to this structure is the impossibility of desire being sated.

The impossibility exists on the narrative level but also in the very theatricality of the piece, which distances the spectator from the stage and from the video: in no sense can Mouth be penetrated. These distancing gestures, which occur simultaneously, are not analogous. The first instance can be read as the refusal of the romanticism of identity, but the second is akin to pornography's inscription of the impossibility of desire being sated because the eroticized mystery of the feminine (the vagina) is not resolved but reinforced. In pornography the vagina is constructed as constantly teasing, beckoning the voyeur but never receiving his penis. In a much more genitally specific way, the stage picture in *Not I* figures the absence of the phallus inscribed in the narrative. The theatricality of the piece demands that the structure of the gaze is not called into question; what is called into question is the allure of Mouth. The teeth, moving with the force of articulation, are menacing—an image of the danger of the feminine. The Mouth, the "godforsaken hole," is the image of castration, for she is both castrated (marked by the absence of the phallus) and potentially castrating. The spectator's position allows the construction of the feminine as alluring and destroying. Such a figuration cannot be construed as feminist.

The audience, watching and hearing *Not I,* is cast in a masculine role. The theatricality of *Not I* frames Mouth, through both the use of light and the fixed position of the actor playing Mouth, and situates the spectators so that our gaze replicates that constructed by pornography. Mouth's narrative is marked by absence—absence which finally amounts to the absence of the Father. We might want to re-consider Brater's contention that " 'she,' even if a fiction, is the fiction of a *real* woman, capable of appearing in courtrooms and shopping in supermarkets, of wandering in fields and loitering in public lavatories"("Dada" 56, my emphasis). Mouth is the figure of a woman written in a scene overdetermined by the Order of the Father. This unproblematized inscription of gender results in her being constituted only in relation to the Father, marked by absence—an absence which is the absence of the phallus.

NOTES

1. Here I play with Enoch Brater's pun of "Mouth (not eye)" in "Dada, Surrealism and the Genesis of *Not I,* " 50.

2. My explanation of Lacan relies on Jacqueline Rose, "Introduction-II," in *Feminine Sexuality* by Jacques Lacan and the ecole freudienne, ed. Mitchell and Rose.

3. Sigmund Freud, "The Ego and the Id," 19:34.

4. Brater, *Beyond Minimalism,* 24. Knowlson and Pilling suggest that the genesis of *Not I* may have been Beckett's visit to Morocco in 1972 or his memory of Caravaggio's *Decollation of St. John,* which he had seen in Valetta Cathedral in Malta (196). Brater lists other sources Beckett has suggested as possible inspiration for the auditor. See *Beyond Minimalism,* 24. [Also see 202 in this volume.—Ed.]

5. For a more extensive discussion of the implications of the male auto-affective gesture see Jacques Derrida, " . . . That Dangerous Supplement."

6. My thoughts on the theatricality of *Not I* were clarified through discussions with Kim Langford of Cornell University, who is working on a study of the male gaze in Beckett's later works.

WORKS CITED

Beckett, Samuel. *Not I.* London: Faber and Faber, 1973.

Brater, Enoch. *Beyond Minimalism.* New York, Oxford University Press, 1987.

——— ."Dada, Surrealism and the Genesis of *Not I.*" *Modern Drama* 18, no. 1 (March 1975).

Cohn, Ruby. *Just Play: Beckett's Theater.* Princeton: Princeton University Press, 1980.

Derrida, Jacques. ". . . That Dangerous Supplement." In *Of Grammatology*. Ed. Gayatari Chakravorty Spivak. Baltimore: The Johns Hopkins University Press, 1976.

Diamond, Elin. "Refusing the Romanticism of Identity: Narrative Interventions in Churchill, Benmussa and Duras." *Theatre Journal* 37, no. 3 (October 1985).

Freud, Sigmund. "The Ego and the Id." *The Standard Edition of the Complete Psychological Works of Freud*. vol. 19. Trans. James Strachey. London: Hogarth Press, 1961.

Gidal, Peter. *Understanding Beckett: A Study of Monologue and Gesture in the Works of Samuel Beckett*. New York: St. Martin's Press, 1986.

Irigaray, Luce. "When Our Lips Speak Together." *This Sex Which Is Not One*. Trans. Catherine Porter and Carolyn Burke. Ithaca: Cornell University Press, 1985.

Knowlson, James, and John Pilling. *Frescoes of the Skull: The Later Prose and Drama of Samuel Beckett*. London: Calder, 1979.

Kristeva, Julia. "The Father, Love and Banishment." *Desire in Language: A Semiotic Approach to Literature and Art*. Ed. Leon S. Roudiez. Trans. Thomas Gora, Alice Jardine, and Leon Roudiez. New York: Columbia University Press, 1980.

Rose, Jacqueline. "Introduction—II." *Feminine Sexuality* by Jacques Lacan and the ecole freudienne. Ed. Juliet Mitchell and Jacqueline Rose. Trans. Jacqueline Rose. New York: W. W. Norton, 1985.

Zeifman, Hersh. "Being and Non-Being: Samuel Beckett's *Not I*." *Modern Drama* 19 (March 1976).

Portrait of a Woman
The Experience of Marginality in Not I

DINA SHERZER

Powerful dramaticule, uncanny theatrical performance, stark visual orchestration of light and darkness, movement and stasis—*Not I* has been discussed by many critics. Enoch Brater (49-59) compares several components of the play with Dada and Surrealist experiments. Ruby Cohn, (69-72, 129-31) focuses on the aural and oral experience created by Mouth's onslaught of words. In "A Poetry of Moving Images" (65-76) Martin Esslin considers that *Not I*, like all other works by Beckett, constitutes a metaphysical meditation on the human condition and that Mouth's plight is thus a metaphor of the suffering of the individual in the world. Because of the staging of a mouth speaking insistently, Linda Ben-Zvi (165) proposes to interpret the play as an animated hieroglyphic, as an icon for Beckett's entire oeuvre. And Katherine Kelly (73-80) sees Mouth as an orphic figure and *Not I* as a disfigurement of Ovid's heroic story.

While these readings are valid and warranted and attest to the power of Beckett's oeuvre to generate many different interpretations, it seems as if critics have shied away from the literal content of the play, from the actual experience of the woman called Mouth. As Esslin writes, Beckett encompasses and molds "that wealth of human suffering, a whole lifetime of human experience into an image so telling, so graphic, into words so brilliantly meaningful that a bare quarter of an hour suffices to communicate it all" (*Not I* 39).

What I propose here is to tease out several effects of meaning in the play—indeed, to expand Beckett's terseness or, as Esslin says, his so brilliantly meaningful words. It seems improper and perhaps even indecent to tamper with Beckett's elegant minimalness and to bring down to the literal what he has raised to the level of the metaphysical. Yet it is appropriate to do so, because in *Not I* several utterances mean more than they say, and furthermore there is meaning in form and in performance. Therefore I focus on the written text of the play, on the performance of Mouth, and on the aural experience that the spectator has in listening to the play. In addition, around *Not I,* I establish a web of other texts which echo, resonate with, and illuminate Beckett's own text.

Beckett always stages characters who are outsiders, like the tramp/ clowns in *Waiting for Godot,* Winnie buried in the sand in some no-man's-land in *Happy Days,* and Hamm, Clov, and Hamm's parents confined to a house on an island in *Endgame.* But in these plays the marginal status of the characters, while being important, is not the main focus of the dramatic action. In *Not I* Beckett centers his play on the experience of marginality.

The first text in my web around *Not I* is the following statement by Beckett himself in which he explains that one inspiration and the source for his play was a familiar sight he knew in Ireland: "I knew that woman in Ireland... I knew who she was—not 'she' specifically, one single woman, but there were so many of those old crones, stumbling down the lanes, in the ditches, beside the hedgerows. Ireland is full of them. And I heard 'her' saying what I wrote in *Not I.* I actually heard it" (Gontarski 132). In *Not I* Beckett has his character Mouth describe herself as an old hag and a wanderer in the same kind of forlorn setting: "walks mostly... walking all her days... day after day;... stare into space... drifting around... day after day... old hag already... sitting staring at her hand... no one else for miles... "(20)

The presence of these women in such a setting is not indifferent. Both the old hag Beckett knew and Mouth live in, and are relegated to, spaces which isolate them and separate them from others. They are outside the boundaries of normal living patterns, outside time, outside society. They are wanderers, drifters, tramps. Such women on the margins conjure up the image of the witch, of the lunatic—two types of individuals who signify exclusion and outsiderhood.

Beckett makes Mouth's anomic status and her marginality become even more apparent during her interactions with "normal" individuals in "normal" settings. Mouth describes these encounters with others as painful experiences:

> how she survived!... even shopping... out shopping... busy shopping centre... supermart... just hand in the list... with the bag... old black shopping bag... then stand there waiting... any length of time... middle of the throng... motionless... staring into space... mouth half open as usual... till it was back in her hand... the bag black in her hand... then pay and go... not so much as goodbye... how she survived!(19)

> ... how she survived!... that time in court... what she had to say for herself... guilty or not guilty... stand up woman... speak up

woman . . . stood there staring into space . . . mouth half open as usual . . . waiting to be led away . . . glad of the hand on her arm . . . (21)

. . . once or twice a year . . . always winter some strange reason . . . the long evenings . . . hours of darkness . . . sudden urge to . . . tell . . . then rush out stop the first she saw . . . nearest lavatory . . . start pouring it out . . . steady stream . . . mad stuff . . . half the vowels wrong . . . no one could follow . . . till she saw the stare she was getting . . . then die of shame . . . crawl back in . . . (22)

In these passages Mouth stresses two things: her abnormal behavior caused by her stigma and the reactions of "normal" individuals toward her. Mouth's stigma makes others treat her as either a non-person or a child—with too much condescendence or pity or as strange and incongruous. With these brief utterances Beckett shows that because of the disparity between Mouth and others there is no possibility of intersubjectivity but rather only rejection and loneliness. Such elements cause readers to apprehend the significance of muteness and of the marginality experienced by Mouth.

Through Mouth's words, Beckett displays a keen sense of what stigma, difference, and rejection mean. In his minimalness he presents the type of experience which concerns such scholars as Victor Turner, Michel Foucault, and Erving Goffman, who have studied marginality in culture.[1]

Mouth's account is the story of a life marked by stigma. She tells how she lived her aphasia and how she suddenly recovered speech. Like all of Beckett's characters, no matter how sorry their plight, she refuses to give up and to sink into despair. Her situation is uncannily similar to that of the woman described in the following text which appeared in France in 1975 in a collection of popular literature, *La Bibliothèque bleue,* edited by Geneviève Bollène:

Marie Grelard, born in 1743 in the Parish of St. Hilaire in Poitou, was attacked by small pox at nine years of age. Ulcers grew on her tongue. This organ deteriorated. . . . Henceforth the girl stopped talking. She emitted only a confused noise like the inarticulate sounds of a mute. But after some time, nature took its course again. First Marie Grelard stuttered; she uttered some words with difficulty. Finally speech returned to her. There are still some sounds that are hard for her to pronounce. . . . Indeed the desire that this girl had to establish normal communication through speaking and the continuous efforts that she made to succeed, have set her muscles in action and have given them movement and dynamism. (23) [my translation]

I found this text quoted in a feminist leaflet, where it represented a metaphor of woman's condition and the feminist awakening. I read it literally here. Marie Grelard is in a predicament similar to that of Mouth. She had her tongue partially cut out. Mouth was aphasic. Both Marie Grelard and Mouth display a persistence, an obstinacy to break the fatality of the body, to change their weakness into force, to liberate themselves by speaking. Both display the desire to establish relations with others, to be related to the world by speaking. Both fight to overcome their stigma and to come out of solitude. This character of a woman, completely marginalized because of some sort of stigma but not giving up, is also found in the novels of Marguerite Duras. The old beggar in *Le vice-consul* has been rejected from her family at an early age because she became pregnant. Duras describes her wandering alone in rice fields and in forests, living in the wilderness where little by little she becomes mute and insane because of fear, hunger, and loneliness. Along with these sufferings Duras describes the resourcefulness of the beggar which allows her to survive and in fact to overcome her negative fate. Beckett, like the anonymous author of the text from the *Bibliothèque bleue* and like Duras, creates a positive image of woman as strong character who is a victim of stigma but refuses to give up.

Part of the portrait of woman that Beckett creates in *Not I* depends also on how Mouth speaks and here the specifics of staging and the quality of the oral performance of Mouth yield meaning. Because in the original version Mouth addresses her words to a silent figure present on stage, it has been suggested that in fact the play is staging a session between analyst and analysand. Because of the intensity of the torrent of words she utters, we can speculate that the spectator is in fact listening to an instance of *abreaction*. Freud formulated his definition of abreaction after dealing with mainly female, hysterical patients. Abreaction is defined as an "emotional discharge whereby the subject liberates himself from the affect attached to the memory of a traumatic event in such a way that this affect is not able to become (or to remain) pathogenic. Abreaction may . . . come about spontaneously, either a short or a long interval after the original trauma" (Laplanche and Pontalis 1). What is emphasized in *Not I* is not the liberation from the memory of a specific traumatic event but the actual verbal outpouring, the description in vivid terms of different moments of Mouth's life. Like the hysterics Freud listened to, Mouth lives her past in her telling. She herself says she is dragging up her past (20). She articulates the expression of her non-being, her marginality, and her suffering through the staccato rhythm of her speech, her pantings, her screams, her pauses, her repetitions, her broken syntax, and her alogical tale. Through her voice the spectator apprehends a body taken over both by torment and by exhilaration—a woman estranged from the rest of the world, expressing an intransitive intimacy, closed in on herself, oriented to her past and her sufferings.

Mouth's performance, in addition to echoing Freud's female patients' outbursts, brings to mind other artistic creations in which a woman is represented in the act of screaming or talking in ways that are felt to be inappropriate and disturbing. Roberto Rossellini's film *Amore* (1948), based on a scenario by Jean Cocteau entitled *La voix humaine,* presents only a woman (Anna Magnani) screaming on the phone to her lover who has left her. This is another instance of a hysterical oral display, whereas in *Not I* speaking is both a relief and a torment. Duras also uses the voice in a similar fashion in her works. The beggar of the *Vice-consul* is mute, but the Europeans hear her singing and she constantly repeats one word—"Battambang"—which is the synecdoche of her whole tragedy, since it is the name of the place where she was born and from which she has been expelled by her mother. This name conjures up and exorcizes her past. In her film *Le Camion* Duras talks about an old woman who perhaps escaped from an asylum and spends her time hitchhiking in order to talk to people. She is garrulous, stringing along unrelated topics. These women characters, like Mouth, need to give themselves an oral and aural satisfaction and release. They are sensitive to the erotics of their own voice.

Ruby Cohn coins the word *theatereality*; used in relation to *Not I* (30-31), it means that the buzzing and the rays that Mouth describes as tormenting her during her muteness are actualized on stage by the buzzing of her words and the ray of light emanating from her lips as she speaks. But there are other aspects of Mouth's performance which create this theatereality and which contribute to making Mouth a marginal being for spectators. The speed and staccato quality of Mouth's speech prevent complete intelligibility. Mouth, though she now can speak, places herself outside normal communication. It is particularly significant that Billie Whitelaw, in an interview with Jim Knowlson (86), talks about the physical pain, the discomfort, and the buildup of tension in the body that the required speed of oral delivery produces. The straining that the actress feels is also felt by the spectators. In fact Beckett plays an ironic twist on spectators, an instance of theatereality par excellence. We are sitting in the dark, we are made uncomfortable, we are disturbed and appalled by this panting voice. We stare at her lips, puzzled, uncomfortable, disturbed by this verbal encounter, just like the individuals Mouth talked to in the bathroom in winter when she had this sudden urge to communicate with others. We think of this woman as hysterical and mad, as a witch babbling in darkness. The first impulse is probably to reject her.

It is apropriate to ask why Beckett chose a woman as his character for *Not I*. Experiences of isolation, rejection, and abreaction can happen to men as well as to women. Marginality, hysteria, and madness cut across gender. What is the difference between a man and a woman in such cases? In Western cultural tradition and convention, the witch is always seen as a woman—an old woman, an old hag babbling in solitude. Hysterical outpourings are connected with women talking about their bodies and their sufferings. Duras is of the opinion that women are more vulnerable, that they can become outsiders more easily, that they are frequently associated with difference and marginality (*Les Parleuses* 49). It might be argued that Beckett chose a woman as his character in *Not I* because he shares with Duras this sociological and anthropological awareness about women, and he therefore felt that a woman would be more true to life—a more believable character.

In *Not I* then Beckett offers not only a surrealist experience and a metaphysical statement about the human condition. He also reaches into the literal world and renders a moving experience of a woman suffering. In his essay "Présentation" Pierre Chabert points out that the genesis of *Not I,* Beckett's recollection of the old hags of Ireland, is most revealing about the playwright's dramatic writing (17). It shows how it is intimately linked to seeing, to space, and to the body. I would add that Beckett's writing owes much to his compassion for human beings and to his uncanny sense of what it means to be on the margins and to be female.

NOTE

1. The anthropologist Victor Turner defines outsiderhood as "the condition of being permanently and by ascription set outside the structural arrangements of a given social system, or being situationally or temporarily set apart from the behavior of status-occupying, role-playing members of the systems" (231). Space is equally an important feature in Michel Foucault's analysis of madness through the centuries. Part of the condition of the insane is that they are relegated to spaces which isolate them and separate them from the sane, the normal individuals. Erving Goffman in his book *Stigma* studies the special relations which exist between normal people and people with stigmas.

WORKS CITED

Beckett, Samuel. *Not I. Ends and Odds*. New York: Grove Press, 1976.

Ben-Zvi, Linda. *Samuel Beckett*. Boston: Twayne, 1986.

Bollène, Geneviève. *La Bibliothèque bleue: la littérature populaire en France du XVIème au XIXème siècle*. Paris: Julliard, 1971.

Brater, Enoch. "Dada, Surrealism, and the Genesis of *Not I*." *Modern Drama* 18, no. 1 (1975), 49-59.

Chabert, Pierre. "Présentation." Special issue of *La Revue d'Esthétique* on Beckett (Spring 1986), 7-21.

———. "The Body in Beckett's Theater." *Journal of Beckett Studies* (1982), 23-28.

Cohn, Ruby. *Just Play: Beckett's Theater*. Princeton: Princeton University Press, 1980.

Duras, Marguerite. *Le Camion*. Paris: Minuit, 1977.

———. *Les Parleuses*. Paris: Minuit, 1974.

———. *Le Vice-consul*. Paris: Minuit, 1964.

Esslin, Martin. "A Poetry of Moving Images." *Beckett Translating/Translating Beckett*. University City: Pennsylvania State Press, 1987, 65-76.

———. "Not I." *Plays and Players* 20, no. 6 (1973), 39.

Foucault, Michel. *Histoire de la Folie*. Paris: 10/18, 1961.

Goffman, Erving. *Stigma: Notes on the Management of Spoiled Identity*. Englewood Cliffs: N.J.: Prentice Hall, 1963.

Gontarski, Stanley. *The Intent of Undoing in Samuel Beckett Dramatic Texts*. Bloomington: Indiana University Press, 1985.

Kelly, Katherine. "The Orphic Mouth in *Not I*." *Journal of Beckett Studies* 6 (1980), 73-80.

Knowlson, James. "Extracts from an Interview with Billie Whitelaw." *Journal of Beckett Studies* 3 (1978), 85-90.

Laplanche, Jean, and Jean-Baptiste Pontalis. *The Language of Psychoanalysis*. New York: Norton, 1974.

Turner, Victor. "Passage, Margins, and Poverty." *Dramas, Fields and Metaphors*. Ithaca: Cornell University Press, 1974, 231-71.

Speaking Parisian: Beckett and French Feminism

ELIN DIAMOND

To associate Samuel Beckett with the controversial feminist theory coming out of France since the early 1970s seems, at first glance, highly improbable. And yet both Julia Kristeva and Hélène Cixous, whatever their fundamental disagreements, refer to the linguistic ruptures and raptures of male high modernists—Beckett, Joyce, Artaud, Genet—and both, along with Luce Irigaray, have written about female sexuality in ways astonishingly compatible with, and contemporary with, Samuel Beckett's late stage plays—*Not I* (1972), *Footfalls* (1976), and, to a lesser extent, *Rockaby* (1982).[1] My brief is as follows: In what we Americans (too reductively) call "French feminism," two foci of discussion and debate have emerged in the last decade as crucial to describing the "feminine" in discourse: the hysteric and the pre-symbolic (or "semiotic") maternal. Each is theorized as a position of resistance to the patriarchal symbolic (the langue we speak and through which we constitute our social and sexual identity). And each—the hysterical and the maternal—"plays" in the words and elisions of Beckett's recent theater.

To place Beckett within theoretical debates about the feminine seems odd only because critics have tended to sanctify the great Author's solitary brilliance, although Beckett's vast literary and philosophical interests are well documented, as is his knowledge of Freud. Moreover, if Beckett's dispossessed speaker/subjects of the late plays and prose seem to defy social, medical, legal, or even metaphoric labeling, they have, despite their fright wigs and great coats, gender. In fact, the displaced sexual signifier is one of Beckett's more playful gestures—Krapp's banana, Winnie's pearls. This essay does not assume a cross-influence among Cixous, Irigaray, and Kristeva (all trained psychoanalysts) and the ascetic Irishman in their midst but takes an intertextual perspective. I will argue that the polemical and performative gestures of French feminist theory are revealingly staged in three late Beckett plays and that, conversely, reading Beckett through a feminist theoretical lens foregrounds often-overlooked features of his gender representations.

Who speaks? Whose language? These fundamental questions of contemporary theory continue to unravel the structures of knowledge, and they come from many quarters—linguists, semioticians, deconstructionists, as well as hysterics and the insistent unheard prompter in Beckett's *Not I*. In *Problems in General Linguistics* (1971; French edition 1966), Emile Benveniste unchains the "I" from the ideology of the Cartesian *cogito*, the humanist fiction of selfhood, to posit an "I" whose only referent is the act of discourse in which it is pronounced. Language, and only language, instantiates an "I" by assuming, relationally, a "you," but both are merely positions, empty spaces, marked by pronominal shifters. "I" is simply the one who "utters the present instance of discourse containing the linguistic instance I" (cited in Silverman, 218). This is, of course, vintage Beckett: "I, say I. Unbelieving" (*Unnamable* 291). The Unnamable's quarrel with any attempt to signify the subject might serve as the anthem of Parisian poststructuralism. Like the Derridean trace, Beckett's Unnamable eludes signifying form (except in the reader's desire) through a seemingly endless writing that tempts, but always forecloses, presence. Paraphrasing the last words from *The Unnamable*, Foucault begins "The Discourse on Language," putting in crisis (and under erasure) his own authority to speak.[2] Parisian poststructuralism shares (has incorporated?) Samuel Beckett's desiring, linguistic homelessness, his wholly unholy deracinated subjects.

After 1968, amidst contests on many fronts, the feminist critique of linguistic gendering forced another crisis of the "I." The symbolic order, Lacan's designation for the (gendered) subject positions in language taken up by the child after the Oedipus, is the Order of the Father—the phallus, the relational signifier by which all meaning is produced. The female child, lacking the organ to exchange for the phallic privilege of subjectivity, cannot assume that "I" without an erasure of her unnamable—because unrepresentable—sexuality. In the early 1970s feminists, having absorbed the lessons of deconstruction, noted that psychoanalysis, the authoritative science of sexed subjectivity, constitutes itself by repressing an Other. Coiled in the heart of psychoanalysis is a lamia, a sick monster—the hysteric. In *La Jeune Née* (1975; *The Newly Born Woman*, 1986), Hélène Cixous and Catherine Clément reread Freud's case histories of hysterics, on which he based his "new science" of psychoanalysis, particularly his "fragment" on Dora. They acknowledge the greatness of the listening doctor who, after the long sad history of medical resentment at resistent, incurable women, hears his own hysteria in his patients' somatic raving and verbal obsessions. Clément and Cixous reconfigure the hysteric as both historically victimized by, and metaphorically destructive of, the patriarchal symbolic, the language of the fathers that brings about her "cure." Freud discovers repression, the cornerstone of psychoanalysis, through his hysterics, who suffer, he first postulates, "from reminiscences" (*Studies* 7). Clément and Cixous insist that psychoanalysis listen to its own reminiscences, to the repressed memory of feminine hysteria that lies at the heart of its formulations. They insist that the inability of the female to say "I"—to represent herself in what Kristeva calls the socio-symbolic contract—is precisely the symptom, incurable in Western culture, that betrays and unravels the patriarchy.

Behind this polemic, the hysteric uncoils and unleashes her anti-language, a derisive somatic mimicry of the father's lexical and syntactic order. Like Cixous's Medusa she is painfully spectacular. "Her body," says Clément, "[is] transformed into a theater for forgotten scenes, [it] relives the past, bearing witness to a lost childhood that survives in suffering" (5).

> out . . . into this world . . . this world . . . tiny little thing . . . before its time . . . in a godfor- . . . what? . . . girl? . . . yes . . . tiny little girl . . . out into this . . . before her time . . . (*Not I* 14)

Beckett's Mouth, both organ of speech and (with its *"fully, faintly lit"* lips) organ of sex, is also the body's metonymic reduction, a pulsing muscle that spews words like excrement, "pouring it out' " in a gasping, spittling deformation of the Father's logos. Symptoms of hysteria surface in Mouth's fragmented case history: withdrawal and silence ("practically speechless . . . all her days" 18), the analgesiac attack ("whole body like gone" 21), the "steady stream" (19) of words that defies comprehension ("no idea what she's saying!" 19), not unlike the polysemic gibberish of Anna O. The "I" that Mouth refuses to utter refers to a female speaker who is neither present nor absent but rather adrift in the elisions between four fragmented reminiscences that will not congeal into meanings: lying face down in the grass; at the supermart; on the bench seeing tears fall; and "that time at court" (21). Like all reminiscences, the latter is preceded by a reprise of the repressed first "scene":

> tiny little thing . . . before its time . . . godforsaken hole . . . no love . . . spared that . . . speechless all her days . . . practically speechless . . . how she survived! . . . that time in court . . . what had she to say for herself . . . guilty or not guilty . . . stand up woman . . . speak up woman . . . stood there staring into space . . . mouth half open as usual . . . (21)

Guilty or not guilty? Standing before the Law of the Logos, the female, by virtue of being born female, is always already guilty, since, the psychoanalytic story goes, she cannot assume subjectivity within the symbolic (she lacks a penis) or outside of it. She has a guilty secret (her sexuality) that is both her disease (the organ of all that spewing) and her resistance to cure. Hysteria, the body talking out of control, "speaks" always of this guilt *and of its resistance*. Clément: "The hysteric is in ignorance, perhaps in innocence; but it is a matter of a *refusal*, an escape, a *rejection*... " (14). Mouth rejects the regulations of discursive logic, which order her to take up a subject position in a language that represses her secret: "what?... who?... no!... she!" (15).

Who speaks? Who listens? The (male?) figure in the priestly djellaba, face averted, listens as though to an analysand, with sympathy, with "*helpless compassion*" (14), silently urging Mouth to staunch her verbal flow with an object-representation—an "I"—however fictional and provisional. The djellaba figure acts the role of mental healer, who cannot modify the culture that makes his patient sick (he is "*helpless*"), but attempts to, as Kristeva puts it, "prevent [her] *jouissance*, [her] truth, and replace it with the plausibility of reasonable discourse" (*Reader* 236).[3] The djellaba figure is not the only one to replace/prevent; he stands in for an absent, much more powerful, censor—a proscriptive voice that Mouth hears reminding her of the buzzing and the flickering light inside her head, that corrects her on empirical details (her age, the position of her body on the grass). Who speaks inside the speaker (Mouth) but the Other—the Law, the Symbolic Order, or (in Beckett, always), God. Mouth dutifully if frantically responds ("who? what?"), corrects herself ("... sixty... what?... seventy?... good God!" 15), and even plaintively asks ("perhaps something she had to... had to... tell... could that be it?" 21). However, intermingled with questions are the signifiers of the hideous hysteric who rejects both the Father's ministrations and his orders; who shrieks with laughter at the "thought" of a "merciful God"; and, most of all, who refuses the ego-agency—that is, *the fiction* of ego-agency—that would quell the violent symptom. Instead the "mouth on fire" with its "steady stream" overcomes the repression barrier and does not cease: "*Voice continues behind curtain, unintelligible*... " (23).

But to imply a marginal narrative of heroic proportions in *Not I*, or in recent feminist theorizing on hysteria, would be utterly simplistic for two reasons. First, as Clément puts it: "The feminine role... of hysteric is... antiestablishment and conservative at the same time. Antiestablishment because the symptoms—the attacks—revolt and shake up the public, the group, the men, the others to whom they are exhibited.... The hysteric unties familiar bonds, introduces disorder into the well-regulated unfolding of everyday life. [But her role is] conservative... because every hysteric ends up inuring others to her symptoms, and the family closes around her again, whether she is curable or incurable" (5).

The gestures of Beckett's djellaba figure, registering compassion (and dismay?) at Mouth's spectacle, fade into immobility, because the curtain will "close around her again, whether she is curable or incurable." The second reason for rejecting a heroic narrative is that in the mise-en-scene of Beckett's *Not I* (and of psychoanalysis) there is no narrative at all, nor are there discrete discourses—a delirious unconscious *jouissance* exploding through a coherent linguistic surface. The signifier is always already a tracery of desire and reminiscence which "speaks," throwing out flickering images of a life, a courtroom, a woman face down in the grass; throwing out responses to unheard prompters; or throwing out, just as "clearly," elisions, those gaps or ruptures in the symbolic which are not small victories so much as evidence of the conundrum of enunciation: the I of discourse is *in* discourse; it is *not I*, it seems, who speaks. *Not I* is a drama of the lacerating encounter with monologic discourse that occurs to every human being, every "tiny little thing." It is also the particularized struggle of the female speaker in that encounter, whose cultural "I" is never herself, but a "no-body, dressed up, wrapped in veils, carefully kept distant, pushed to the side of History and change, nullified, kept out of the way, on the edge of the stage . . . " (*Newly Born Woman* 69).

The critique of patriarchal language and law through the figure of the hysteric is limited by the onus of her disease. Feminist theory has embraced a more significant human role—one impossible to marginalize, however silenced she has traditionally been. The mother, or more accurately the maternal function, because of her "pre-Oedipal" or pre-cultural role in nurturing, gendering, and socializing the infant, has become a metaphoric lever for dislodging patriarchal structures. In Kristeva's formulations through the 1970s, the pre-Oedipal—or to use her terms, the *semiotic* or *chora*—is central to her theory of artistic subversion. Kristeva locates the semiotic in the pre-verbal moment of mother-child bonding, when the child is most dependent on the maternal body, when instinctual drives are channeled and organized, when vocal/kinetic rhythms are unconsciously absorbed. Modernist writing, in its alliteration, repetition, melody, harmony, signifies not a referent but "the influx of the semiotic" into the symbolic (*Revolution* 62). The artist's (incestuous) appropriation of an "archaic, instinctual, and maternal territory . . . " (*Desire* 136) produces "an irruption of the drives in the universal signifying order . . . " (*Revolution* 62). Importantly, Kristeva sees the semiotic as a *dialectical* interference (*Revolution* 24); the patriarchal symbolic is necessary to break the mother-child dyad, that space of non-differentiation (Lacan's Imaginary), to release the child—however problematically for the female—into separation and signification. Radically different is Hélène Cixous's concept of *"l'écriture feminine,"* a writing empowered by a "woman-voice," a maternal muse that the female writer ingests to create her own song for other women (in Stanton 167). This maternal voice is, like Kristeva's semiotic, the "song before the law, before ... the symbolic" (167), but it brooks no interference from the Symbolic, the law of the Father. In this deep auditory intimacy, "the voice is the uterus" which, merging with the breast, creates an absolute convergence: "Voice. Inexhaustible milk. Is rediscovered. The lost mother. Eternity: voice mixed with milk" (167).[4]

M. Mother. [*Pause. No Louder.*] Mother.
[*Pause.*]
V: Yes, May.
M: Were you asleep?
V: Deep asleep. [*Pause.*] I heard you in my deep sleep. [*Pause.*] There is no sleep so deep I would not hear you there. (*Footfalls* 44)

Beckett's *Footfalls,* emerging from darkness and a single chime, between May ("M") and her mother's voice ("V"), stages a crisis posed by feminist theories of the maternal: how celebrate and separate from the mother's body? The obsessive May, "revolving it all" in her "poor mind" as she paces and "wheels" nine steps to the right and left, exists entombed with(in) her Mother's voice. No milk, metaphorical or otherwise, flows between the ninety-year-old "V" and the spectral May with her *"dissheveled"* grey hair, her *"worn grey wrap ... trailing"* (42) over unseen feet. Maternal rhythms have atrophied into a menopausal parody of the death drive: a linear repetitive dance whose steps the mother ghoulishly calls: "But let us watch her move, in silence. [*M paces. Towards end of second length.*] Watch how feat she wheels [*M turns, paces. Synchronous with steps third length.*] Seven eight nine, wheel" (45). The mother's voice says that she cannot remember how "it" started but, in response to an invented (rational) interlocutor, she notes the time May sleeps and when she "tries to tell how it was ... It all ... It all" (46).

The "it" that May rehearses is displaced into a story fragment set in a small church—a "sequel" that contains pacing and references to "His poor arm" and "a semblance" (47)—but how connect "it all"? The sign of the dismembered god (the "poor arm") is seen through flickering candles, and a ghostly vision or "semblance" that is there and not there, like May herself as she slips across pronouns. With that slippage, language breaks into a seductive "tangle" of alliteration—"light" "like"; "moon" "through":

A tangle of tatters. [*Pause.*] A faint tangle of pale grey tatters. [*Pause.*] Watch *it* pass—[*pause*]—watch *her* pass before the candelabrum how its flames, their light... like moon through passing rack. [my italics] (47)

Another narrative frame retrieves or, rather for the first time, produces a new object—an imaginary May called Amy and a mother called Mrs. Winter, who has seen something "strange" at church. Amy, the reticent storyteller explains, cannot confirm her mother's vision, because though her mother "distinctly" heard her praying, Amy was "not there." Analogously, immediately, the created "it," the object/story, vanishes, swallowed back into the first dialogue which, in turn, is swallowed up by M's voice as she repeats her mother's lines: "Will you never have done... revolving it all?" (48)

"You put yourself in my mouth, and I suffocate. Continue to be also outside. Keep yourself/me also outside. Don't be engulfed, don't engulf me, in what passes from you to me" (in Gallop 114). These lines are from *Et l'une ne bouge pas sans l'autre* (1979), a sixteen-page text by Luce Irigaray that both marks and tries to rupture the paralyzing bond between mother and daughter. Jane Gallop extrapolates from this paralysis a speculation about the anxiety of/between women concerning phallic privilege—who has it and will it threaten the integrity of she who does not? Perhaps this "it" has something to do with May's "it"—the privilege to escape from the mother-daughter dyad. Is May's pacing perhaps *not* the result of a mysterious "it," some veiled trauma about ghostly semblances, but rather the very image of that engulfing bond that keeps mother and daughter in paralysis so that "one can't move without the other"? Is that "it"? Gallop's analysis of the phallic mother—she who engulfs, who is in command and all powerful—belies Cixous's vision of the deep, productive (milk-giving) intimacy between the mother's voice and the listening daugher/writer. Beckett's *Footfalls,* itself an unstable, overdetermined "it," partakes of and produces both visions, for V, the mother's voice, both controls and is subsumed by May's monologue, in which she is still "revolving it all... in [her] poor mind" (48).

The phallic mother, both seductive and destructive, makes an appearance in Beckett's *Rockaby* (1981) in the shape of an old woman dressed in gaudy feminine finery. As she rocks and is rocked, she conflates child and mother into one stage image. W (Woman in the rocker) hungrily addresses an unseen V ("her recorded voice" 9) with the childlike demand, "More." V offers a rhythmic Beckett babble of truncated repetitive phrases that seem to signify regret at approaching death. But V closes with "rock her off," / "fuck life" (20). This image of the crone/mother who rejects life, or would end life, is Beckett's radical contribution to [the] feminist discussion of the phallic mother—she who, as mother and primary nurturer, seems omnipotently in control of life (she is the rocker) but who, as a female subject, cannot emerge from her internal monologue to change or control her representation (she is rocked). Furthermore, the phallic mother's power is defined—and circumscribed—by her body's sexual rhythms: her rocker, Beckett says, is "controlled mechanically" (12).

Kristeva praises the "literary avant-garde for introducing ruptures, blank spaces, and holes into language . . . [for this] calls into question the very posture of mastery" (in Marks and de Courtivron, 165). Samuel Beckett's own posture as venerated twentieth-century avant-garde author has been continually to link mastery to failure, speech to silence, syntax to gap. He has, in other words, "feminized" his writing, permitted the other to invade his discourse; and at this historical moment, as Parisian women theorists have been writing (of) the feminine, the Irish-Parisian writer has theatricalized their theory, ruptured and challenged *their* discursive mastery through powerfully denatured stage images.

NOTES

1. In Julia Kristeva's *Revolution in Poetic Language* (a shortened translation of her doctoral thesis *La Revoluion du Langage Poétique*, 1974), modernist writing exemplifies what she calls semiotic *pulsion*—the rupturing effects of bodily drives as/in the rhythms, repetitions, elisions, and word play of poetic language since Mallarmé (Artaud particularly exemplifies, in this and other works, linguistic rupture, *jouissance*, hysteria). In "The Father, Love, and Banishment" (in *Desire in Language*, first published in *Cahiers de l'Herne*, 1976, reprinted in *Polylogue* 1977), Kristeva looks at the interplay of (paternal) meaning and (maternal) *jouissance* in Beckett's "First Love" and *Not I*. The latter play enters Kristeva's discussion of narcissism in ego development in "Freud and Love: Treatment and Its Discontents" (in *The Kristeva Reader*, also in *Histoires d'Amour*, 1983). Hélène Cixous wrote her dissertation on Joyce (*L'Exil de James Joyce, ou l'art du remplacement*, 1972), but Genet is usually her exemplary male writer, one whose text "divides itself; pulls itself to pieces, dismembers itself, regroups, remembers itself . . . a proliferating, maternal femininity" (in *The Newly Born Woman*, 84; originally *La Jeune Née*, 1975, a title which puns on Genet's name). Luce Irigaray's *Speculum of the Other Woman* (*Speculum de l'autre femme*, 1974, her doctoral thesis) focuses on Freud and Plato, rather than on male poets and novelists, as a means of retrieving the repressed feminine in master discourses. Although she never mentions Beckett, Irigaray shares his fascination with mimetic doubles and, as we will see, with the suffocating power of maternal possession.

2. Foucault (unwittingly?) misattributes the source of these lines, claiming to cite "the voice of Molloy" (215).

3. As the spittle gathered at the corners of Billie Whitelaw's mouth during the televised version of *Not I,* the metaphor of verbal stream as orgasm (one meaning of *jouissance*) was, to say the least, palpable.

4. Domna Stanton, quoting from Hélène Cixous's *Illa.*

WORKS CITED

Beckett, Samuel. *Three Novels: Molloy, Malone Dies, The Unnamable.* New York: Grove Press, 1965.

———. *Ends and Odds* (containing *Not I, Footfalls,* among others). New York: Grove Press, 1977.

———. *Rockaby and Other Short Pieces.* New York: Grove Press, 1981.

Cixous, Hélène. *Illa.* Paris: Editions des Femmes, 1980.

———, and Catherine Clément. *The Newly Born Woman.* Trans. Betsy Wing. Minneapolis: University of Minnesota Press, 1986.

Foucault, Michel. "The Discourse on Language." Trans. Rupert Swyer. In *The Archaeology of Knowledge.* New York: Harper and Row, 1972.

Freud, Sigmund. *Studies on Hysteria.* New York: Basic Books, 1955.

Gallop, Jane. *The Daughter's Seduction: Feminism and Psychoanalysis.* Ithaca, N.Y.: Cornell University Press, 1982.

Irigaray, Luce. *Et l'une ne bouge pas sans l'autre.* Paris: Minuit, 1979.

Kristeva, Julia. *Desire in Language.* Trans. Thomas Gora, Alice Jardine, Leon Roudiez. New York: Columbia University Press, 1980.

———. *Revolution in Poetic Language.* Trans. Margaret Waller. New York: Columbia University Press, 1984.

———. *The Kristeva Reader.* Ed. Toril Moi. New York: Columbia University Press, 1986.

Marks, Elaine, and Isabelle de Courtivron. *New French Feminisms: An Anthology.* New York: Schocken Books, 1981.

Silverman, Kaja. *The Subject of Semiotics.* New York: Oxford University Press, 1983.

Stanton, Domna. "Difference on Trial." In *The Poetics of Gender.* Ed. Nancy K. Miller. New York: Columbia University Press, 1986, 157–82.

Female Subjectivity in
Not I *and* Rockaby

LOIS OPPENHEIM

> For what is this colored plane, that was not there before. I don't know what
> it is, having never seen anything like it before. It seems to have nothing to
> do with art, in any case, if my memories of art are correct.
>
> Samuel Beckett, *Three Dialogues with Georges Duthuit*

Ever since the first philosopher of art inquired into the creative production of meaning, investigation into the problem of reference has faith-
fully proven to be the sine qua non of any metacritical treatise aiming
to illuminate the expressive function of art. For creativity—whether
viewed as the emotive expression of something within (and otherwise
ineffable) or as the articulation, through abstraction, of something without—never takes place outside some kind of referential field, one in
which perception, however transformed in the act of imaginative play, is
the predominant force. Though literary criticism has, in recent years,
moved well beyond the reductionist thinking on linguistic meaning
most significantly advanced by the Saussurian notion of the arbitrary
relation of signifier to signified,[1] perception continues to remain all too
often unacknowledged as the implicit (if surreptitious) and unavoidable
recourse of all meaningful expression. In hermeneutic analysis, however,
where the work of art is evaluated in accordance with its disclosure of
truth, it must be said that interpretation depends not on an assumed
restriction of an aesthetic object by itself to itself but on the mutual implication of empirical or perceptual intersubjective fields of reference. So
too in deconstruction—where a "releasing" or "decentering" of the
work seeks to disprove any notion of a unification of referential fields by
substituting for it a plurality of truths which, ultimately, call into question the very idea of truth itself[2]—a contemplation of perceptual reference, though within the restricted framework of its eventual undoing,
must be recognized as supporting any thinking on the interpretation of
meaning.

To the extent that any statement on the production of meaning necessarily consists in circumscribing the perimeters and functioning of human perception, we can say that all critical interpretation with an epistemological bent necessarily carries within it an awareness (however clandestine) of the illusion of representation in art. The feminist critical effort, for one, has significantly contributed over the last decade to the recognition of this illusion insofar as the notion that the world is never fully identical with itself in any formalization of "reality" is supported by the feminist critics' appraisal of the perception of self as a key factor in the creative process. That the question of reference is inseparable from art's relation to self-perception—and, thereby, to questions of social and cultural identities and their internalization by the speaking (or otherwise creative) subject—attests to an ontology of art that allies the feminist critical endeavor with that of the philosophical critic working within the phenomenological tradition. To the degree that the feminist critical revolution is grounded in the belief that the question of aesthetic meaning defies explication on the level of abstraction, where critical practice has maintained it from formalism to post-structuralism, it is contiguous with the aims of a phenomenological hermeneutics which resituates the artist and viewer, or writer and reader, on the level of an intersubjective participation in the constitution of the work of art. In its effort to expose what Elaine Showalter has called "the misogyny of literary practice"—"the stereotyped images of women in literature as angels or monsters, the literary abuse or textual harassment of women in classic and popular male literature, and the exclusion of women from literary history"[3]—feminist criticism is committed to a transformation of existing paradigms that is comparable to the phenomenologist's effort to eliminate all presumption or presupposition from the aesthetic experience which gives credence to the notion of a representational function of art. In sum, meaning—and, in particular, linguistic meaning—is apprehended by feminist and phenomenological critic alike on the order of praxis where, in the case of linguistic praxis, it is a particular use of language determined by the speaking subject's pre-cognitive perception of herself in relation to the world, that is the focus of interpretation.

The incompatibility of the feminist and phenomenological critics' recognition of the significance of self-perception in the creative process, with the notion of art as the re-production or re-presentation of a reality existing outside of or prior to it, is affirmed by the entire modernist perspective in art and literature. For modernism may be seen as the creative effort to come to terms with the referential failure of art as representation, the absence of any real relation of the materiality of art or language to the external world over and above the perception of the self's mode of inherence within it. And of the practitioners of modernism, none, perhaps, has been more acutely aware than Samuel Beckett of the limitations of any art to circumvent the failure of representational reference. ("The history of painting," Beckett has said, "is the history of its attempts to escape from this sense of failure, by means of more authentic, more ample, less exclusive relations between representer and representee . . . "[4])

Beckett's thematization of the failure of art in his creative work is, of course, well-documented. In his three dialogues with Georges Duthuit on the painters Tal Coat, André Masson, and Bram van Velde, however, Beckett explicitly names referential failure, or the "incoercible absence of relation,"[5] as the origin of the failure of art to express anything but the certitude of the impossibility of expression. All art for Beckett is referential only insofar as it is self-referential, the replication of the experience of its own singular origin: the projection, as opposed to representation, of the self as a Being-in-the-world. This circularity is difficult to grasp, for it owes its complexity to the temporality of art—that which prevents our ever conceptualizing of art as totalization, objectivation, or reproduction.

It is not our purpose here, however, to consider art as temporalization or, for that matter, to treat at greater length Beckett's notion of the failure of representational referentiality, a failure stemming for Beckett, as for the phenomenological or feminist critic, from the impossibility of any apprehension of the world apart from a perception of the self within it. Rather, it will be our aim to explore, from the perspective of the inability of art to refer representationally or reproductively to the world conceived as existing outside of self-perception, a question which may be formulated as follows: if meaningful (aesthetic) communication necessarily implies not merely the penetration of reality as the sum of objective phenomena by human perception but the perception of self in relation to that reality, a pre-cognitive self-awareness, is the aesthetic presentation of consciousness in *the act of self-perception*—as found in certain of the recent plays by Beckett in which the focus is precisely on the self or speaking subject *as the very object of perception*—immune to the failure of symbolic representation? Otherwise stated, does the "I" of Beckett's characterizations—as revealed in *Not I* and *Rockaby,* for example—achieve a truly symbolic or representational function or, rather, is it subject, despite its auto-interpretive and self-reflexive constitution, to the same limitations as any aesthetic form or structure?

To respond, we will situate the question in the context of a dialectical interplay in these two texts between anonymity and individuation wherein the speaking subject alternatively loses herself within the universal structures of Being and identifies herself through the differentiation of her ego from all that it is not. In the perspective of this dialectic, the two monologues display both an ontological discourse preceding gender identification—one in which the transcendental imagination has primacy over social, historical, and cultural determinants—and a distinctly female discourse supporting, on the one hand, the designation of the two primary personages as women and, on the other, feminist analyses of the language as evidence of male hegemony of the cultural order.

In recognizing the predominant role of self-perception in both feminist and phenomenological criticism, we are led to consider the question of a body politic in both the delineation of the ontological structures of Being-in-the-world and the demarcation of an inherently feminine element in Beckett's languge. We might begin by noting that, though much has been offered in the way of critical interpretation of Beckett's preoccupation with the dismembering of the body, little, if anything, has been written on disembodiment as such in Beckett's texts. This reflects the objectifying and positivistic tendencies of our critical traditions which seek to identify, from the perspective of stasis as opposed to process, symbolic and other signifying structures as the principle components of textuality. Inquiry into the phenomenon of disembodiment, however, should serve to uncover in Beckett's two plays the imagistic rendering—in the sense of Paul Ricoeur's *metaphore vive,* or living metaphor—of isolation as both an ontological deprivation—a violation of being with others as a primary structure of Being-in-the-world—and a devaluation by a male-centered culture of the female experience.

Considering the first, we recall that the disembodied (taped) voice of the old woman in *Rockaby,* the real monologist despite the presence of the woman on the stage, reveals the fundamental synonymy of life and words with which Beckett is consistently concerned. Here the dramatic monologue, unfolding *outside* the body, articulates—as ontological deprivation—an anonymous self in isolation from an anonymous Other and, thereby, the impossibility of any unified or integrated identification of the self by the self apart from its relation to, and differentiation from, those surrounding it.

Similarly, in *Not I,* Mouth emerges as this "tiny little girl" projected "before her time" into this "godforsaken hole" that is, simultaneously, the fathomless space of our world *and* that orifice whose very presence *is* the *dramatis persona* herself. Her image, in other words, is constituted by a confluence of theme and structure: the unification of "something"—namely, sound and meaning—with its opposite, "nothing"—ellipsis, lacuna, the unsaid—which prevents the reader from attributing to the text either truly symbolic or metonymic functions. That Mouth is but a ve-hicle of articulation and physically, in her disembodiment, nothing more renders her the metaphoric equivalent of the *potentiality* of meaningful expression. The disembodied personification of the transcendental power of language allows the word to *uncover,* in the projection of meaning, what it simultaneously *conceals* within the materiality of expression: the wholeness of Being. In her disembodiment, therefore, Mouth is posed on the creative horizon as the anonymous configuration of the transcen-dental consciousness.

The ontology of Being-in-the-world, the anonymity of existence qua existence, however, is not disclosed in the disembodiment of either Mouth or the old woman in the rocker independently of its relation to the individuation of female identity. Considered not on the order of lan-guage as representation, where each of the two monologues would be thought to contain clues to the unconscious as shelter of the repressed feminine, but, rather, on the order of language as intentionality, where ego and world are fused within the very utterance itself, the old wom-an's discourse, like that of Mouth, *inscribes* (as opposed to symbolizes) *the female identity within the appropriation of the world to the self that is the individuating function of expression.*[6] To support this claim, we might look to three possible interpretations of the disembodiment pre-eminent in these plays to which current feminist critical thinking might give rise.

In the first, *the analysis of the disembodied discourse would focus on a discourse of disembodiment:* interpretation, in other words, would center on a linguistic awareness of a body politic in which subordination breeds imperfection. In this perspective, both the division between the physical presence of the old woman and her soliloquizing (taped) voice and the detachment of Mouth from any body whatsoever would be viewed as metaphors for woman, as explored by Luce Irigaray in *Specu-lum de l'autre femme,* defined in the Platonic and Freudian traditions—at once deformed (the castrated male) and irrational. The old woman, then, would be the marginalized figure of incompletion, having been cast off—or, to paraphrase the last lines of her monologue, "rocked off"—by a world in which isolation, or psychic death, is the price paid for difference. The figure of alteration or mutation, she would be seen in this light as ventriloquizing her own vulnerable existence, as the pa-thetic stand-in for herself. The vocal displacement would thus serve as a persistant reminder of the fragmentation of women's identification by a patriarchal determinism of the social and cultural orders. So too Mouth, the personified *hole,* would be seen as the configuration of absence, fe-male genitalia inhabited by a non-ego, a "not I." And her language, with its broken syntax, its explosive and rhythmic babble, would be said to convey the nonsensical, as contradictory, constitution of one created not in any cultural or theological tradition of her own image but in that of her male counterpart.

All that is most often considered evidence of both characters' determination to efface any relationship with the past, of the "disassociation of the self from the category of individualilty,"[7] of the thematization, in sum, of the dissolution of an ego incapable of integration, which would, in light of this thinking, be resituated on the order of female subjugation.[8] Clearly, Beckett would be lauded by proponents of such an interpretatiion, if not for his practise of a "gynetext"[9] or the presence of a female vision in a male or female authored fiction, then for his dramatic imaging of the female victim of the psychological, cultural, and social constraints placed on her by a masculine semiotic order.

Jacques Derrida's notion of phallocentrism, as it is explored, for example, in Susan Gubar's highly intelligent essay, " 'The Blank Page' and the Issues of Female Creativity," offers further insight into the question of the relation of women to language that might yield a second—and opposing—interpretation of Beckett's preoccupation with disembodiment. Derrida's model of what Gubar describes as "the pen-penis writing on the virgin page" exemplifies a tradition of the reification of woman that might allow us to take Beckett to task for his portraits of Mouth and the old woman as "secondary objects lacking autonomy"— seeking, outside themselves, in the third-person pronominal expression of the self, confirmation of their proper identities.[10] In the context of Gubar's illustration of woman's self-image as cultural, and thereby textual, artifact, Beckett's careful synchronization of the aurally perceptible voice with the visually perceptible woman in *Rockaby* may be considered an all-too-accurate depiction of male "authorship"—the divided, and thus incomplete, and passive female as the object of male manipulation and creativity.

A third possible feminist-inspired interpretation of the function of disembodiment in these two plays views the old woman's dichotomized self and Mouth's disincarnation neither in terms of a deformation of the male prototype nor as parable of reified woman but as metaphoric correlates of the non-individuated or symbiotic experiencing of the world characteristic of the pre-Oedipal child. In this perspective, the old woman's taped voice—which repeatedly proclaims the search "for another/ another living soul/one other living soul/going to and fro/all eyes like herself . . . ," the search "for another/another like herself"[11]—would express the need, comparable to that of the small child, to unite with the identity of another (the mother) on whom it depends for its limited sense of self. In Jacques Lacan's rewriting of Freud, this symbiosis is termed the "imaginary." At a crucial point in the child's development, Lacan's *stade du miroir* (mirror stage) gives way to the formation of an integrated or unified self-image—a source of delight to the transforming ego whose existence is confirmed by its specular reflection. The old woman's taped voice, however, would be seen in such an analysis as articulating not the fulfillment of the individuation process but rather its interruption. This deprivation of individuation might be illustrated in the increasingly passing resignation of the old woman to her separation from the outside world:

> rocked
> with closed eyes
> closing eyes
> she so long all eyes
> famished eyes
> all sides
> high and low
> to and fro
> at her window
> to see
> be seen
> till in the end
> close of a long day
> to herself
> whom else
> time she stopped
> let down the blind and stopped
> (*Rockaby* 19)

The woman's non-individuated self, projected through the rhythmic, but otherwise barely cohesive, expression of the taped voice, is driven by the unorganized forces that constitute a pre-symbolic or semiotic residue. For Kristeva and others, semiotic expression—as found in both of the inconsistent and uncertain monologues in question—is inherently feminine. Originating in the pre-Oedipal phase, the semiotic has as its reference the female body of the mother, whereas the symbolic centers on the so-called Law of the father.[12] To the degree that the discourse of Beckett's shattered female subject may be likened to the infantile or not yet symbolically meaningful utterance of Kristeva's semiotic, it appropriates, through its association with "another" female "like herself," a vision which, in the ultimate fulfillment of individuation, would unfold not as a uniquely female voice but as the representation, in fixed sign and symbol, of accepted cultural (phallocentric) meanings.

Evidence of this semiotic in *Not I* might be the unintelligible sounds produced by Mouth behind the curtain both prior to and immediately following her soliloquy; the plurality of meanings of the "godforsaken hole" (genital, cosmic, oral), none of which is symbolically rendered but rather imaged in the unmediated expression of a free-floating syntax whose persistant disruption and rearrangement playfully negate all assumed semantic hierarchies; and the screams which ironically interrupt the only quasi-historical account of her inability, on that April morning, to "make the sound . . . not any sound . . . no sound of any kind . . . no screaming for help for example . . . "(*Not I* 218). The endless repetition of Mouth's tale of that April morning—implying not a temporality conceived according to our habitual chronology of a passage from past to present, and from present to future, but an existential or lived time, an eternal present—serves to create *a confluence of narrative and metanarrative, a congruence of fictional time and temporalizing fiction*, that provokes a deliberate confusion of text with reality.

It is in this loosening of temporal and semantic restrictions, then, that the feminine "essence" could be said to reside, for if the semiotic is, as defined by Terry Eagleton, "fluid and plural, a kind of pleasurable creative excess over precise meaning,"[13] it is clearly characteristic of the feminine imagery and female-body languge that authenticates Mouth's discourse.

Our discussion of *Rockaby* and *Not I* focuses specifically on the function of disembodiment because this phenomenon offers access—through the plurality of non-representational or non-symbolic interpretations— to both the ontological structure of Being-with (Heidegger's *Mitsein*: the existential situation of "I" as a "Being-with Others"[14]) and the feminine that inhabits both texts. Space permitting, an in-depth analysis of the language of each play could support the elucidations of disembodiment as *the fragmentation of female subjectivity* through deformation (castration), reification (subordination), and the semiotic (the reverse and severely incapacitated side of the politically and psychologically symbolic linguistic order). And a more comprehensive identification of the interrelation between the anonymity of an ontological discourse preceding gender identification and the individuation of a uniquely feminine presence could be made. Our purpose here, however, was to point to the convergence of feminist and phenomenological critical thinking residing in that non-reductive view of textuality as the intersubjective awareness of self (that of author, character, and reader alike) in relation to the world which precludes representational analysis.

In her recent paper, "From Position to Intervention: Feminist Theoretical Practice," Sharon Willis reminds us that "the problem . . . of a text's relation to lived social reality . . . is haunted by questions of identity and of the material body." Our investigation of female subjectivity in Beckett's two plays, the virtual detachment of voice from the speaking subjects' physical presence, supports Willis's recognition that the problem of referentiality is informed by the "economic and political distribution of power" that "maps the body" and causes us, as individuals, to "inhabit partial bodies, bodies politicized and fragmented. . . . "[15]

That we were led to consider this disincarnation of the self-perceiving subjects precisely in the context of an ontological deprivation, a fundamental isolation of the self from the Other that impedes an integrated self-image through the absence of identification and differentiation, however, also confirms the phenomenological critic's notion of referentiality as the fusion of ego and world in a relation of intentionality.

In an analysis of a poem by Mallarmé, for example, phenomenological critic Jacques Garelli uncovers a metamorphosing process that allows the poet, through his subjective investment of the objective world, to extend—in the creative linguistic expression of this ego-world fusion—*beyond* the limitations imposed on his understanding of self by his corporal existence.[16] In the light of such a metamorphosis, the repression and alienation circumscribed by Beckett's two female characters' inability to assume the first-person pronominal identity reveals not a total dissolution of the ego, as the representationalist thinker would have it, but the annihilation of individuality in the *ubiquity* of Being-in-the-world. Both the feminist critic's emphasis on the politics of language and the phenomenological critic's effort to display the ontology of language, then, come together in a dialectic of anonymity and individuation which—in the abolition of the one by the other in their mutual (creative) sublimation (a process characteristic of the Hegelian *Aufhebung*)—simultaneously appropriates two primary dimensions of lived experience.

We return now to our initial question concerning the possible immunity of the speaking subject's positing of self in *Not I* and *Rockaby* to the failure of representational referentiality. There is the absence of any real beginning in each of the plays; in *Not I* it is the unintelligible sounds made by Mouth from behind the curtain, and in *Rockaby* it is the use of a connecting word *till*—"till in the end/the day came," a preposition having, as the second word of the play, no preceding element to which to relate what follows. This absence projects readers or viewers—like the "tiny little thing" that was Mouth—" . . . out . . . into this world . . . ," this narrative world, *in media res* and implants them, ipso facto, on the level of the intentional functioning of language) and given Beckett's privileging of what we have identified, with Kristeva, as a language of the semiotic—a persistent disruption of meaning, a valorization of the euphonic, a play of subliminal forces that rupture the stability of semantic norms— leads us to conclude that the objectivation of the ego that occurs in Mouth and the old woman's substitution of "she" for "I" is the meta- phoric transcription, as opposed to symbolic representation, of the in- tentionalizing structure of consciousness. Thus the renunciation of "I" serves to negate a concretized pure subjectivity—*whether female or anon- ymous, individuated or ubiquitous*—in favor of the transcendental func- tioning of a perceptualizing ego ("I," as process not stasis, perceiving itself as "she"). And thus Beckett's presentation of the act of self- perception—insofar as it displays not only a cognitive or ideational pos- iting *but also a pre-cognitive or subliminal awareness of the self in relation to the world*—is subject to the same limitations of symbolic representation that are the origin of both the self-reflexive (or self-referential) and auto- interpretive functions of any work of art.

NOTES

I would like to express my gratitude to the National Endowment for the Humanities and Professor François Rigolot for enabling me to continue my Beckett research at Princeton University in the summer of 1986.

1. As has been shown by Jacques Garelli, Saussure himself, though very much despite his efforts to the contrary, reintroduced reality—and hence percep- tual referentiality—into his definition of the sign precisely, though ironically, in his designation of it as "unmotivated" or unnatural. See Garelli, "The Ontology of Reference," trans. Lois Oppenheim, in *The Favorite Malice,* ed. Thomas Har- rison (New York: Out of London Press, 1983), 97-113, particularly 100-102.

2. Cf. John D. Caputo, "Telling Left from Right: Hermeneutics, Decon- struction, and the Work of Art," paper presented at the American Philosophical Association, December 1986; published in the *Journal of Philosophy* 83 (Nov. 1986), 682.

3. *Feminist Criticism,* ed. Elaine Showalter (New York: Pantheon, 1985), 5.

4. Samuel Beckett, *Proust and Three Dialogues with Georges Duthuit* (Lon- don: John Calder, 1965), 125.

5. Ibid.

6. The juncture of feminist and phenomenological criticism would seem to reside in the problem of linguistic reference insofar as it is conceived by feminist and phenomenological critics alike according to a network of "truth" (political and cultural for the one, existential and ontological for the other) that inscribes itself at the heart of an individual's meaningful expression. Even Jacques Lacan echoes the feminist and phenomenological theses on this point: "The language of man, this instrument of his lie, is transversed through and through by the problem of his truth" ("Propos sur la causalité psychique," *Ecrits* [Paris: Seuil, 1966], 166; cited in Garelli, "The Ontology of Reference," 107).

7. Robert Champigny, "Adventures of the First Person," in *Samuel Beckett Now,* ed. Melvin J. Friedman (Chicago: Chicago University Press, 1975), 119-28, cited in Keir Elam, "*Not I,* Beckett's Mouth and the Ars(e)/Rhetorica," in *Beckett at 80/Beckett in Context,* ed. Enoch Brater (New York: Oxford University Press, 1986), 135.

8. Mouth's inability to know herself as *whole,* to project herself in the context of completion, would be viewed, in this perspective, as the result of her transmutation of a male paradigm. And her entire monologue would be seen as the expression of a profound and painful awareness of life's sin against her. We recall that the thought of merciful God inspires a "good laugh" and that the realization of her lack of suffering is accompanied by that of her lack of pleasure. See *Not I,* in *The Collected Shorter Plays of Samuel Beckett* (New York: Grove Press, 1984), 217.

9. In "Is There a New Novel Today?" Leon Roudiez identifies "some of the salient features of the gynetext" while acknowledging the problems associated with the use of this term. See *Three Decades of the French New Novel,* ed. Lois Oppenheim (Urbana: University of Illinois Press, 1986), 166-71, and n. 35.

10. Susan Gubar, " 'The Blank Page' and Female Creativity," in *Feminist Criticism,* ed. Showalter, 295.

11. Samuel Beckett, *Rockaby* (New York: Grove Press, 1981), 10.

12. See Terry Eagleton, *Literary Theory* (Minneapolis: University of Minnesota Press, 1983), 188.

13. Ibid.

14. The structure of *Mitsein* is outlined by Heidegger, above all, in pt. 1, ch. 4 of *Being and Time,* trans. John Macquarrie and Edward Robinson (New York: Harper and Row, 1962).

15. Sharon Willis, "From Position to Intervention: Feminist Theoretical Practice," paper presented at the Modern Language Association, December 1986.

16. Jacques Garelli, "Le 'Avoir Lieu' du Lieu," in *Artaud et la question du lieu* (Paris: Jose Corti, 1982), 131-38.

Beckett's Eh Joe: *Lending an Ear to the Anima*

ROSETTE LAMONT

Written in English for Jack MacGowran in April-May 1965, Beckett's *Eh Joe*, "a piece for television," was first presented on BBC2 July 4, 1966. It could be considered a forerunner of the "dramaticules" composed for the stage, radio, and film in the seventies and eighties. Grouped together under the expressive heading, "Beyond Minimalism," they are described by Enoch Brater as "not drama in the shape of poetry, but poetry in the shape of drama."[1]

Less "abstract and geometric" than the recent "performance poems,"[2] *Eh Joe* is Beckett's small-screen haiku on the subject of love's death-bearing failure. It is a tragic variation on *Krapp's Last Tape* with the essential difference that Joe is not listening to his own voice—as does Krapp when he establishes a confrontation between his past and present self—but to that of a woman who might be his conscience, the aural concretization of his anima.

In his *Aion*, C. J. Jung describes the woman figure of the anima as one of the archetypes of the collective unconscious—a perilous illusionist who draws man "not only into life's reasonable and useful aspects, but into its frightful paradoxes and ambivalences where good and evil, success and ruin, hope and despair counterbalance one another."[3] This challenging force is, according to Erich Neumann, the Great Mother as Kali the Devourer or the Gorgon. An analytical psychologist renowned for his theory of feminine development, Neumann explains that "consciousness sees the unconscious as feminine and itself as masculine" but that "since the liberation of the male consciousness from the feminine-maternal unconscious is a hard and painful struggle for all mankind, it is clear that the negative elementary character of the Feminine does not spring from an anxiety complex of the 'men,' but expresses an archetypal experience of the whole species, male and female alike."[4] This dangerous force which unleashes primordial fears draws the psychic traveler into the underworld. While it enchants with its incantatory powers—like the

singing, winged female Sphinx whose riddle Oedipus is able to solve—it
also swallows the unsuspecting hero into its yapping, yawning gullet,
the gate to the womb of death.

As in countless fairy tales, the anima confronts the hero with a series
of trials he must undergo along the path to self-realization. This is
the function of "the *transformative character* of the feminine." While appearing hostile, it is bent on wreaking a positive change through
the intensification of personality. The soul-image is experienced by
man as feminine, a crystallization of his own "inner femininity and
soulfulness."[5]

One of the fascinating devices Beckett uses for his television piece is
the utter silence of his protagonist. We watch his face register the
"mounting tension of listening" to the "low, distinct, remote" and relentless voice of a woman who is presumably a ghost[6]—one of the dead
who, like Joe's parents, come to haunt him in his solitude—or possibly a
former lover he has not seen for many years. After Joe has been shown
full length in the opening sequences, inspecting his small room, closing
himself in, checking the cupboards and the underside of his bed, the
camera comes in for a series of closeups of his face, nine moves checked
each time by the resumption of Voice's intrusion. In his directions,
Beckett stresses that the camera never moves while the voice is heard.
The voice becomes a technical device, on a par with the dolly. However,
whereas the latter brings us closer to the suffering protagonist, as
though inviting us to enter his mind and share his delirium, the first
blocks this motion, drawing attention to itself as an independent force.

Joe is listening not merely to a story but, as Enoch Brater points out,
"to language . . . a language which . . . creates a story in which he is the
protagonist."[9] In this sense Joe is an image for the writer, for Beckett,
for whom words shape action and thought. The monologue becomes a
dialogue with self.

As early as 1959, in his radio sketch *Embers,* the dramatist portrays a
lonely man who cannot stop speaking to himself. He hopes to drown
out with his voice the pounding of the sea or perhaps to summon his
dead father, who drowned years ago during an "evening bathe (taken)
once too often" (93). Principally, he likes telling himself stories. He
says: "I usen't to need anyone, just to myself, stories, there was a great
one about an old fellow called Bolton, I never finished it, I never finished any of them, I never finished anything, everything always went on
for ever" (94). Once upon a time, he used to talk to a woman who lived
with him, a certain Ada by whom he had a child, little Addie. Conversation with her is described as a form of hell: "small chat to the babbling
of Lethe about the good old days when we wished we were dead" (96).

In the second half of the short play, Ada's ghost comes to haunt Henry, the protagonist. He wants to know whether "the hole is still there." "What hole? The earth is full of holes," Ada remarks with startling empiricism (101). Henry provides the exact reference in time and space: "Where we did it at last for the first time" (101). Is he speaking of a hollow in the ground or of a more intimate aperture? Beckett's Shakespearian love of puns leaves the matter wide open. As to Ada, who assures him that "the place has not changed" (101), she sounds like an old crone listing her surviving assets. What has not changed at all is Henry's weird habit of talking to himself out loud. Ada threatens that, with time, no one will speak to him. "You will be quite alone with your voice, there will be no other voice in the world but yours" (102).

Beckett's Joe is another avatar of the protagonist of *Embers*. The voice he hears is an echo of his own probing of his past. Memory stirs imagination, which, although dead, continues to imagine. The ironic, shrewish tone of a self-assured woman suggests one who knows Joe as well as he knows himself. Only at the very end will she tell him something that seems to take him aback. Yet it is possible, even likely, that this story issues from the protagonist's vivid sense of remorse, a reliving of events reported to him but obviously unwitnessed by any living being.

Although only one woman addresses Joe in his head, this is the tale of two women: the tough survivor and the tender victim. Together they represent two complementary aspects of womanhood: the bitch and the angel. As to Joe, he has loved and betrayed both of them. His punishment is his haunted solitude.

According to her own definition, the woman's voice issues from "that penny farthing hell" Joe calls his mind (*Eh Joe* 202). Nor is she the first invisible presence to have come haunting him. For a long time, as she reminds him, he heard the voice of his dead father. Following his mother's demise, her voice streamed down from the heavens she had been taught to believe in: "Look up, Joe, look up, we're watching you" (203). It was no easy matter to succeed in "throttling the dead in his head," committing what he called "mental thuggee" (203).

Having killed off his parents' articulate ghosts, Joe remains alone until the voice of his conscience, or of his subconscious, takes over. We can safely assume that this is not the first time Joe hears the woman's voice. Something about the expression of the actor (MacGowran, Jean-Louis Barrault in the French version) conveys his fearful expectation. Moreover, as soon as the taunting begins, we, the viewers, understand the reason Joe had for securing his room. The "louse" the woman refers to in her first series of questions is herself, or perhaps Joe himself ("There might be a louse watching you"[202]).

The insidious, low voice is like a sharp knife turning in the wound of Joe's mind and heart. It taunts him with the lovelessness of his present condition, with the grotesque exception of "that slut that comes on Saturday" (203), a service for which Joe has to pay. He—that "lifelong adorer" (203), the cowardly Casanova who always made his escape before marriage, like Gogol's anti-hero in the short play *The Wedding*—is now sitting in "his stinking old wrapper hearing himself" (203). What does the woman mean by "hearing himself," when in fact she is doing the talking? Clearly, by listening to her Joe is lending an ear to his inner self—his anima.

Indeed, the voice draws Joe in the direction of "life's frightful paradoxes and ambivalences."[8] The speaker reminds him that they were lovers, "holding hands exchanging vows" (203). Joe had admired her powers of elocution, the speeches delivered in a voice "like flint glass" (203). Something of the hardness is still there, if not in the ghostly whisper then in the angry clarity of the woman's intellect, in her relentless ability to pass judgment. She recalls her lover's cowardice, his broken promises: "The best's to come" (202), he had assured her, helping her into her coat and out the door. "In the end" (202), the best was to come for her, in the shape of another man, "preferable in all respects . . . Kinder . . . Stronger . . . More intelligent . . . Better looking . . . Cleaner . . . Truthful . . . Faithful . . . Sane" (204). Could there be a better way to tell a betrayer what one thinks of him? This list of virtues indicts Joe's obverse lacks. It culminates in the accusation of insanity, not easily contested by one who hears voices.

Voice strips away every shred of illusion, compelling the listener to sacrifice whatever aggressive male character he may have considered once as his prerogative. In this sense the ghostly woman is the castrating, punishing Terrible Mother. Erich Neumann speaks of the mysteries of transformation operated by the Great Goddess as Lady of Beasts and Men. As such, "she confers no birth and no life without pain."[9] Joe's mounting suffering is part of the intimate process of psychic growth—a trial which will reach its unbearable climax in Voice's final story.

That story deals with the pure, intense love Joe inspired in a very young, highly spiritual woman. It is impossible to tell from Voice's account whether the young woman preceded or followed her in Joe's affections. Voice knows all there is to know about "the green one . . . the narrow one . . . Always pale" (205), but this might be the result of a superior vision, acquired in the Beyond, rather than that of time sequence. Time and space are left quite vague in *Eh Joe*. What is most striking is the fact that the two loves of Joe are diametrically opposed to one another. If Voice is a lioness, the girl with the pale eyes—"spirit made light" (205), as Joe described them, to whom? most probably only to himself—is a doe.

The adventure itself is perfectly banal, worthy of a soap opera. Once again Joe fled from marriage, commitment. Once again he promised that the best was to come while "bundling her into her Avoca sack" (205). A ticket "for the first morning flight" (205) was in his pocket at that time. The rest is the detailed description of the abandoned girl's suicide. What makes it moving is the wealth of tiny facts reported by Voice: the girl's acute fear of pain, her inability to slash her wrists with the Gillette Joe recommended "for her body hair" (206). Although determined to do away with herself, the young woman is groping for a way. Sleeping pills do not seem sufficiently effective. She has decided to combine these with drowning, but she will only achieve her aim after she has put herself into a deep sleep. Her face in the water, "a few feet" (206) from the incoming tide, she awaits the end.

Voice forces Joe to see—to envision the scene as though he had been there, as though he had been inside the young woman's suffering mind and body. She forces the listener to perform that leap of the imagination which takes us out of ourselves, allows us to coincide entirely with another being. It is more than empathy; it belongs to the special realm of art. No longer a shrewish female intent on mocking Joe, Voice is the artist, the writer, who is able to perform this miracle of understanding. The word *imagine,* in italics in the text, comes back again and again, forcing its way into the man's consciousness: "All right . . . you've had the best . . . now *imagine* . . . Before she goes . . . Face in the cup . . . Lips on the stone" (206). Twice more she asks him to imagine the girl's hands, touching the stones as the water rises, as sleep takes over. The conclusion: *"There's love for you"* (207)—the kind of love Voice and Joe did not have for each other, the kind of love most people never possess. Having fled from "the best," having failed to recognize it, Joe is now living in hell, not "the penny farthing hell" of his mind but metaphysical, theological Hell, the realm of infinite, eternal despair.

The banality of the story is an essential component of the writer's message. Most of us are blind to happiness, blind to the rare possibilities life offers us. This blindness brings us to the dreadful gate which opens upon the abyss. As the camera travels closer and closer, to the face, into the face and eyes of the listener, we follow the latter's labyrinthine path into the deepest form of suffering, the *prise de conscience,* as the French say, from which there is no escape. It is the very movement of tragic recognition. Joe's silence is as eloquent as Oedipus's heart-rending cry.

Nor is the number of camera moves ("nine slight moves in towards the face" [201]) accidental. The numeral nine has often been associated with death. Thus, the form coincides with the subject: the process of leaving this life, the parallel phenomenon of gaining understanding. The modern medium of television provided Beckett with the perfect metaphor for this inexorable apprehension. It allowed him to draw the viewer into the secret recesses of a fellow human being's mind.

In *The Broken Window: Beckett's Dramatic Perspective,* Jane Alison Hale states: "The originality of *Eh Joe* resides ... primarily in the new form and technology in which Beckett envelops his character's perceptual processes."[10] She agrees with Martin Esslin's comment, in his "Beckett and the Art of Broadcasting," as to the impact of the more concentrated television image—an effect unachievable upon the larger cinema screen.[11] Enoch Brater makes much the same point in *Beyond Minimalism:* "The 'grey rectangle' brings the strange into the comfortable room of the viewer, alongside the dirty dishes and the personal computer. Intruding its presence into the safety and security of a world we like to think we control, Beckett's television image invades our reality and makes it part of its own."[12] To take a frequently debased medium, such as television, and make of it the instrument of the most subtle kind of analysis, the most fundamental of revelations, is the kind of task Beckett likes to set for himself. All tools invented and used by people hold in themselves as many possibilities as the human creature: they can corrupt, but they are also able to enlighten.

Both Joe and the viewers receive enlightenment from Voice's tale of two women, herself and the other. In mythic terms, the older and younger women, although unrelated by blood, assume the Demeter/Kore archetypal situation. Erich Neumann states that the mother-daughter unity was "the central content of the Eleusinian mysteries."[13] The matriarchal oneness of the two females annulled the male incursion into the group. Because Demeter and Kore are the two poles of the Eternal Feminine, the mystery of their fusion celebrates a renewal independent of male sexuality. Thus, the magical unity of the older and younger female serves as a guide to the male psyche.

With her powerful, almost virile, grasp of language encased in a flint glass voice, the ghostly monologuist suggests *da priestess-guide,* the representative on earth of the Demeter principle. On the other hand, the young suicide seeking a difficult path to the underworld is a clearly recognizable Kore. The attributes of the Feminine are there on the fateful night—the moon, "going off the shore behind the hill" (*Eh Joe* 206), and the palpable presence of the watery element, the lapping sea between the rocks. The girl's pale green eyes suggest the clear water of a pool. Voice turns the rapier of remorse in Joe's heart as she reminds him of "the look they shed before ... The way they opened after" (206).

These are the very eyes of the girl old man Krapp loved and foolishly rejected to pursue his oeuvre. In Box three, on spool five, he finds again the blissful moment in the past when he and his girl, lying at the bottom of a small boat, allowed the water to move them "up and down, and from side to side" (*Krapp's Last Tape* 60). Gaston Bachelard's analysis of elemental imagery in literature may help us decipher the strange mixture of sensuality and spirituality in this scene. In *L'eau et les rêves* Bachelard writes: "Of the four elements only water is able to rock. It is the *rocking element*. This is one of its feminine features: it rocks like a mother."[14] In the life of the selfish bachelor Krapp, a man involved principally in abstruse intellectual pursuits, this will prove to have been the only moment when he achieved a profound union with a woman. As he recalls the scene on tape, he describes how he bent over the girl in the boat to shade her face from the light. The younger man on the tape says: "They [her eyes] opened. Let me in . . . I lay down across her with my face in her breasts and my hand on her" (61). The lover's position also suggests that of a suckling babe. This is one of the most lyrical scenes in Beckett's work.

We have no reason to assume that Krapp's friend took her life. It is a different thing with Joe's girl, unable to carry on with her existence. Written almost ten years after *Krapp's Last Tape*, the television play presents the same conjunction of water, sexuality, and loss. As the abandoned girl walks to the shore, swallowing the contents of a tube of sleeping pills, she trails "her feet in the water like a child" (*Eh Joe* 206). Later, lying face down to await the rising tide, "she scoops a little cup for her face in the stones" (206). The cup is the reverse image of the mother's breast; from this concave breast the young suicide will drink the bitter sea water of her death. To loosen her lips she speaks the name of the beloved, "*Joe, Joe*" (206). Although he found out about the girl's death by reading an announcement "in the *Independent*" (205), Voice completes the story for him. She relates in unsparing particulars the ways the girl devised to "go young" (205). "No old lip from her," Voice jokes sardonically. Indeed, the old lip is that of Demeter/Voice.

In order to avoid simplifying Beckett's pattern in this play, we turn once again to Erich Neumann's splendid book, *The Great Mother*, to the concluding pages in which he treats the figure of ultimate wisdom, the Sophia. He writes: "The dual Great Goddess as mother and daughter can so far transform her original bond with the elementary character as to become a pure feminine spirit, a kind of Sophia, a spiritual whole in which all heaviness and materiality are transcended."[15] By the use of myth as a decoding device, it is possible to recognize the ultimate fusion of the two women of Voice's story. The fragility and sensitivity of the young Kore, goddess of the underworld, comes to complement the earthy resilience of Demeter. Together they fashion the Goddess of the Whole. Their lesson is visibly not wasted on Joe, who reflects the intense suffering and illumination which comes from discovery. Nor can it fail to transform the viewer of Beckett's television piece, irrevocably altered by the art of Beckett's language, which conveys the haunting image of human blindness and inhuman pain.

NOTES

1. Enoch Brater, *Beyond Minimalism: Beckett's Late Style in the Theater* (New York: Oxford University Press, 1987), 17.

2. Ibid., ix, 165.

3. C. J. Jung, *Aion: Researches into the Phenomenology of the Self,* trans. R. F. C. Hull, Bollingen Series 20, vol. 9, pt. 2 (New York: Pantheon, 1959), 13.

4. Erich Neumann, *The Great Mother: An Analysis of the Archetype,* trans. Ralph Manheim, Bollingen Series 47 (Princeton, N.J.: Princeton University Press, 1972), 148.

5. Ibid., 28, 33.

6. Samuel Beckett, *Eh Joe,* in *The Collected Shorter Plays* (New York: Grove Press, 1984), 202, 201. All further references to plays in this collection will appear in the text, giving the title of the play and the page.

7. Brater, *Beyond Minimalism,* 85.

8. Jung, *Aion,* 13.

9. Neumann, *The Great Mother,* 279.

10. Jane Alison Hale, *The Broken Window: Beckett's Dramatic Perspective* (West Lafayette, Indiana: Purdue University Press, 1987), 103.

11. Martin Esslin, "Beckett and the Art of Broadcasting," in *Meditations: Essays on Brecht, Beckett, and the Media* (New York: Grove Press, 1982).

12. Brater, *Beyond Minimalism,* 84.

13. Neumann, *The Great Mother,* 307.

14. Gaston Bachelard, *L'eau et les rêves, essai sur l'imagination de la matière* (Paris: Librairie José Corti, 1942), 177. The passage was translated from the French by the writer of this essay.

15. Neumann, *The Great Mother,* 325.

Women in Beckett's Radio and Television Plays

KATHARINE WORTH

It is a rather curious fact that women began to come into their own in Beckett's theater at about the time he discovered the attraction of writing for radio. Perhaps something in the nature of the medium—its ability to create ambiguous distances, maybe—fitted in with his attitude in those days about the presentation of women characters in his plays. Earlier on, there had been little or no place for them. *Waiting for Godot* is without women even as topics of conversation (when Pozzo refers to the process of giving birth he uses the sexless pronoun: "They give birth astride of a grave." *Endgame* admits a woman, significantly a mother, but Nell's is a thin, depressed role compared with that of her fellow dustbin dweller, and she is ushered out of the action well before its end with Hamm's matter-of-fact order, "Go and see is she dead."

When the tape recorder enters the scene with *Krapp's Last Tape,* a very different female image is conjured up for the first time. Youthful beauty now appears, in stark contrast with the image of the dying mother and (a harsher comparison) the older woman who gives Krapp his meagre sexual pleasure, the "bony old ghost of a whore." Fanny is an "old" ghost but they are all ghosts, really, dependent for their existence on Krapp's bitter-sweet recording of them. The female life in the play comes to us only by courtesy of a man's memory or imagining: it has still no robust voice of its own, though already there can be glimpsed possibilities for a much wider range of women characters than the first plays allowed.

With *All That Fall* all that changed. Maddy Rooney is master of the scene which she creates for us out of air. She is also, though a thing of air, one of Beckett's most resoundingly physical characters. She entered his imagination in an aggressively physical way in his "nice gruesome idea full of cartwheels and dragging feet and puffing and panting."[1] And throughout the play there is a rollicking emphasis on her overwhelmingly capacious female presence. Dan Rooney is sardonic about her "two hundred pounds of unhealthy fat" but not more frank than she is herself in her rueful summary of her condition: "a hysterical old hag... destroyed with sorrow and pining and gentility and church-going and fat and rheumatism and childlessness."

"Destroyed" she may be but her sexuality is still vital, as the wicked little episode with Mr. Slocum suggests: she never fails to pick up a bawdy double entendre, and she enjoys a good giggle when he heaves her up into his car by following (with seemingly enthusiasm) her unabashed instruction, "Get your... shoulder under it." In her openness to all she meets on her Gothic journey to the railway station, her concern for living things, including the hen that Mr. Slocum runs over in their precarious passage, and in her preoccupation—even obsession—with childbirth and childlessness, she is a kind of earth mother, warm-blooded and warm-hearted but capable of ruthlessly unsentimental realism, as in her final comment on the hen, after all her grieving: "They would have slit her weasand in any case."

She is also, despite her histrionics and grotesqueries, a mater dolorosa, ever grieving for "little Minnie" as for all the others we hear of in the course of the action who suffer from loss or affliction, especially to do with procreation. Her relationship with her blind husband, like much else in her behavior, is almost a parody of femaleness. "Be nice to me, Dan, be nice to me today," she implores the sardonic man who depends on her to "uphold" him in the way the "Lord" seemingly does not. But she is not seen consistently in a parodic light. It is she who sets the melancholy leitmotif that underlies the farce of the goings on. Her opening line is a call for sympathy for the human race, we may feel, by the end of the play. "Poor woman. All alone in that ruinous great house," she cries, and in comes the music of Schubert, the sombre and haunting "Death and the Maiden" to reinforce and extend her cry.

So she has that sort of power. She also has the power to make us "see" what she sees: "the entire scene, the hills, the plain, the racecourse with its miles and miles of white rails and stands." Amusingly she commands the air, calling up sound effects—"brief wind" coming in on cue when she mentions wind—and imposing her perspective on the scene, despite Dan's masculine tendency to dismiss it. And behind it all is her uneasy awareness that she is trapped in some illusion. She knows what it is to feel "not there," tells Miss Fitt, who saw only "a big pale blur" when looking supposedly in Maddy's direction, that she has "piercing sight," adding characteristically "if you only knew it."

Maddy does know such things: she is all the more master of the action for being so aware of the illusion. Her ability to play with it, to see and hear herself in wry perspective as one "struggling with a dead language," places her in a category previously reserved for the male characters in Beckett's theater. This was a tremendous step which seems to owe something to radio's power to convey bounding physicality without any sacrifice of visual spareness and sparseness.

Something of the Maddy spirit survives in Ada of *Embers* (1959), though she is no longer in a producing role. Like the young beauties of *Krapp's Last Tape* she is dependent on a male storyteller to bring her to life. Unlike them, however, she has a voice of her own—one by no means altogether pleasing to the man who calls her up, as he tells us with humorous vivacity just before he summons her: "Ada too, conversation with her, that was something, that's what hell will be like . . . "

Why then does he summon her? The answer is that he needs her: he has come to an impasse in the process in which he is endlessly engaged: evoking shades of memory and spinning stories obscurely connected with them. He has called his father and he has introduced the story of the two old men, Bolton and Holloway, but nothing happens; he cannot advance in either direction. So he turns to Ada. There is a suggestion in this that she has a muse-like function, a hint stressed in the sound of her voice—"low and remote throughout"—and in the curious fact that she has been present in some mysterious way before he spoke her name. "Some little time," she tells him when he asks her how long she has been there.

It could be said, of course, that she has been "present" only in the way that everything appears to be, in Henry's memory, waiting in limbo for the moment of full recall. But that theoretical interpretation does not give enough weight to the presence Ada creates for herself as a radio character who is immensely *there*. She is there in a much fuller sense than the other female voice in the play, that of little Addie, a kind of dream child whose real existence, even as an object of memory, is always in doubt. In producing this play, with Elvi Hale as Ada, I found it natural, for instance, to have Addie's voice projected by Ada in the tiny scenes with her Music and Riding Masters.[2] Addie seems no more there as an independent being than she is in Henry's long monologue at the start of the play, when he mimics her responses to his irritated invitations to her to "Go on when you're told and look at the lambs." But Ada could never be refused a voice of her own.

One reason for that is the personality she conveys, on what might be called the realistic level of the play. It is a strong, rather tart, humorous, and wry personality. She is something of a nagger, bossing Henry for his own good, as in the absurd conversation about warm underwear when she persists in wanting to know if he is wearing his "jaegers," for protection against the chilly beach. He fights back with a comical display of exasperation—"I put them on again and then I took them off again and then I put them on again and then I"—but she will have none of that. "Have you them on now?" she asks in her matter-of-fact way, bringing about his total collapse from fine frenzy into the meek, "I don't know." This sequence in performance always draws laughter, in my experience, laughter of a rather rueful kind, perhaps, with a note of fellow feeling. For this is certainly a recognizable marital situation, the basis of many a more conventional comedy. Henry's relationship with Ada has a good deal of the filial in it: this is one of the ways in which he needs her—and resents her.

"Don't," the maternal warning cry, is a sound so associated with her that it is used as a key at one point to unlock a memory of a very different kind. "Don't wet your good boots" says the Ada talking to the Henry complaining of his "old bones." And on Henry's presumably vexed repetition of "don't," in comes a surge of new sound—a rougher sea and the voice of Ada "twenty years earlier" calling "don't" in the tone of a girl responding conventionally to the ardent advances of a would-be lover. From the moment of youthful exaltation, when "don't" was a word charged with sexual feeling, we return to the "don't" of later times, with Henry (we imagine) held in an ecstasy of memory and Ada using the fraught word in sadly prosaic and minatory fashion: "Don't stand there gaping."

There are many debits against Ada in Henry's account. She has little or no sympathy with his word spinning, thinks he should seek medical advice about his eccentric talking habits which Addie used to notice as a small child: "Mummy, why does Daddy keep on talking all the time? She heard you in the lavatory. I didn't know what to answer." She has no apprehension of his obsessive dread of the sea, for her a "lovely peaceful gentle soothing sound." So, she is weak on imagination, at least of the inner torments of others. Yet it is clear that she is also a source of strength and has her own kind of understanding. It is she who provides Henry with the melancholy phrase he uses to end the play. The sea, she tells him, is noisy only on the surface: "Underneath all is quiet as the grave. Not a sound. All day, all night, not a sound." "Not a sound" is the last sound we hear from him.

In these shifts into reflection, as in her care for the more mundane aspects of Henry's life, Ada establishes herself as a pivot of his creativity as well as his memory. In fact, these two faculties cannot be separated, as Beckett takes pains to remind us on one occasion through Ada's casual reference to Holloway, who is for her the doctor whom Henry in real life should consult. For him, he is a figure in the fiction he is weaving (about an old man called Bolton and a doctor called Holloway). Ada's memories are thus part of his invented world, a part he can reach only when she acquires the kind of near-independent existence she has in the play. She is necessary to him in the creative sphere despite all the irritations associated with her memory. Through her he hopes to get closer to his father, which means also, we deduce, to the father figures in the Bolton/Holloway story. Toward the end of the play she is working hard for him, summoning up memories: the family going bathing, Henry's father slamming a door (something already noted by Henry) and pausing in his journey to sit on a rock and look out to sea. The way she "sees" him then is something Henry has not observed. He listens avidly as she describes the stillness of the seated man, "the great stillness of the whole body as if all the breath had left it."

Ada remains true to her down-to-earth nature in her attitude to her own reflections and intuitions. "Is this rubbish a help to you, Henry?" she asks, obligingly offering to continue if it is. But the fact that she seems not to set a high value on the narrative process in which they are both involved does not lessen the importance of her contribution to it. Perhaps if she had remained in the scene Henry would have been able to finish his story. As it is, he is left unable to continue when she departs, as mysteriously and abruptly as she came, on a characteristically matter-of-fact note: "Then I think I'll be getting back."

It is the muse departing, we might say. A muse in lower case, disconcertingly without pretensions and obscurely involved in the whole of the story-teller's life, so deep in it that it is impossible to draw a line to mark where memory ends and fiction begins. Crucially she is poles apart from the man who summons her up: it is because of this—because of her "otherness," her femaleness, it might be said—that he needs her so much, to fill out his story. Poets' muses have usually been female: Beckett provides a droll modern twist in insisting (at least in this and the previous radio play) that femaleness should have its full weight, including the maternal and other aspects which irritate the male beneficiaries.

In one of the other radio plays, *Words and Music* (1962), a more romantic version of inspiration appears, though only as an image. The face of the beautiful dark-haired girl, seen "from above" in a silver light, is the image the conductor-character, Croak, has been trying from the start to evoke. He has failed to persuade his servants, Words and Music—both, it may be noted, male—to carry out his muttered wish to see the "face." They persist in their standarized doodlings, requiring no labor. Only when Croak gives the order to contemplate "Age"—an unwelcome theme—are they compelled to commit themselves to painful creative effort, an effort finally rewarded by the "little poem" which brings satisfaction, if only fleetingly, to all. In the evocation of unloved age, woman figures in unromantic aspect. The "hag" who "puts the pan in the bed" is at the opposite pole from the lovely girl in the moonlight. Yet Croak cannot come at the one without the other, nor can he reach his ultimate goal, the image of the well where it is "all dark," without the double image of woman summoned up by Words and Music. Woman here is seen as both object of desire and inspiring or supporting force. The "hag" too is a necessity. "Hag" is indeed a word of power, with a suggestion of dread in it, such as attaches also to the beauty in the moonlight. Words has to control his feeling on approaching that subject by cultivating a style of clinical detachment which does not last, so overwhelming is the desire released. I have needed to touch on the images of women in *Words and Music,* even though they never materialize as characters, because they call up such concepts as "muse," "anima," "inspiration." And these terms seem especially appropriate to Beckett's representation of women in the radio, and still more, in the television plays as a group.

In turning to the television plays, perhaps one's first impression is of a ghostliness which fits well with words like *anima* or *muse.* The woman in *Eh Joe* (1966) is nameless and invisible. Yet she is undoubtedly, overpoweringly there, the unexpected, dreaded voice that drives Joe to "imagine" what he would rather not. Like Ada's in *Embers*, it is a low, remote voice that seems to come half out of memory, half out of some indefinable sphere where memory and fiction merge. The difference here is that Joe has not called her up—has indeed done his utmost to shut her out—yet she makes her way in and must be listened to. The emphasis is on the almost purely painful aspect of the creative process. For those of us watching the play, however, the effect, though intensely moving, includes surely an element of exhilaration. It comes, as so often in Beckett's oeuvre, from the power of the "story" that is brought alive for us. We seem to be taken by the voice of the invisible speaker to the inner realm behind the face of the mute listener where actions of dire weight have been recorded: a man has betrayed two women, a girl has committed suicide. From this not-uncommon material, Joe and the voice between them evoke for us an experience so strange and deep that we are able to imagine "better" the inner life of others. We come in the end to appreciate not only the events the voice tells of—sometimes with wry humor—but also something of the spiritual world which surrounds and underlies the act of creativity. The experience is not to Joe's comfort but may be perhaps to ours. The destroyed girl, after all, has been lifted up from the misery of her ending into a kind of immortality. She survives in the form that Joe has been led by the voice to bestow on her: she is "spirit made light."

The sense of some female force driving the action emerges in a different form in a later television play, *Ghost Trio* (1977). Again the woman is confined to a voice, a voice that may or may not be heard by the man whose movements she describes; we have no means of telling. He seems to do only what she prescribes for him, though once he performs an action that surprises her; he retains some freedom. To her, however, belongs the "pre-action," as Beckett calls it. She is the expositor and perhaps the animator, pointing out features of the image the viewer should be observing: the "familiar room," "the indispensable door," the "colour grey." There is clearly an element of self-reference and mild self-mockery here on the author's part. And he has entrusted it to a female voice, almost as though amusedly acknowledging the role of the "anima" in the act of composition.

The desirable aspect of the female image cannot in this play be wholly separated from its commanding, driving aspect. The male figure in the room is waiting for some "she" who does not come. He waits in silence except for the music which from time to time relieves him and promises (we may imagine, since it is the music of the *Ghost Trio*) some ghostly visitation. Is it the voice of the animator he is waiting for, the voice that has ceased to sound? Or some other woman from a life outside the room, a ghost of memory? As ever, we cannot tell: we sense only the painful and poignant force of the longing and its ability to create a dimension of unearthly calm, like the music of the *Ghost Trio* itself.

Finally, in . . . *but the clouds* . . . the apotheosis of woman is achieved in the summoning up of a being described only as W. This being, evoked by ritual and weary labor in the "dead of night," manifests itself only as a face. Its lips move, murmuring words that can only be heard by the viewers when the vision has faded and the magician, M, projects them, as it were, on her behalf. They are the words of a poet, one close to Beckett's heart. Even for those who do not recognise them as the closing lines of W. B. Yeats's *The Tower,* the poem in which he "makes" his soul, there is a resonance from the exquisite image of the bird's sleepy cry "among the deepening shades" which confers a kind of supernatural status on the apparition. Not quite a character, she is, like other women in these plays of the air and screen, both an object of desire and a force beyond desire. Woman is clearly seen at last as the creative inspiration without which the poet cannot complete his acts of evocation.

NOTES

1. Beckett to Nancy Cunard, 5 July 1956, quoted in D. Bair, *Samuel Beckett* (London: Cape, 1978), p. 474.

2. *Embers,* issued by the University of London Audio-Visual Centre in 1975, was produced by Katharine Worth and directed by David Clark. Patrick Magee played Henry and Elvi Hale was Ada.

Not I:
Through a Tube Starkly

LINDA BEN-ZVI

Reversing the usual order in a Beckett play, *Not I* begins with sound rather than action: a voice, unintelligible but faintly heard, emanating from behind a curtain for ten seconds. As the houselights dim and the curtain rises, an image appears, a human mouth "faintly lit from closeup and below" off center, suspended eight feet above a blackened stage. From this orifice pours forth, in breathless gobbets of sound, at great speed, a fifteen-minute tale of birth, solitude, silence, fear, guilt, and loss. The words are barely audible, the image barely discernible; but the power of the vision is unforgettable. *Not I* is ur-Beckett, the image that underlies all other Beckett works: a mouth, unable to stop, unable to get "It" right or "I" acknowledged, attempting to talk itself—in this case herself—into sense, attempting in the process to find an author of the words and of the self, and failing in both endeavors.

"I'm a big talking ball, talking about things that do not exist, or that exist perhaps, impossible to know, beside the point," the Unnamable says in his own monologic rush toward a closure that eludes him at the end of Beckett's trilogy, written in 1950. Talking is his only recourse, yet his monologue is constantly tinged with the recognition that words change nothing because language can offer neither the surety of the world nor even of the speaking self: "I seem to speak, it is not I, about me, it is not about me."

The "not I" to which the Unnamable refers becomes the ostensible speaker of the 1972 play, the medium and gender changed, the image the same: a "cretinous mouth, red, blubber and slobbering in solitary confinement." The live mouth, miniscule and helplessly dangling against the blackness of the stage, is a metonymic icon for the otherwise invisible speaker, the "tiny little thing" emitted into the world, and for the failure of the verbal act itself.

In the original stage version Mouth is not alone. Beckett's stage directions call for an Auditor, a figure of indeterminate sex, draped in a djellaba with hood, standing on an unseen podium four feet high, "shown by attitude alone to be facing diagonally across stage intent on Mouth, dead still throughout but for four brief movements where indicated." The figure fulfills several roles: intermediary between the audience and Mouth, offering mute compassion for the tale heard; traditional choral device calling attention to the play as play; draped cleric who can gesture but not alter; analyst who can listen but not heal. Although the Auditor enriches the possibilities of the dramatic piece, in the staged play the figure has proved problematic, in some productions dwarfing Mouth more than the relative positions would indicate, in others becoming lost in the space of a large hall or unseen by large portions of the audience. In 1975, when Beckett directed a French version, *Pas Moi,* with Madeleine Renaud, he omitted the figure because of these technical difficulties; and though the Auditor has been reinstated in subsequent performances, the positioning and gestural movements have never quite worked.

What does work is the visual power of the image of Mouth. Theater critics have often commented on the revolutionary nature of Beckett's use of stage space in *Not I,* his act of reconstituting the very heart of drama—action—making language not merely a vehicle for thought but the source of the action itself. A mouth that conveys words becomes the only visible image on the stage and its movements—lip pressing lip—the only stage action.

Not I, like other Beckett plays, offers more than a compelling use of the stage; it also concretizes a central issue in contemporary society: the connections linking language, self, and gender. In every Beckett work characters recognize, as the Unnamable does, that all one has is words, and they are "lifeless things." In that novel, and in many of Beckett's earlier writings, the relation between self and language is described in male terms. Even though the Unnamable is portrayed as a gelatinous ball, he is still given penis and spats to mark his gender. What makes *Not I* different and opens up the possibilities of new analyses is the fact that the speaker is female, and the search for self through language is constituted in terms of the female experience.

It is, therefore, not surprising that *Not I* has aroused the interest of feminist critics, particularly French feminists grounded in both Freudian and Lacanian psychoanalysis, whose works have concentrated on the relationship between gender and language, the place of woman in the dominant male discourse, and female attempts to establish identities in a patriarchal society. In a 1976 essay entitled in English "The Father, Love, and Banishment," Julia Kristeva connects the speaking Mouth with an earlier avatar, the narrator in Beckett's short story "First Love," a figure banished by the death of the Father. She finds both reacting to the power of the paternal agency. The latter creates his narrative as a means of identifying with the order of the Father, the symbolic order of language. The former refuses narration and sense, but indicates through her acquiescence to the internalized prodding of the Questioner—whom Kristeva labels the Father—the dominance of the patriarchal, the inability of the female to avoid the shaping force of this imbibed male voice and its debilitating effects, causing the speaker to efface the ego and remain forever "not I."

In an entirely different approach, Peter Gidal, in his book *Understanding Beckett,* sees the fragmented discourse of Mouth not as the failure or effacement of the female but as her victory. Beckett, he argues, achieves the feminization of Mouth, the Auditor, audience, and writing itself, since the outpouring of Mouth displaces the coherent form of accepted, i.e., male, discourse, subverts the expectations of listeners who desire art to be coherent, reveals to them in the process their own predilections, and makes the struggles of Mouth the shared central experience of all, thereby displacing the traditional patriarchy as the dominant mode of experience and logical, rational discourse as the primary basis of art.

Both Kristeva and Gidal take their points of departure from two very different forms of *Not I.* For Kristeva the work exists as text, a piece of writing presenting a condition so far removed from its original medium on the stage that she can conflate the persona Mouth with the male figure of the earlier fiction and not even acknowledge the obliteration of the intended sex in the work as Beckett wrote it. For Gidal *Not I* must be first approached as a play, its intended medium, and his own arguments are predicated on the original Billie Whitelaw production in London, the photographs of which accompany his discussion and serve as referents for his argument.

What makes *Not I* so interesting and unusual in the Beckett canon is the fact that it exists in yet a third form: television film. It is possible, therefore, to discuss the issues of female inscription, as Kristeva and Gidal do, in relation to this medium as well, which offers new possibilities of analysis.

In one of the few instances where Beckett has willingly allowed a work written for one medium to be transposed to another, he gave permission to the BBC in 1975 to film Billie Whitelaw in a specially made-for-television version of the play, directed by Bill Morton. At first attempting to keep the veracity of the staged performance, the director filmed Mouth in her stationary position against a field of black, with the Auditor in the camera range. However, the reduced dimensions of the television screen made the intended balancing of Mouth and figure awkward, and the effects distorted, so the original visual imagery was reversed: Mouth's placement shifted from a distantly perceived speck in the void to a closeup filling the screen, an all-consuming gaping maw, if still cretinous, no longer "tiny little thing." The Auditor was abandoned.

Billie Whitelaw remembers being furious when friends who had attended a performance of *Not I* at the Royal Court Theatre in London came backstage and asked her if Mouth had been videotaped, since they assumed the image flickering in the dark was not "real." In the case of the television production, that is precisely what happens: the "reality" of Mouth is gone, along with the presence of that live, albeit effaced, actor who stands and suffers behind her. Instead of presenting a figure who has gone through the torture Whitelaw describes, television offers the mechanical reproduction of the event, the camera freezing the moment, acting as a bridge between the viewer and the image mechanically captured on the screen: a new, mechanical Auditor.

On television Mouth becomes the object perceived by the unremitting stare of the camera, which is both the pursuer, though stationary, and the perceiver, imposing its angle of vision on Mouth, caught in its gaze, and on the viewer, who sees only what the mechanical apparatus allows. This mechanical means of reproduction thus adds another dimension to the work and to critical responses to it. Instead of offering helpless compassion at the sight of the searing Mouth, as the Auditor or the audience did in the presence of the live, suffering actor, the camera unflinchingly, unfeelingly records the scene of pain. No longer able to hear and see—no longer human Auditor—it is transparent receptor and conveyor, the unremitting eye/I, the ultimate voyeur.

In "The Work of Art in the Age of Mechanical Reproduction," Walter Benjamin noted that "the audience's identification with the actor is really an identification with the camera," the result being a dehumanization of the actor in the process. "For the first time—and this is the effect of the film—man has to operate with his whole living person, yet forgoing his aura. For aura is tied to his presence; there can be no replica of it" (228–29). Not only is film less "human" than the stage, but Benjamin describes it as less "magical" than other art forms—for instance, painting. Equating the painter to a magician and the cameraman to a surgeon, he sees the latter as "distancing himself from the subject," while at the same time dismembering, offering "multiple fragments which are assembled under a new law."

Although Benjamin's intentions are to demystify art, not to denigrate film, and to suggest the lineaments of the "new law," he cites those dislocations caused by mechanical reproduction, quoting at length the play-wright Pirandello's words on the new silent film form: "The film actor feels as if in exile—exiled not only from the stage but also from himself. With a vague sense of discomfort he feels inexplicable emptiness: his body loses its corporeality, it evaporates, it is deprived of reality, life, voice, and the noise caused by his moving about, in order to be changed into a mute image, flickering an instant on the screen, then vanishing into silence" (229).

The first element, then, in the shift of *Not I* from stage to television screen is the loss of—to use Benjamin's word—"the aura" of the live actor, who may be "she" as well as Benjamin's generic "he." The actor in the stage performance, enacting the suffering of being in the attempt to voice self, is lost in the television version. Mouth is no longer the palpitating, vulnerable presence suffering before the gaze of the Auditor and/or the audience. She is the fixed image incapable of alteration and of respite. The pain becomes one of embarrassment, the gigantic mouth trapped and naked, writhing before the indifferent perceiver.

In feminist terms, the nature of Beckett's icon also shifts; Mouth now becomes not only grotesque in her all-consuming size, and less "real"; she becomes more obviously a fragmented female body part used, as it so often is in a materialist society, as signification not of self but of non-being, an object, particularly on that most depersonalizing of all media, the TV. In close-up Mouth on television resembles a vagina. A pulsating orifice attempting to give birth to the self, the image marks an elision of mouth and vagina, the female reduced to genital identification, more blatant but no less familiar than the use of female body parts in this and other consumer media. Since the Auditor is also absent, the camera taking the place, compassion gives way to the stare, and the act becomes voyeuristic, the female as vagina reduced to a pornographic entertainment or a hard sell.

In the process of this transformation from stage to screen, the possible victory that Gidal describes, the refusal of Mouth to play by the rhetorical and narrative rules, giving the linguistic finger to the patriarchal hierarchies of discourse, alters as well. The emphasis is less on the monologue itself and its fragmented words than on the physical apparatus of speech-making—lips, teeth, saliva, tongue—captured by the mechanical apparatus of the television camera. Woman in the process is less heroic enunciator of her own hysteria and her own refusal than she is talking machine, already dismembered, taking up a familiar position on the tube: as object. The effect is to reinforce both the psychological dilemma of the female as Other, outside the symbolic order of the male, an absence, lacking both a penis and a persona, and as materialist emblem, vagina cum mouth, served up and magnified, all-consuming to the all-consumer.

In relation to *Not I* and the positioning of the female both in the materialist society and in language itself, it is true that the film version allows for a "deepening of apperception," which Benjamin says film can offer, but with the result that the objectification of woman, woman as Other/as mouth/as vagina/as pornographic image, is heightened; and the possibilities of escape—that tenacity which the flickering, live mouth seems perhaps capable of exercising—is lost. The image no longer flickers to the beholder as it does on the stage; its distortions are rather those of the medium itself. And while Mouth says the same words in both versions, language itself plays a different role. The droning of the barely visible image of the stage version, almost humorous in its insistence on being heard and seen in a cavernous theater, becomes on the small screen the gigantic aperture, pouring out its "spiel"—as just another talking head, just another genital display, reduced by the gaze of the camera into the very object whose tale she tells.

I thank Stan Douglas, who first commissioned this article for the Vancouver Art Museum.

WORKS CITED

Beckett, Samuel. *The Collected Shorter Plays*. New York: Grove Press, 1984.

Benjamin, Walter. "The Work of Art in the Age of Mechanical Reproduction." *Illuminations*. Trans. Harry Zohn. New York: Harcourt, 1968.

Gidal, Peter. *Understanding Beckett: A Study of Gesture in the Works of Samuel Beckett*. New York: St. Martin's Press, 1986.

Kristeva, Julia. "The Father, Love, and Banishment." *Cahiers de l'Herne* (1976). Rpt. in *Desire in Language: A Semiotic Approach to Literature and Art*. Ed. Leon S. Roudiez. New York: Columbia University Press, 1986.

Whitelaw, Billie. Interview with Linda Ben-Zvi. 11 December 1987.

Appendix

The following is an excerpt from Beckett's unpublished *Dream of Fair to Middling Women,* printed here (with the author's permission) for the first time. Accompanying it is a reproduction of a painting of Peggy Sinclair—the probable model for the Smeraldina-Rima in *Dream*—a cousin of Beckett, whom he visited in Kassel, Germany, during the years 1928 to 1932. Peggy Sinclair died of tuberculosis at the age of twenty-two on May 11, 1933.[1] In the original portrait, Peggy's coat is navy blue; the beret, top, and skirt are shades of light green; the scarf is green and red plaid; the belt and chair are red; and the background is dark green.

The images of woman and the language of the work have striking resonances in later Beckett writings. The two selections which follow it illustrate the recurrence of the themes and Beckett's development as an artist in his handling of the material. The former was suggested by Beckett when I asked him which piece of writing he would choose to include in a book on women in his writing; the latter is one of the most lyrical sections in the Beckett canon.

from *Dream of Fair to Middling Women*

Shall we consider then in the first instance that powerful vedette that we have been hearing so much about, the Smeraldina-Rima? Shall we? To begin with, then, there was the Dublin edition that bewitched Belacqua, the unopened edition, all visage and climate: the intact little cameo of a bird-face, so moving, and the gay zephyrs of Purgatory, slithering in across the blue tremolo of the ocean with a pinnace of souls, as good as saved, to the landing-stage, the reedy beach, bright and blue, merging into grass, not without laughter and the old K'in music, rising demitonically, we almost said: diademitonically, to the butt of the emerald sugarloaf. When she went away, as go she did, across the wide waters Hesse to seek, again Hesse, unashamed in mind, and left him alone and inconsolable, then her face in the clouds and in the fire and wherever he looked or looked away and on the lining of his lids, such a callow wet he was then, and the thought or dream, sleeping and waking, in the morning dozing and the evening ditto, with the penny rapture, of the shining shore where underneath them the keel of their skiff would ground and grind and rasp and stay stuck for them, just the pair of them, to skip out on to the sand and gather reeds and bathe hands, faces and breasts and broach the foothills without any discussion, in the bright light with the keen music behind them—then that face and site preyed to such purpose on the poor fellow that he took steps to reintegrate the facts of the former and the skin of the zephyr, and so expelled her, for better or worse, from his eye and mind. (101)

from *Words and Music*

Age is when to a man
Huddled o'er the ingle
Shivering for the hag
To put the pan in the bed
And bring the toddy
She comes in the ashes
Who loved could not be won
Or won not loved
Or some other trouble
Comes in the ashes
Like in that old light
The face in the ashes
That old starlight
On the earth again.[2]

from *Krapp's Last Tape*

I said again I thought it was hopeless and no good going on and she agreed, without opening her eyes. [*Pause.*] I asked her to look at me and after a few moments—[*Pause.*]—after a few moments she did, but the eyes just slits, because of the glare. I bent over to get them in the shadow and they opened. [*Pause. Low.*] Let me in. [*Pause.*]   We drifted in among the flags and stuck. The way they went down, sighing, before the stem! [*Pause.*] I lay down across her with my face in her breasts and my hand on her. We lay there without moving. But under us all moved, and moved us, gently, up and down, and from side to side.[3]

Portrait of Peggy Sinclair, painted by Karl Leyhausen, Kassel

NOTE

1. To learn more about Beckett's connection to Kassel and to the Sinclair family, see Gottfried Büttner's chapter, "Beziehungen Becketts zu Kassel" in *Beckett und die Literatur der Gegenwart,* Anglistische Forschungen Heft 196 (Heidelberg: Carl Winter Verlag, 1988), 292. Dr. Büttner's study offers first-hand accounts from Kassel residents about the Sinclair family, particularly Peggy, as well as Beckett's connections with the Sinclairs, Kassel, and German culture. The painting of Peggy Sinclair was first published with this essay. Permission to reprint the portrait has kindly been given to me by the private owner in Kassel, who wishes to remain anonymous.

2. *Words and Music,* in *The Collected Shorter Plays of Samuel Beckett* (New York: Grove Press, 1984), 131.

3. *Krapp's Last Tape,* in *The Collected Shorter Plays,* 63.

Contributors

JAMES ACHESON is senior lecturer in English at the University of Canterbury in Christchurch, New Zealand. He is co-editor of *Beckett's Later Fiction: Texts for Company* (1987) and author of a forthcoming book on Beckett's drama and early fiction. A member of the editorial board of the *Journal of Beckett Studies,* he recently co-edited a special Australian issue of the journal with Professor Colin Duckworth.

DAME PEGGY ASHCROFT, one of the most honored and respected actresses on the British stage, portrayed Winnie in *Happy Days* at the National Theatre in London in 1976, under the direction of Peter Hall.

SHARI BENSTOCK is professor of English at the University of Miami and a major feminist critic. She has written extensively on James Joyce; her recent book is *Women of the Left Bank,* a study of expatriate American writers in Paris.

LINDA BEN-ZVI, professor of English at Colorado State University, has recently published *Samuel Beckett* for the Twayne English Authors Series. She has also written on O'Neill, Pinter, and the philosophy of language and is presently completing a biography of Susan Glaspell.

SUSAN BRIENZA, who has taught in the English Department at UCLA, has published *Samuel Beckett's New Worlds;* she has also written on Sam Shepard and on modern drama in various journals.

BRENDA BYNUM is an Atlanta-based actress and director associated with the Alliance Theatre, Theatre Emory, and the Emory University Department of Theatre and Film Studies, and the T. H. E./Southern Poet's Theatre. She has appeared in *Not I, Happy Days,* and has directed *Come and Go.*

CAROL HELMSTETTER CANTRELL is professor of English at Colorado State University. She has published on Ezra Pound and other modern writers. She is now working on feminist epistemology and modern writers.

PIERRE CHABERT is a distinguished French actor and director associated with the Théâtre du Rond-Point. He has appeared in several Beckett works, including *Krapp's Last Tape,* and he has adapted *Company* for the stage. He has also written on acting and directing Beckett.

RUBY COHN, professor of dramatic literature at the University of California, Davis, has written several books on Beckett, including *Samuel Beckett: The Comic Gamut, Back to Beckett,* and *Just Play,* and she has edited *Disjecta,* a collection of Beckett's critical writings, as well as two casebooks on *Waiting for Godot.*

ELIN DIAMOND, a 1987 Mellon fellow at Harvard, is associate professor of English, Rutgers University. She has published a book on the theater of Harold Pinter entitled *Pinter's Comic Play.* She is presently completing a book on feminist theater.

MARTIN ESSLIN, who since his retirement from the BBC Third program has been teaching at various American universities including Stanford University, has published extensively on modern drama, including books on Pinter, Brecht, and Artaud, as well as the influential *Theatre of the Absurd,* in which he devotes a chapter to Beckett.

MARTHA FEHSENFELD is co-author of *Beckett at Work* and has written on Beckett for *Modern Drama* and other periodicals. She is co-editing Beckett's letters.

GUDREN GENEST, an actress from Berlin, played Nell in the 1967 Berlin production of *Endgame,* directed by Beckett.

PETER GIDAL is a leading avant-garde filmmaker whose *Materialist Film* has just been published in London by Routledge and Kegan Paul. His book *Understanding Beckett* was published by St. Martins Press/Macmillan in 1986.

LAWRENCE GRAVER is Kenan Professor of English at Williams College. He has co-edited *Samuel Beckett: The Critical Heritage* and has written extensively on modern literature.

NANCY ILLIG has played several Beckett roles: *Play,* 1963; *Happy Days,* 1964, and *Come and Go,* 1966—all in Ulm, under the direction of Deryk Mendel. She was also Voice in the 1966 Stuttgart production of *Eh Joe,* directed by Beckett. She most recently performed *Happy Days* in Lübeck in 1983.

IRENA JUN, a versatile Polish actress, has appeared in eight Beckett plays including *Play, Not I, Footfalls, Rockaby,* and *Endgame* as well as the televison plays *Eh Joe, Ghost Trio,* and *... but the clouds ....*

ROSETTE LAMONT, professor of French and comparative literature at the Graduate Center of the City of New York, is editor of the *Twentieth Century Views*

Collection of Essays on Eugene Ionesco and has written on contemporary drama in leading drama journals, book collections, and most recently as contributing editor on theater for the *New York Times*.

ANTONI LIBERA is Beckett's Polish translator and has directed many Beckett productions in Poland and, recently, in London.

CHARLES R. LYONS, chair of the Theater Department at Stanford University, has written books on Shakespeare, Brecht, and Ibsen. His most recent book is a critical study of the theater of Samuel Beckett, published by Grove Press.

HANNA MARRON, the "first lady of the Israeli stage," is co-founder of the Cameri Theatre. She played Winnie in *Happy Days* and Maddy Rooney in *All That Fall*.

ANGELA MOORJANI is chair of the Department of Modern Languages and Linguistics at the University of Maryland–Baltimore County. She has written on modern fiction and has published a book entitled *Abysmal Games in the Novels of Samuel Beckett*.

KRISTIN MORRISON is the author of *Canters and Chronicles: The Use of Narrative in the Plays of Samuel Beckett and Harold Pinter*, published by the University of Chicago Press. She has also published on Irish literature in various journals and is currently finishing a book on the fiction of William Trevor.

SHIVAUN O'CASEY produced, directed, and did the scenic design for *Happy Days* in 1987 at the Samuel Beckett Theater in New York—her directorial debut.

AIDEEN O'KELLY, for many years a leading member of the Abbey Theatre, Dublin, starred in *Happy Days*, directed by Shivaun O'Casey.

LOIS OPPENHEIM, who teaches French at Montclair State College, has edited a collection of essays on the Nouveau Roman, published by the University of Illinois Press.

LOIS OVERBECK, in the English department at Spelman College, has edited the *Beckett Newsletter*, is consultant to the Beckett Radio Project, and organized Beckett/Atlanta in 1987. She is currently co-editing Beckett's letters.

RUBIN RABINOVITZ; professor of English at the University of Colorado, has written *The Reaction against Experiment in the English Novel, 1950-1960; Iris Murdoch*, and most recently *The Development of Samuel Beckett's Fiction*.

MADELEINE RENAUD, one of the most renowned French actresses and co-founder of the Renaud-Barrault Theatre in France, gave the first performance in

French of *Happy Days,* with her husband, Jean-Louis Barrault, as Willie, in a production directed by Roger Blin and assisted by Beckett, presented at the Odéon Theatre in Paris in September and October 1963. She was also V in *Pas* (*Footfalls*) with Delphine Seyrig as M.

EVA KATHARINA SCHULTZ performed Winnie in *Happy Days* at the Schiller Werkstatt Theatre in 1971, directed by Beckett.

DELPHINE SEYRIG, an actress of French stage and screen, appeared in two Beckett plays—*Comédie* (*Play*) in 1964, under the supervision of Beckett, and *Pas* (*Footfalls*), in 1978, directed by Beckett.

DINA SHERZER, co-editor of *Beckett Translating/Translating Beckett,* has also written *Structure de la trilogie de Beckett: Molloy, Malone meurt, L'Innomable* (1976) and, more recently, *Representation in Contemporary French Fiction.*

BILLIE WHITELAW, known for a wide variety of stage and film parts, is the actress most closely associated with the female roles in Beckett. She has played all of Beckett's stage women except Nell in *Endgame. Footfalls* was written for her.

ANN WILSON teaches in the Department of Drama, University of Guelph, Ontario. She is working on a feminist reading of the plays of Sam Shepard.

KATHARINE WORTH has recently retired from the department of Drama and Theatre Studies in Royal Holloway and Bedford New College, University of London. A frequent contributor to collections on Beckett, she has edited *Samuel Beckett: The Shape Changer* and is the author of *Revolutions in Modern English Drama.* She has also produced new versions of his television play, *Eh Joe,* and his radio plays *Words and Music, Embers,* and *Cascando.* Her recent adaptation of *Company* received one of the "Fringe Firsts" at the 1987 Edinburgh Festival.

Index

Abbey Theatre, 35
Adorno, Theodor W., 126
Aion (Jung), 228
A la recherche du temps perdu, 74
Allen, Jeffner, 121
All My Sons (Miller), 46
All Strange Away, xii, 112
All That Fall, x, 7, 46, 47, 107, 113, 146,
   165, 172, 236
Arikha, Avigdor, 143
Artaud, Antonin, 208
"Assumption," 68, 70, 74, 76, 103
Atwood, Margaret, 118

Bachelard, Gaston, 234
Bair, Deirdre, 68
Barber, Francis, 162
Barrault, Jean-Louis, 15, 230
Barthes, Roland, 134, 148
Beckett, May, 148
Beckett, Samuel. *See* individual works
Benveniste, Emile, 209
Ben-Zvi, Linda, 201
Betrayal (Pinter), xiv
Beyond Minimalism (Brater), 233
Blin, Roger, 15
Bollène, Geneviève, 203
Book of Job, 146
Bordo, Susan, 122
Brater, Enoch, 191, 193, 201, 228, 233
Bruce, Brenda, 11
... but the clouds ..., 17, 47, 242
Büttner, Gottfried, 27, 244, 246

Calmative, The, 61, 72–73, 113

Cameri Theatre, 41
Carmichael, Polly, 162, 163
Catastrophe, xiv
Chabert, Pierre, 5, 206
Chaikin, Joe, 53
Chekhov, Anton, xv, 30
Cixous, Hélène, 139, 208, 209, 210, 213
Clément, Catherine, 209, 210, 211
Coat, Tal, 219
Cocteau, Jean, 205
Cohn, Ruby, 201, 205
Come and Go, x, 51, 52, 164, 170
Comédie, 18
Commedia (Dante), 135
Company, 102, 113, 148, 150, 151, 154, 157
Coward, Noel, 7
Craig, Gordon, 29

Dante, 72, 95
Death of a Salesman (Miller), xv
"Death and the Maiden" (Schubert),
   165, 237
Dedalus, Stephen, 68, 69, 70
Demeter/Kore Myth, 233, 234, 235
Derrida, Jacques, 179, 181, 182, 183, 222
Descartes, 119, 120, 179, 180, 208
Desmoulins, Mrs., 162, 163
Dialectic of Enlightenment (Horkheimer
   and Adorno), 126
Diamond, Elin, 192
Discourse on Language, The (Foucault), 209
Divine Comedy (Dante), 88
Dream of Fair to Middling Women, xi, xii,
   92, 109, 114, 115, 243–44
Duras, Marguerite, 21, 204, 205, 206

Duthuit, Georges, 217, 219

Eagleton, Terry, 224
Effi Briest (Fontane), 76
Eh Joe, 3, 6, 7, 26, 47, 228–35, 241
Elam, Keir, 167
Eleuthéria, 61, 164–65
Ellis, Havelock, 93
Embers, 6, 7, 229, 230, 238, 241
End, The, 113
Endgame, xiv, 3, 27–28, 47, 160, 165, 202, 236
End of the Beginning, The (O'Casey), 31
Enough, xi, 62, 63, 64, 113, 143
Esslin, Martin, 201, 233
Expelled, The, 72, 113

Fehsenfeld, Martha, 32, 40
Female Body in Western Culture, The, xv
Femme Fatale, 162–69
First Love, 61, 62, 63, 64, 72, 73, 76, 82, 85, 86, 94, 100, 102, 113
Fizzles, ix
Fizzle 3, 113
Fizzle 4, 113
Fizzle 6, 113
Fizzle 8, 113
Fletcher, John, 92
Fontane, Theodor, 76
Fool for Love (Shepard), xiv–xv
Footfalls, ix, 3, 6, 9, 10, 19, 31, 46, 47, 49, 50, 61, 143, 146, 148, 168, 169, 170, 171, 208, 213, 214
Foucault, Michel, 153, 203, 209
Frayn, Michael, 9
Frazer, Sir James G., 136
Freud, Sigmund, 73, 209, 222
From an Abandoned Work, 113
Fugard, Athol, 52

Gallop, Jane, 214
Garelli, Jacques, 225
Genet, Jean, 208
Ghost Trio, 47, 65, 187, 241–42
Gidal, Peter, 193, 195, 198
Gilbert, Sandra, 175–76
Glückliche Tage (Hübner), 55–56
Goethe, Johann Wolfgang von, 63
Goffman, Erving, 203
Golden Bough, The (Frazer), 136

Govrin, Michal, 42
Great Mother, The (Neumann), 234
Gregory, Lady Augusta, 30
Grelard, Marie, 204
Griffin, Susan, 121, 122, 123
Grotowski, Jerzy, 47
Gubar, Susan, 175, 222
Guggenheim, Peggy, 92

Hale, Elvi, 238
Hale, Jane Alison, 233
Hall, Peter, 11, 12, 14
Happy Days, xi, 3, 4, 5, 6, 10, 11, 13, 14, 16, 22–23, 24, 25, 26, 30, 31, 34, 35, 36, 39, 40, 41, 42, 43, 44, 45, 47, 51, 52, 53, 54, 55, 56, 57, 107, 113, 143, 146, 165–66, 172, 173, 176, 177, 179, 181, 182, 183, 202
Heartbreak House, 81, 89
Heidegger, Martin, 224
Heraclitus, 72
Horkheimer, Max, 126
How It Is, xiv, 66, 112
Hübner, Alfred, 55
Human Wishes, xi, 162, 163, 164, 170

Ibsen, Henrick, xv
Ill Seen Ill Said, ix, 102, 113, 134, 138, 142, 143, 146, 147, 148, 150, 151, 152, 154, 156, 157, 158, 159, 160
Imagination Dead Imagine, 102, 113
Interpretations of Dreams, The (Freud), 73
Irigaray, Luce, 197, 208, 221

Janeway, Elizabeth, 91–92, 99
John, Augustus, 29
Johnson, Samuel, 162–63
Jordanova, L. J., 120
Joyce, James, 68, 74, 107, 208
Jung, C. J., 135, 228
Juno and the Paycock (O'Casey), 29

Kean, Marie, 35
Kelly, Katherine, 201
King Lear, 146
Klein, Melanie, 148
Knowlson, James, 31, 75, 174, 179, 196, 197, 205
Krapp's Last Tape, 46, 68, 74, 76, 228, 234, 236, 238, 244

Kristeva, Julia, 194, 208, 211, 212, 213, 215, 223

La bibliothèque bleue (Bollène), 203, 204
La Camion (Duras), 205
Lacan, Jacques, 179, 209, 222, 223
La Jeune Née (Cixous and Clément), 139, 209–11, 213
Lamont, Rosette, 40
Landscape (Pinter), 42
"Law of Genre, The" (Derrida), 182
Lawley, Paul, 166–67
Lawrence, D. H., 68, 69, 99, 101
L'eau et les rêves (Bachelard), 234
Les beaux jours, 15
Le temps retrouvé, 74
Levett, Dr. Robert, 162, 163
Levy, Ori, 177
Libera, Antoni, 47, 48
Lie of the Mind, A (Shepard), xiv–xv
"L'Isolement" (Lamartine), 61
Lloyd, Genevieve, 120
Lonsdale, Michael, 18
Lost Ones, The (Le dépeupleur), 64, 92, 102, 103, 113
"Love and Lethe," 93
Lukács, Georg, 154
Lyons, Charles, xii

MacGowran, Jack, 10, 30, 228, 230
Madwoman in the Attic (Gilbert and Gubar), 175, 176
Magee, Patrick, 10, 30
Magic Flute, The, 37
Magna Mater myth, 134–39
Mailer, Norman, 101
Mallarmé, Stéphane, 225
Malone Dies, ix, 100, 101, 110, 111
Man and Superman (Shaw), 85, 86
Masson, André, 219
Mendel, Deryk, 24, 25, 26
Merchant, Carolyn, 120
Mercier and Camier, 42
Miller, Arthur, xv, 46, 101
Milton, John, 175
Mitchell, Breon, 164
Molloy, 101, 108, 110, 118, 119, 122, 123, 124, 125, 128, 134, 135, 137, 138, 139, 190

More Pricks Than Kicks, xii, 81, 82, 84, 85, 87, 88, 89, 91, 92, 93, 94, 95, 96, 102, 106, 107, 108, 109, 111, 114, 115
Murphy, 70–72, 76, 84, 87, 91, 92, 93, 96, 97, 98, 100, 102, 107, 109, 112, 114, 143

Neumann, Erich, 228, 231, 233, 234
Neville, John, 14
Not I, ix, 4, 6, 9, 10, 47, 50, 51, 53, 61, 107, 146, 154, 157–58, 160, 167, 168, 187, 188, 189, 190, 191, 193, 195, 196, 197, 198, 199, 201–2, 204, 206, 208, 209, 212, 217–26
nouvelles, xvi, 72

O'Casey, Sean, xvi, 29, 30, 34, 35
O'Casey, Shivaun, 35, 39
Oedipus at Colonus, 64
Ohio Impromptu, 65, 143, 187
O'Kelly, Aideen, 30, 31, 32, 33, 53

Paradise Lost (Milton), 175
Paradiso (Dante), 88
Pas, 18, 20
Perloff, Marjorie, 145
Piece of Monologue, A, 9, 50, 143, 150, 154, 156, 157, 158, 160
Pilling, John, 196, 197
Ping, xii
Pinter, Harold, xiv
Play, xiv, 6, 47, 61, 143, 166, 167
Pleasure of the Text, The (Barthes), 148
Plowright, Joan, 11
Poetics of Gender, The (Wittig), 172
Portrait of the Artist as a Young Man (Joyce), 68, 69
Postcard, The (Derrida), 181
Proust, Marcel, 68, 74, 75, 76
Proust, ix
Purgatorio (Dante), 88

Quadrat 1 + 2, 66

Read, David, 144
Renaud, Madeleine, 18
Residua, 143
Ricks, Christopher, 147
Ricoeur, Paul, 220
Road to Mecca (Fugard), 52

Rockaby, xv, 6, 8, 10, 47, 61, 143, 148, 150, 154, 157, 158–59, 160, 170, 171, 187, 208, 214, 217–26
Rossellini, Roberto, 205
Rubin, Gayle, 121
Rudman, Michael, 9
Rule and Exercises of Holy Dying (Taylor), 163

Salome, Lou-Andreas, 188
Schneider, Alan, 6, 56
Schopenhauer, Arthur, 68, 71
Serreau, Jean-Marie, 18
Shaw, George Bernard, xvii, 29, 30, 64, 81, 82
Shakespeare, William, 10, 11
Shepard, Sam, xiv–xv, 101
Showalter, Elaine, 218
Silence (Pinter), 42
Silver Tassie, The (O'Casey), 29
Sinclair, Peggy, 243, 245
"Smeraldina's Billet Doux, The," 96, 109
Speculum de L'autre Femme (Irigaray), 221
Smith, Dorothy, 117–29
Spinoza, Baruch, 68, 71
Stanislavski, Konstantin, 31
Stock, Werner, 177
Suleiman, Susan Rubin, xv, 148
Surfacing (Atwood), 118
Symbols of Transformation (Jung), 135
Synge, John Millington, 30

Taglíaferri, Aldo, 136
Taylor, Jeremy, 163
Texts for Nothing, 113
That Time, 50, 143, 154
Thomas, Dylan, 107
Thrale, Mrs. Henry, 162
Three Dialogues with Georges Duthuit, 217, 219

Tower, The (Yeats), 242
Trilogy, The, 111, 142
Turner, Victor, 203, 206

Ulysses (Joyce), 57, 107
Unnamable, The, 108, 110, 111, 112, 151, 155, 209

van Velde, Bram, 219

Waiting for Godot, ix, 9, 27, 33, 165, 166, 171, 202, 236
Walkowitz, Judith, 94
Warrilow, David, 4, 9
Watt, 91, 92, 94, 99, 100, 101, 108, 112
Wedding, The (Gogol), 231
"*Wet Night, A,*" 81
What Where, xvii, 187
White, Ruth, 56
Whitelaw, Billie, xvi, 3–10, 12, 55, 187, 191, 205
Wilhelm Meister (Goethe), 63
Williams, Anna, 162
Willis, Sharon, 224–25
Wittig, Monique, 172, 178, 184
Woman and Nature: The Roaring Inside Her (Griffin), 122
Women in Love (Lawrence), 69–70, 99
Woolf, Virginia, xv
Words and Music, 61, 65, 240, 241, 244
Wordsworth, William, 72
Worstward Ho, xii, 113, 150, 151, 152, 157

Yeats, W. B., 30, 242
"Yellow," 85

Zeifman, Hersh, 190